D1005799

HEAR MY SAD STORY

HEAR MY SAD STORY

The True Tales That Inspired
"Stagolee," "John Henry,"
and Other Traditional
American Folk Songs

Richard Polenberg

Cornell University Press   *Ithaca and London*

Copyright © 2015 by Cornell University

All rights reserved. Except for brief quotations in a review, this book, or parts thereof, must not be reproduced in any form without permission in writing from the publisher. For information, address Cornell University Press, Sage House, 512 East State Street, Ithaca, New York 14850.

First published 2015 by Cornell University Press

Printed in the United States of America

Library of Congress Cataloging-in-Publication Data

Polenberg, Richard, author.

   Hear my sad story : the true tales that inspired "Stagolee," "John Henry," and other traditional American folk songs / Richard Polenberg.

      pages cm

   Includes bibliographical references and index.

   ISBN 978-1-5017-0002-6 (cloth : alk. paper)

   1. ·Folk songs, English—United States—History and criticism.   I. Title.

   ML3551.P65 2015

   782.42162'13009—dc23   2015016652

Cornell University Press strives to use environmentally responsible suppliers and materials to the fullest extent possible in the publishing of its books. Such materials include vegetable-based, low-VOC inks and acid-free papers that are recycled, totally chlorine-free, or partly composed of nonwood fibers. For further information, visit our website at www.cornellpress.cornell.edu.

Cloth printing   10 9 8 7 6 5 4 3 2 1

For Margo, Nina, Mia, and Leo

Contents

Acknowledgments

I am indebted to friends, relatives, and colleagues for their detailed and supportive comments. For their good advice I wish to thank Paul Cashman, Anne Marie Cummings, Dr. Howard Feinstein, James Ferwerda, Dr. Michael Goodfriend, Joseph Halpern, David A. Kaplan, Walter LaFeber, John Malcolm Miller, R. Laurence Moore, Isabel Rachlin, Dr. Michael I. Resnick, Gene Robinson, Mindy Roseman, and Toby Walker.

I am also grateful for the suggestions I received from my children—Lisa, Amy, Michael, and Jesse—from my sister, Judith Resnick, and from my wife, Joan Spielholz.

Michael J. McGandy, Max Porter Richman, and Ange Romeo-Hall of Cornell University Press were most helpful.

My research was supported, in part, by the Colonel Return Jonathan Meigs First (1740–1823) Fund, the Marie Underhill Noll Chair, and the Steven H. Weiss Presidential Fellowship.

For several years I have taught at the Auburn Correctional Facility through the Cornell Prison Education Program. I have read some of the chapters to the men in my classes, and I thank them also for their advice.

PROLOGUE

The Streets of Laredo

"I can see by your outfit that you are a cowboy,"
These words he did say as I boldly walked by
"Come sit down beside me an' hear my sad story,
I'm shot in the breast an' I know I must die"

In the winter of 1875–1876, a young man named Francis Henry (Frank) Maynard, only twenty-one years of age, was working as a cowboy near Medicine Lodge, a tiny village in southern Kansas. While he was there he heard some ranch hands singing a song called "The Dying Girl's Lament." So Maynard used a tune from an old Irish ballad, "The Bard of Armagh," modified the lyrics of yet another Irish song, "The Unfortunate Rake," did considerable rewriting, and came up with a song called "The Dying Cowboy." In his original version, the first line was "As I rode down by Tom Sherman's bar-room," and the singer was not a "cowboy" but rather a "ranger"—someone who herded cattle on the open range. Then some cowboys who liked the song altered it a bit and changed the locale from Tom Sherman's barroom, one of the toughest saloons in Dodge City, Kansas, to "the streets of Laredo."

In the spring of 1876 Maynard headed to Texas to work as a cattle driver and found that a version of his song had already begun to make the rounds. A year or so later he returned home to Kansas, fell in love, got married, and by 1887 he and his wife had settled in Colorado Springs, Colorado. In 1911 he published the verses of "The Dying Cowboy" along with his other poems in a slender paperback booklet he issued himself called Rhymes of the Range and Trail. He remained in Colorado Springs, working as a carpenter, for the rest of his life.

Like "The Streets of Laredo," the songs in this book are ballads that tell narrative stories, nearly always about individuals but every so often about groups, or events, or institutions. Ballads can be traced back many hundreds of years, but they became popular in England during the eighteenth century. Often based on folktales, and generally transmitted orally, the lyrics frequently changed over the years. One of the earliest ballad collectors, Francis James Child (1825–1896), was a professor of rhetoric and oratory at Harvard University who published (posthumously) a multivolume work titled The English and Scottish Popular Ballads. The Child ballads, as they came to be known, included songs about hardships, outlaws, feuds, rebellions, romances, superstitions, ghostly apparitions, historical events, political conflicts, love, and tragedies. Child even devoted an entire section to "love-ballads not tragic."

"At a more favorable time the whole subject may be resumed," Child stated, "unless some person better qualified shall take it up in the interim." That well-qualified person was the British scholar Cecil Sharp (1859–1924). A graduate of Cambridge University, Sharp traveled to Australia, where he spent a decade teaching music theory, and on his return to England in 1889 he turned his attention to folk songs and folk dances. In 1911 he founded the English Folk Dance Society. In a video recording made in 1912, Sharp can be seen folk dancing with a few friends, and more than a century later, in 2014, a tribute was paid to him (available on YouTube) at the Folk Awards ceremony at the Royal Albert Hall.

From 1916 to 1918, Sharp made four lengthy visits to the United States, collecting an enormous number of songs—more than fifteen hundred in all—in the southern Appalachians: Virginia, West Virginia, North Carolina, Kentucky, and Tennessee. He traveled with Maud Karpeles, herself an avid collector and also a fellow folk dancer. When he arrived at Asheville, North Carolina, in July 1916, Sharp began collecting lyrics from young and old alike, songs such as "Cumberland Gap," "Johnson Boys," and "Sourwood Mountain." Remarkably, he obtained seventy songs from one woman, including versions of "Lamkin," "The Cherry Tree Carol," "The False Knight on the Road," and "The Grey Cock." Sharp found a teenage boy who "sang Mathy Groves very beautifully." In only nine weeks, he collected four hundred songs from sixty-seven men, women, and children. "I just love the people and the talks I have with them in their cabins," he said, and by early 1919, having returned to England, he wrote: "I am often dreaming about America and the wonderful time I had there and the invaluable experience I gained there."

Most of the people who appear in this book were contemporaries of Child and Sharp, and nearly all the songs about those people were already being sung during the lifetimes of the two renowned collectors. Many of the songs describe tragic events. Some are about murders, often resulting from love affairs gone wrong. Others tell of criminals who had to live outside the law or chose to do so. Still other songs describe calamities: railroad crashes and shipwrecks, natural disasters and industrial accidents. And some portray the brutal treatment of prisoners or the executions of criminals and radical critics of American society.

Virtually all the songs were written either while the events themselves were unfolding or very shortly thereafter. The lyrics often provide important information about those incidents and the circumstances in which they took place. The songs naturally reveal the outlook of those who wrote them, sang them, and listened to them. The songs also tried to teach lessons, either by condemning those who committed wicked acts or by praising those who behaved valiantly and sometimes even heroically. To understand how people lived in the past I utilize the songs' lyrics, which are as trustworthy as most sources on which historians traditionally rely.

———————

I have always loved these old songs and enjoy singing and playing them on the guitar and banjo. In the summer of 1957, as a college student, I traveled with my best friend to Asheville, North Carolina, to attend the Mountain Dance and Folk Festival, which had been founded and was still being directed by Bascom Lamar Lunsford. For a reason I no longer remember, I telephoned him, hesitantly, for he was reputedly a man with many prejudices. (He did not allow blacks to perform at the festival.) Born in 1882, Lunsford had worked as a fruit-tree salesman, teacher, and lawyer, and during World War I he had kept himself busy tracking down draft evaders. Known for having written "Good Old Mountain Dew" ("They call it that good old mountain dew / And them that refuse it are few"), he eventually recorded more than 330 traditional songs for the Archive of American Folk Song at the Library of Congress.

One of the most respected performers at the festival was "Aunt" Samantha Bumgarner. Born in 1878, she was, in 1924, the first woman to make a recording with the five-string banjo, and in 1928, the year the festival began, she made her first appearance on the stage. In 1935, sixteen-year-old Pete Seeger, attending the festival with his father, heard her play and decided, then and there, that he would take up the banjo. In June 1939 Franklin and Eleanor Roosevelt arranged for her and other traditional singers to perform for King George VI and Queen Elizabeth at a White House concert of American music. I found Aunt Samantha's number in the phone directory, made a call, and she graciously invited us to visit her and swap some songs.

Nearly eighty years of age, she settled down in a rocking chair on her front porch, wearing high-top button shoes and a long granny dress, and played her banjo, on which were painted bees, butterflies, and flowers. She had been married, but her husband had passed away years before. Her repertoire included "Worried Blues" and "Cindy in the Meadows," but she began by singing a song she had recorded many years earlier: "Fly around my pretty little miss / Fly around my daisy / Fly around my pretty little miss / You almost drive me crazy." She passed away little more than three years later on Christmas Eve in 1960. I have included her photograph in the chapter on John Hardy.

Leaving the festival one evening we heard a five-string banjo, and there, standing outdoors, by himself, was tall, lanky George Pegram Jr., playing and singing "Old Reuben": "If this train runs right, I'll be home Sunday night / I can hear Old Reuben when she pass / Poor Reuben, poor Reuben, oh Reuben ain't got no home." In 1941, during the attack on Pearl Harbor, Pegram had lost the sight in one eye; now he worked in tobacco fields, sawmills, and furniture factories, and also performed at Asheville. Riverside Records had recently brought out Banjo Songs of the Southern Mountains, an album that included several of his songs with accompaniment by the harmonica player Walter "Red" Parham. Lunsford, who had a testy relationship with Pegram, nevertheless made time for him at the festival, and he now delivered an impromptu performance, including a version of "John Henry."

We encountered other musicians, too, on our visit to North Carolina, including "Fiddlin'" Clarence Greene, who along with his son came to our hotel room, where, luckily, we had a tape recorder. He was sixty-three years of age, and even without any liquid refreshments—we were in a dry county!—he agreed to sing some songs for us. A superb fiddler and guitar player, he had, in the late 1920s, recorded more than two dozen songs for eleven different record companies. In 1928 and 1929, he had also participated in the Columbia Records field studio sessions held in Johnson City, as well as the Victor Talking Machine Company's sessions in Bristol, Tennessee. His recording of "Johnson City Blues" was later imitated—often note for note—by guitar players, and, as a member of Byrd Moore's Hot Shots, he recorded a version of "The Ballad of Frankie Silver." That tragic story, and the song written about it, can be found in chapter 6.

In the summer of 1957, the color line was still tightly drawn in the small towns and rural areas of western North Carolina, as it was throughout the South. (Early that fall, bitter controversies would erupt over public school desegregation, and federal troops would be sent to several southern cities, notably Little Rock, Arkansas.) But exceptions to the regime of Jim Crow could sometimes be made for the sake of music. Late one afternoon we were trading songs with several white musicians, many of them farmers, who suggested we meet a black man, Dee Brown, who was an outstanding guitar player. After the sun had gone down, and night had fallen, they somehow got word to him, and he joined us. He was a gifted musician, despite having lost two fingers in an accident, and as he played—one song was "Raise a Ruckus Tonight"—we looked on admiringly, and, if memory serves, sang along with him. Later he left as quietly and as unobtrusively as he had arrived.

———————

Quite a few of the songs in this book, more than half in all, describe events that took place in only three states: North Carolina, West Virginia, and Missouri. Like a great many people, the men and women about whom these songs were sung moved about from place to place, but they generally resided either in those states or elsewhere in the South: Tennessee, Kentucky, Georgia, Alabama, Mississippi, Virginia, and Louisiana. Migration and mobility have always been central features of American life, so even individuals who resided in the West or East had usually traveled widely or had journeyed from town to town.

All of the songs, at some point, were transcribed and eventually appeared in print—in broadsides, in newspapers, in journals, and certainly in books—but often the lyrics and even the tunes varied, sometimes quite considerably. As the years passed, verses might be added, or altered, or even dropped. At times, people in different parts of the country might well sing their own, favored versions, and even adapt the lyrics to their own personal circumstances. But whatever the version, the songs' messages did not fundamentally change. Their essential meaning remained constant.

Hear My Sad Story traces the roots of many of these songs and describes the circumstances under which each was written and first recorded. Some of the songs—"Frankie and Johnny," "Jesse James," "John Henry," and "Casey Jones"—are famous, known by countless numbers of people. Others, however—"Engine 143," "Duncan and Brady," "Pearl Bryan," and "Cole Younger"—are less well known, at least outside folk-song circles. I have deliberately omitted songs that are fictitious or even lack a credible basis in reality. Every song in this book is truthful, is grounded in historical fact, and illuminates the social history of the times.

The songs tell how the American legal system worked and, in some instances, failed to work, for men and women, many of whom were poor, or African Americans, or immigrants, as well as for others who for one reason or another simply ran afoul of the law. More than half the chapters involve trials, often for murder, and guilty verdicts sometimes produced appeals to higher courts, including the United States Supreme Court. Other chapters concern deeds that perhaps should have been judged by the courts but in fact never were. Yet the crimes that were committed—as well as the evidence presented at the trials, the courtroom procedure, the conduct of the judge, the verdict of the jury, and the punishment meted out—all found their way into lyrics.

Most people seem to like singing these songs, sad though they may be, and derive comfort and pleasure from singing them. Hearing others sing them can also be enjoyable, rather like witnessing a tragedy on the stage or watching a heartrending movie. At some point everyone experiences misfortune, or heart-break, or the loss of loved ones, and one way to cope with grief, to confront sorrow, is to seek solace in music. These stories and songs tell of tragic, sometimes heartbreaking, events, but reading the stories and hearing the songs may enlarge our capacity for compassion and understanding.

The songs in this book, while written at different times, always told people's stories, often rather sad, about love and loss, work and struggle, hope and fear. A long time ago, a noted folklorist suggested that these ballads should be collected to ensure they would never be lost or forgotten. The songs, he said, the newer as well as the older versions, were "the product of the people." Indeed they are and should always serve to remind us of our shared humanity.

St. Louis

CHAPTER 1

ST. LOUIS BLUES (1914)

I hate to see de eve'nin' sun go down
Hate to see de eve'nin' sun go down
Cause my baby, he done lef' this town

William Christopher Handy wrote "St. Louis Blues," but he spent very little time in that city and a most unhappy time at that. In 1892, when he was nineteen years old, he and a few friends made their way to Chicago, hoping to find work at the World's Fair Columbian Exposition. But the fair was postponed for a year, and Handy ended up nearly three hundred miles away in St. Louis, "down and out" (as he put it): hungry, homeless, penniless, and lice-infested. He had to sleep in vacant lots, in poolrooms, or on the cobblestones of the Mississippi's levee. Twenty-two years later, however—successful, married with a large family, and living comfortably in Memphis—he wrote his famous song. To compose it, he left home and rented a room over a bar on Beale Street, explaining: "I could feel the blues coming on, and I didn't want to be distracted, so I packed my grip and made my getaway." In the course of a single restless night he wrote what would become one of the most often-recorded songs of the first half of the twentieth century, second, in fact, only to "Silent Night."

Handy was born in 1873 in Florence, a small town in northern Alabama, less than a decade after his parents had been freed from slavery. His father, Charles Bernard, was a farmer and a minister in the African Methodist Episcopal Church. His mother, Elizabeth Brewer, had also somehow managed to acquire an education. Handy attended racially segregated schools, but his passion was music: as a teenager he saved enough money—$1.75—to purchase a cornet, only to incur his father's wrath ("Son, I'd rather see you in a hearse. I'd rather follow you to the graveyard than to hear that you had become a musician"). In his family, Handy said, it was the church that mattered and not music, unless, of course, music served a religious purpose. He nevertheless befriended a black fiddle player, who taught him many songs, and on graduating from high school Handy left Florence to find work as a musician with a blackface minstrel company.

In 1893, after his ill-fated stay in St. Louis, Handy headed to Evansville, Indiana, where he found a job playing his cornet in a brass band while earning extra money as a janitor. Soon he met Elizabeth Price, and they were married in 1896. Then, that summer, he traveled to Chicago to join Mahara's Mammoth Colored Minstrels, a troupe under white management that traveled throughout the South and also performed in Canada, Mexico, and Cuba. Handy finally began to earn good money, as much as $200 a month, even splurging on a new gold-plated trumpet. The show, which included a female impersonator, would parade through the streets of a town, circling the public square in hopes that onlookers would pay admission to see the evening performance. Here is a contemporary account: "The street parade is in full dress, silk hats and eight silk banners bearing various designs, with six Mexican-dressed drum majors and pickaninny drum corps, six walking gents with white Prince Albert suits and

W. C. Handy, ca. 1893. Courtesy of the Alabama Music Hall of Fame.

white silk hats, kid gloves and canes, with W. A. Mahara and his St. Bernard dog, Sport, in the lead of the parade."

As the band traveled through the South, it sometimes faced danger. In Tyler, Texas, in 1900, when several musicians came down with smallpox and news of the illness spread, whites chased the entire troupe to the outskirts of town, threatening to burn their railroad car and lynch the performers. In 1902, in New Madrid, Missouri, one of the musicians, Louis Wright, cursed a group of whites that had insulted him and his girlfriend. When angry men came after him, he drew his gun and fired at them. Backed by police officers, a group of whites assembled, began whipping members of the band, and finally located Wright: "The law gave him to the mob," Handy wrote in his autobiography. "He was lynched, his tongue cut out and his body shipped to his mother in Chicago in a pine box." On one occasion, white thugs pointed a rifle at Handy; on another, whites riddled his railroad car with bullets as it sped along. There was a hidden compartment under the floor of the train known as the "get-away," which contained provisions, "not to mention a small arsenal." Handy recalled: "I had my own private collection of arms, a Winchester 44, a Smith and Wesson and a Colt revolver."

> If I feel tomorrow lak ah feel today
> Feel tomorrow lak ah feel today
> I'll pack up my trunk, and make ma git away

In the fall of 1900, Handy returned to Florence and joined the faculty of the State Agricultural and Mechanical College for Negroes. He taught music for two years, leaving, however, after angering the college president by arranging a concert of ragtime music. He briefly rejoined Mahara's troupe and then in 1903 took a job in the small town of Clarksdale, Mississippi, as director of a black Knights of Pythias band. And it was there, he said, at a railroad station in Tutwiler, waiting for a train to take him back to Clarksdale, that he first heard the blues. He saw a "lean, loose-jointed Negro" playing a guitar, fretting the strings with a knife blade. "His clothes were rags, his feet peeked out of his shoes," Handy recalled—in what became his most frequently quoted comment—and he was singing "goin' where the Southern cross' the Dog"—a reference to where the tracks of the Southern Railroad crossed those of the Yazoo and Mississippi Valley Railroad.

The singer repeated the line three times, Handy continued, "accompanying himself on the guitar with the weirdest music I had ever heard." Soon afterward, Handy heard other black musicians playing the blues at a dance in Cleveland, Mississippi. "A long-legged chocolate boy"—he was twenty-one-year-old

Prince McCoy, though Handy did not identify him in his autobiography—led a three-piece band consisting of a guitar, a mandolin, and a bass. Members of the audience were enthusiastic, Handy said, and soon began tossing coins to the performers. Shortly thereafter, he started to write blues lyrics of his own, recalling: "That night a composer was born, an *American* composer."

In 1905 Handy moved with his wife and family—by now there were three children—to Memphis, bought a small house in an area known as "Greasy Plank," and formed a band. For several years, he hired musicians to play for dances, often on Mississippi riverboat excursions. Then, in 1909, he wrote a campaign song for Edward H. "Boss" Crump, who was running for mayor. (At the time, Crump supposedly said—naturally, he denied making the remark— "If you put Judas Iscariot on the ballot, he'd get a thousand votes in Shelby County.") Crump was duly elected—with strong support from those blacks who were still allowed to vote in the city—took office in 1910, and held the position for five years. One of Handy's verses in "Mr. Crump" was

> Mr. Crump don't like it, ain't gonna have it here
> Mr. Crump don't like it, ain't gonna have it here
> Mr. Crump don't like it, ain't gonna have it here
> No barrelhouse wimmen, God, drinkin' no beer
> Mr. Crump don't like it, ain't gonna have it here

Years later, Handy rewrote the song, calling it "The Memphis Blues," and added the catch line, "Mr. Crump can go and catch hisself some air!"

Comfortably settled in Memphis, where he would remain for the next ten years, Handy went to see the mayor, hoping to obtain his permission to publish the song, which he eventually titled "Memphis Blues (or Mr. Crump)." "I told him it would be all right," Crump said. But by 1912, having had no luck finding a publisher, Handy made what his biographer David Robertson called "the worst business decision of his life," selling his rights to the song to a deceitful white music publisher for a paltry fifty dollars. So a year later, when public demand led to the printing of an additional fifty thousand copies, Handy received no royalties. Before long, a white man—in blackface—was performing the song on a national tour with lyrics that differed from those that Handy had composed. Although Handy was not credited as the song's author, his name was included in the verse: "I never forget the tune that Handy called the Memphis Blues."

At the time, the city was a hub of the blues, and Handy was one of many composers who were making use of the new musical form. As Lynn Abbott and Doug Seroff have noted, Handy's autobiography "conspicuously avoided mentioning the continuous barrage of professional blues-based activity that was ringing from the little vaudeville theaters within earshot of his Beale Street office. If Beale Street really could talk, it would speak not of a single father figure but of a groundswell *movement* in which commercial possibilities for the blues were explored by a host of aspiring entertainers." Those entertainers included the pianist Cornelius Taylor, often known as "Old Folks," and a husband-and-wife comedy team, Willie Perry and Susie Johnson, who went by the names of Long Willie and Little Lulu, or the "Too Sweets." Music could be heard in five theaters in a two-block area of North Memphis, and, indeed, all over town.

Even as he was making a name for himself in the music business, Handy acquired a partner: Harry H. Pace, the son of a Georgia blacksmith, who had been working as a bank cashier. A graduate of Atlanta University, Pace had once been associated with W. E. B. Du Bois in publishing a black weekly newspaper. In 1907 he met Handy, and the two men decided to create the Pace and Handy Music Company. They remained associates even when Pace later moved to Atlanta. (In the 1920s, Pace, a successful entrepreneur, would form a record company, and he later founded the Northeastern Life Insurance Company.) Soon they were jointly copyrighting and marketing songs, chiefly blues, rags, and an occasional march—such as Handy's "Hail to the Spirit of Freedom"—with Pace often writing the lyrics and Handy the music.

The most famous song the firm published was "St. Louis Blues," for which Handy wrote both the words and the music. He described its genesis in his auto-biography: One day in 1914, he claimed, he felt gloomy and down in the mouth. So, not wanting to be distracted by his wife and children, he rented a room over a bar on Beale Street. In composing the song, he said, he imagined the time, more than twenty years earlier, when he was homeless, wandering the streets of St. Louis, "broke, unshaven, wanting even a decent meal . . . without a shirt under my frayed coat." And he conjured up the memory of a woman "stumbling along the poorly lighted street" murmuring, "Ma man's got a heart like a rock cast in de sea."

So, he said, he decided to create a blues song that would "combine ragtime syncopation with a real melody in the spiritual tradition." He also wanted to use the black vernacular, the rhythms of the tango, and an unusual chord—a G seventh rather than a G—to begin the verse. His goal, he said, was "to use all that is characteristic of the Negro from Africa to Alabama." Further, he wanted to convey a spiritual effect by shifting, atypically, from the subdominant C chord to the tonic G. The song began with the line, "I hate to see de eve'nin sun go down," and as Handy's biographer said, no other American lyricist "so effort-lessly and so confidently employed the language that real people, white or black, used in the United States at that time."

William Christopher Handy, July 17, 1941. Courtesy of the Library of Congress.

Saint Louis woman wid her diamon' rings,
Pulls dat man 'roun by her apron strings
'Twant for powder an' for store-bought hair,
De man ah love would not gone nowhere, nowhere
Got de Saint Louis Blues jes as blue as ah can be
That man got a heart lak a rock cast in the sea

Handy reported that his wife was upset by his disappearance for an entire day, but the members of his band seemed to enjoy his predicament.

The lyrics of "St. Louis Blues" were far bolder and more daring than any of Handy's earlier compositions. In one line—"Cause I'm most wile bout ma jelly roll"—Handy even used the slang term for a woman's sex organ. Elsewhere, he employed the phrase "ball the jack" ("A black headed gal makes a freight train jump the track / But a long tall gal makes a preacher ball the jack"), a commonly used euphemism for sexual intercourse; that it was a man of the cloth who was engaged in the act added a purposefully irreverent touch. Other phrases, such as "Blacker de berry, sweeter am de juice," were similarly suggestive. Yet despite his use of slang, Handy did not employ the hackneyed language of the black minstrel show. To the contrary, "the words do not convey ignorance, helplessness, or foolishness. The song is the plaint of someone who is hurting, but there is a frankness and toughness in the telling about it."

Once he had completed the song, Handy wrote in his autobiography, "time and chance were conspiring to snatch me away from Memphis." The episode that appears to have triggered his decision was his presence at the aftermath of a particularly horrific lynching. In May 1917, a thirty-eight-year-old black woodchopper, Eli Persons, was charged with the rape and murder of a sixteen-year-old white girl, Antoinette Rappal. On May 21, while he was being transferred from the Tennessee State Prison in Nashville to Memphis, a lynch mob seized him. A crowd, numbering perhaps five thousand men, women, and children, then turned out, in a carnival-like mood. A black journalist reported: "Persons was chained down, had a large quantity of gasoline poured over him, and set alight." The mob "cheered gloatingly as the match was applied." Then, Persons's body was decapitated and dismembered, and portions of his remains were taken to Memphis, where his head was thrown from a car at a group of African Americans.

Handy was there. He related that one morning he "noticed a crowd of Negroes gathered around a skull" that had been severed from a body (he called the victim "Tom Smith"): "The eyes had been burned out with red-hot irons. A rural mob, not satisfied with burning his body, had brought the skull back to town and tossed it into a crowd of Negroes to humiliate and intimidate them." Handy reported his reaction, a mixture or horror, anger, and depression: "All the savor had gone out of life. For the moment only a sensation of ashes in the mouth remained." He thought back to other acts of brutality he had witnessed in the South, the outrageous crimes, the viciousness of white mobs, and the unwillingness of white law enforcement authorities to intervene: "I appealed to the town marshal for protection," he recalled about one incident. "He scoffed at my plea and went to the aid of the man who had struck me." Handy also recalled having had to hide deep in a field to avoid a mob. So he made up his mind to escape from the South, and in 1918 he did: he moved to New York City, settling in Harlem, with his family following a year later.

His first few years in New York, however, turned out to be personally and financially stressful. Harry Pace left to form his own company, Black Swan Records, and by 1922 Handy began to lose his eyesight; in fact, for two years, following an unsuccessful operation, he could hardly see. Since his songs were not selling well, he was forced to borrow money. Fortunately, though, he became friends with Edward Abbe Niles—a Rhodes scholar who had studied at Oxford, received a law degree from Harvard in 1921, and went to work on Wall Street—who took over the management of his finances. In 1926 Niles also edited and wrote an appreciative introduction to *Blues: An Anthology*, a collection of Handy's musical compositions. "Handy's talk exhibits such qualities of humor, of comprehension, and of nobility, that to hear it is to long to repeat it," Niles wrote, adding, in a later edition: "He is an artist, a trouper, a citizen, and a gentleman."

Handy was not present when the earliest recordings of "St. Louis Blues" were made: in December 1915 by a band directed by Charles A. Prince; in September 1917, by Ciro's Club Coon Orchestra, an African American band located in England; or in July 1918 by the vaudeville singer Al Bernard. But he was associated with Marion Harris (originally Mary Ellen Harrison), a twenty-four-year-old white singer who recorded his song in April 1920. She had earlier made recordings of "I'm a Jazz Baby" ("I'm a jazz baby / I wanna be jazzin' all the time!") and "I'm a Jazz Vampire" ("For I'm the meanest kind of jazz vampire / I'm the wicked vampire of the jazz"). "She sang blues so well," Handy said, "that people sometimes thought that the singer was colored." (Later, Harris toured with vaudeville shows, moved to England in the 1930s, and perished, tragically, in a fire—she fell asleep with a lit cigarette—at a New York City hotel in April 1944.)

Handy finally recorded his own instrumental version of the song in 1922, and dozens of other recordings would follow over the next two decades, by artists as diverse as Bessie Smith (1925); "Fats" Waller, who played a pipe organ solo (1926); Rudy Vallee and his Connecticut Yankees, who decided to change the phrase to "St. Louis man" (1930); Paul Robeson (1934); Django Reinhardt (1935); Benny Goodman (1939); and Earl "Fatha" Hines (1940). In July 1954 Louis Armstrong and his orchestra recorded the most wonderfully compelling version of "St. Louis Blues" with the vocalist Velma Middleton. The album included a brief interview with Handy by the producer, George Avakian.

Handy spent his final years in New York City, always remaining actively involved in music. In 1929, he served as musical director for the sixteen-minute film *St. Louis Blues*, in which Bessie Smith, making her only such appearance, sang the song while pretending to be in a speakeasy. True to his upbringing, Handy remained a steadfast Republican, although he sympathized with certain liberal causes, including that of the loyalists in the Spanish Civil War, and he condemned what he believed to be the frame-up of the Scottsboro boys. In 1939 he was honored at the New York City World's Fair for his contributions to American culture. Two years later he published his autobiography, *Father of the Blues*, after having been persuaded not to use his original title, "Fight It Out," by his friend the author James Weldon Johnson. Another Harlem author, Arna

Bontemps, assisted in the writing. Handy continued to travel and to perform, until in 1943 he lost his footing and tumbled from a subway platform, suffering serious injuries and permanently losing his sight. In 1948 he invited a friend for dinner but confessed that he was "seventy-four years old and so blind that I cannot see what the chicks look like." Perhaps so, but in 1954, many years after his wife had died, Handy married Louise Logan.

Two years later, the *New York Times* reported that he remained in good health, well enough to attend an outdoor performance, and that he "smiled and nodded approvingly from his wheelchair. He was especially happy when the Stadium Symphony, under the baton of Leonard Bernstein, played his famous piece." That famous piece, of course, was "St. Louis Blues," written more than forty years earlier by a man who, having felt the blues coming on, had holed himself up in a dingy room over a bar in Memphis. Eventually, Handy's composition became one of the most recorded of all songs, two different versions of which would be inducted into the Grammy Hall of Fame. In fact, more than eighteen hundred jazz or jazz-related versions were eventually recorded. There is, it seems, no end to how many recordings will eventually be made, which is as it should be. Handy died in 1958, but as he had written in one of his early blues,

> Do say the word and give my poor heart ease
> The blues ain't nothing but the fatal heart disease.

CHAPTER 2

DUNCAN AND BRADY (1890)

Well it's twinkle, twinkle little star
In walked Brady with a shining star
And Brady says, "Duncan you are under arrest"
And Duncan shot a hole in Brady's breast
Cause he been on the job too long

On Monday evening, October 6, 1890, two men got into a sparring match outside a saloon at 715 North Eleventh Street in St. Louis. The combatants, Luther Duncan and Bob Henderson, were African Americans, as were nearly all the people who crowded around to watch. The owner of the saloon, Charles Stark, was also there, and so was Luther Duncan's younger brother, Harry. Then someone called the police, the Duncan brothers ran into the saloon, and soon a gunfight broke out, leaving several men wounded and one—a policeman named James Brady—dead. Harry Duncan was arrested, charged with the murder, tried, and found guilty. His appeal reached the United States Supreme Court but was eventually rejected. In July 1894 he went to the gallows.

At the time, St. Louis was the fourth-largest city in the nation. With a population of 450,000, it ranked behind only New York City, Chicago, and Philadelphia. In the ten years since 1880, the city had grown by more than one hundred thousand inhabitants. African Americans, numbering thirty thousand, made up somewhat more than 6 percent of the population. They resided chiefly in low-income neighborhoods, one of which was known colloquially as the Bloody Third, a district where Irish Americans resided in "Kerry Patch" and African Americans dwelt in "Clabber Alley" or "Wildcat Chute." Politicians in those areas went by such colorful nicknames as John "Pull-'Em-In" Pohlman or James "Jimmy De Mule" Gillespie. Even Missouri governor William J. Stone, who was responsible for approving Harry Duncan's execution, was informally known as "Gumshoe Bill."

Patrolman James Brady, St. Louis Police
Department, October 6, 1890.

The sparring match that began about 8:30 that Monday evening might have ended uneventfully had not someone summoned the police. Officer John J. Gaffney, who patrolled the beat, quickly appeared on the scene. He claimed that he ordered the onlookers to disperse and to clear the way for passersby, as well as told the fighters to quit. "You know this will not do," he said, whereupon Luther Duncan "put up his fists and shoved against the officer." "If you don't go away, I will have to take you away," Gaffney said, to which Luther replied, "You can go to hell, you can't take me away." Gaffney grabbed Luther's arm, but Harry Duncan "struck Gaffney a violent blow in the face and eye." Then the brothers hustled him through the crowd, where he was kicked and punched, "and finally his baton was wrested from him, and with this the Duncan brothers beat him over the head and left him lying unconscious on the street." Someone in the crowd cried, "Let's kill the son of a bitch while we're at it."

Regaining his senses, Gaffney said, he fired his pistol in the air to attract other policemen, and then followed Luther into Charles Stark's saloon, although he was so dazed that someone had to open the door for him. Spying Luther in the billiard hall, which was six to eight feet higher than the barroom floor, he climbed the stairs, saying "I want you." But as he was descending with Luther in tow, Harry struck him "a violent blow on the head," knocking his hat off and sending him "reeling and bleeding, with a great gash cut over his eye and on his head, down the north stairway." As Luther fled the scene, Gaffney asserted that Harry wrenched his weapon from him.

That was Gaffney's version of events, but Harry Duncan told quite a different tale. The crowd in front of the saloon had not gathered to see a fight, he said, but had been attracted by—a talking parrot. Moreover, the "trouble" between Luther Duncan and Bob Henderson was trivial, over and done with by the time Gaffney arrived. Neither Harry nor his brother wanted any trouble, but Gaffney assaulted him anyway. After defending himself, Harry entered the saloon with his brother. But Gaffney followed them, drew his pistol, pointed it at Harry and cursed him out: "You black son of a bitch, I'll blow your head off." To protect himself, Harry claimed, he knocked the officer down with a billiard cue, took his pistol, and started to leave the saloon.

Two other officers, Daniel P. Maloney and John Conners, having heard the gunshots, then entered the saloon and saw Gaffney, "the blood streaming down his forehead and face and he exclaimed to them that he was nearly killed." The saloon owner, Charles Stark, shouted, "Here is the man who did it." Maloney ordered Harry Duncan to surrender, but Duncan raised his gun, fired at Maloney and Conners, and crouched behind a counter, continuing to exchange fire with the officers. Just then another policeman, James Brady, entered, and demanded that Duncan surrender. The officers testified that Duncan "thereupon sprang up, suddenly, shot Brady, who fell over dead," while they "fired at defendant, and slightly wounded him in the side, and he immediately dropped again behind the counter." When he saw Duncan trying to slip away, Conners covered him with his revolver, saying, "You make a move with that gun and I will kill you." Duncan allegedly said, "I've killed one; I'm satisfied," dropped his pistol and gave himself up.

Naturally, Duncan again offered a much different account. He admitted that he tried to keep firing his gun but "it would not go off. There wasn't no more leads in it. I throwed up my hands to them; here is a shot I got through my finger. . . . I dropped that revolver right here underneath the bar, and crawled on under the show-case." There he remained until Stark pointed a pistol at him and told him to surrender. As he emerged, he saw Brady lying dead on the floor. At his trial, and throughout the appeals process, he would insist and his lawyer would endeavor to show that it was Charles Stark, the saloon owner, and not Harry Duncan who fired the shot that killed James Brady.

> Brady, Brady, Brady, you know you done wrong,
> Walkin' in the room when the game was goin' on
> Knockin' down windows, breakin' down the door,
> Now you're lyin' dead on the barroom floor
> Cause he been on the job too long

The man who surrendered and was taken into custody was twenty-seven. His name was William Henry Harrison Duncan. He was born in Columbia, Missouri, in 1863. His parents, Frederick and Sarah, were former slaves who had been given the surname of the man—Garrett Duncan—who owned them. Frederick, born into slavery in Virginia, eventually acquired a parcel of land; one of his jobs was hauling students' trunks to and from the University of Missouri. He died, though, when Harry was only one year old. Harry's mother, Sarah, was also born in Virginia and worked as a washerwoman. Harry had two younger sisters, Barbara and Kate; his brother, Luther, two years his senior, told the census taker he was a "huckster."

Harry Duncan left home when he was in his teens and moved to St. Louis, where he found work as a bootblack and a barber. As the years went by, he earned a reputation as a "sport, a jolly fellow, a swell dresser, a ladies' favorite, but, above all, he was a magnificent singer." So deep was his voice, and so resonant, that people said he could reach notes lower than anyone else. Although he eventually got a job as a railway porter on a Pullman car, he also had a career on the stage as an actor and singer. Later, in prison, he would sometimes be heard singing his favorite songs, "My Mother's Picture" and "Nigh to the Grave."

Once in custody, Duncan was taken in handcuffs to the coroner's inquest held at Brady's home. Only thirty-one at the time of his death, Brady had left a wife, Nora, and four small children. The newspapers reported that Nora "hugged her infant to her breast and gathered her little ones about her," looked at Duncan, and said, in a voice that may well be imagined, "You murderer, you robbed these children of their father." Shortly thereafter, in January 1891, a grand jury indicted Harry Duncan on the charge of first-degree murder. Pleading not guilty, he asked for a change of venue, and the proceedings were moved to Clayton, a suburb west of St. Louis. The trial was scheduled for early November 1892.

Duncan's attorney was Walter Moran Farmer, the first African American to graduate from Washington University Law School in St. Louis. He received his law degree in 1889. Actively involved in national Republican Party politics, he was a member of the St. Louis Committee of Five, a group that supported racial justice and denounced lynching. An advocate of peaceful protest, Farmer nevertheless stated that "patience has its limits, and it may be that the patience of the Negro race in America has become exhausted." Farmer was the first black lawyer to argue before the Supreme Court of Missouri, and one of the first to argue before the United States Supreme Court; both appearances were on behalf of his client, Harry Duncan.

The trial began on November 2, 1892, before Judge W. W. Edwards. A Republican, first appointed a United States attorney by Abraham Lincoln, he had served on the bench for more than twenty-five years. Chester H. Krum, a prominent lawyer and graduate of Harvard Law School, presented the case against Duncan, assisted by William Zachritz. The judge requested that armed guards in the courtroom keep an eye on the defendant because, if the charges were true, he "is a desperate and dangerous character." Judge Edwards also ruled that the prosecution could show that, at the time of his arrest, Duncan had concealed saws on his person that could be used to break out of prison. The judge also upheld the prosecution's objection to admitting Stark's statement that he "had done some shooting there that night" on the grounds that it was the "merest hearsay." For good measure, the judge added that even if Stark had admitted killing Brady, "evidence of such admission would still have been hearsay."

The prosecution's case relied primarily on the testimony of the policemen involved in the shootout. Officers Maloney and Conners testified that they had seen Duncan shoot Brady and that he had admitted as much to them after his arrest: they repeated Duncan's statement, "I shot him with the gun I took away from Gaffney. I had no other gun." While on the stand, the policemen were asked about the getaway material Duncan was hiding when he was transported to Clayton for the trial: "several small steel saws were found concealed in one of his slippers, wrapped in a cloth, and these were shown to the jury."

> Brady, Brady carried a forty-five,
> Said it would shoot half a mile
> Duncan, Duncan had a forty-four,
> That's what laid Mr. Brady so low
> Cause he been on the job too long

When Duncan took the witness stand, he repeated his earlier story: that Officer Gaffney had assaulted him, followed him into the saloon, cursing, and with his pistol drawn. Purely to protect himself, he had knocked the officer down with a billiard cue, taken his pistol, and tried to leave. But then Officers Malone and Conners entered with their guns drawn "and opened fire upon defendant at once, and without a word." So Duncan returned the fire "and exhausted the chambers." He raised his hands, trying to surrender, but the officers continued firing. "He ran behind the counter, and crawled under it, and while there was shot twice by the officers, leaning over." From behind the counter, he saw Brady enter the room "but did not shoot at him." In fact, Duncan said, he did not even move from behind the counter until he surrendered. Emphatically denying that he had confessed to the officers, he justified his possession of the saws on the ground that "he did not intend to use them unless he were convicted."

Trying to make a case for his client's innocence, Farmer claimed that Duncan's revolver was out of ammunition before Brady was shot. He also got Officer Maloney to admit that he had not bothered to recover the murder weapon, and in fact it was never found. "Why after you had gotten hold of him, did you not go back and get the revolver?" Farmer asked, and Maloney replied: "I don't know as we gave the revolver a thought at the time. We wanted to be sure of him." When Conners took the stand he was asked, "What did you do with the revolver that Duncan threw away?" His reply was: "I didn't bother it. . . . I thought I had better secure the man. I took him out."

Farmer also tried to show that the angle of Brady's fatal wound could not have come from Duncan's hiding place, but must have come from Stark's position. He even attempted to call a witness to testify that Stark had fired his pistol in the bar that night, but the judge upheld the defense's objection to allowing the testimony. (Mysteriously, Stark was himself never called to testify at the trial. But a story was told that he had a parrot, which would tell anyone who passed by: "Stark did it. Stark did it." Rumor had it that Stark killed the bird and replaced it with another.) When Farmer called a witness to the stand who declared that he had seen Stark shoot Brady while Duncan was hiding behind the counter, the prosecutor derided the testimony, pointing out that the witness, who was serving time in prison on a murder charge, was untrustworthy, and questioning why it had taken him so long to come forward.

When the trial concluded, Judge Edwards instructed the jury. To sustain the charge of murder in the first degree, he explained, jurors would have to find beyond a reasonable doubt "all the elements of willfulness, premeditation, deliberation, and malice aforethought." Were they to conclude, however, that Duncan was acting peaceably "and that he was assaulted, shoved or struck by the policeman Gaffney, then he . . . had the right, in law, to resist . . . by such means and in such manner as was necessary to repel his assailant." True, Gaffney had the right to arrest someone who broke the law, but he "had no right to assault or beat or strike or shove . . . Duncan, if he . . . was conducting himself in a peaceable and law-abiding manner."

Not only did an officer have no right to compel anyone who was acting peaceably in public "to move or to go away at the bidding of the said officer," the judge explained, but an individual also had a right to "resist force by force, meet violence with violence," and protect himself from bodily harm, even to the extent of "taking the life of his assailant, whether he be an officer or private citizen." If Duncan was hiding behind the bar, and the police fired at him, then he "was justified in returning the fire" and protecting himself "even to the taking of life." If indeed the police had assaulted Duncan, followed him, and began shooting at him, then he "had the right to exercise the right of self-defense, and to repel force by force, and violence by violence." Lastly, the judge explained that "a brother has a right to defend a brother" if it were reasonable to believe he was in danger of great bodily harm or death from an assailant.

Once Judge Edwards had delivered his instructions, it did not take long for the jury to find Duncan guilty and impose the death penalty. The judge set an execution date in February 1893, but Farmer appealed to the Supreme Court of Missouri, and it granted a stay. On May 16, however, that court, in a decision by Chief Justice Thomas A. Sherwood, upheld the verdict. Yet another execution date was fixed, in June, but again Farmer appealed, this time to the United States Supreme Court. Months passed before the justices heard the case, but on March 12, 1894, the Court rejected Duncan's appeal, citing a lack of jurisdiction.

The issue Duncan's attorney brought before the Court chiefly involved a procedural question. Farmer argued that when the Missouri Supreme Court decided the case in 1893, only three justices had voted; but in 1890, when the crime was committed, the state constitution had provided for adjudication by five justices. The recent amendment to the state constitution, which permitted a ruling by fewer justices, violated the United States Constitution's ban on ex post facto laws, or so Farmer claimed. He also argued that the state court had denied Duncan due process and equal protection, and had also violated the Fourteenth Amendment's ban on abridging the privileges and immunities of citizens.

Supreme Court of the United States, 1894. Courtesy of the Library of Congress.

Chief Justice Melville W. Fuller—who two years later would write the opinion in *Plessy v. Ferguson* upholding "equal but separate facilities" for blacks and whites—handed down the decision, which, while hardly a model of lucidity, nevertheless rejected Duncan's plea. Fuller held that the objection to the state constitution had not been raised in a timely fashion but only "after judgment, and after an application for rehearing had been overruled, and only then in the form of a motion to transfer the cause." For the Court to deny Duncan's claim, therefore, "was in no aspect equivalent to a decision against a right under the Constitution of the United States specially set up or claimed at the proper time and in the proper way." As to the provisions of the Fourteenth Amendment, "due process of law and the equal protection of the laws are secured if the laws operate on all alike, and do not subject the individual to an arbitrary exercise of the powers of government." Fuller also denied that the amended state constitution was, "as to Duncan, ex post facto, and therefore void," since states' decisions to abolish—or create—courts, so long as protections are maintained, "are not considered within the constitutional inhibition."

So all Duncan's avenues of legal appeal were at an end. In July, awaiting execution, he was interviewed by a reporter for the *St. Louis Chronicle*. Reiterating his innocence, he said he had seen Charles Stark fire the shot that killed James Brady, and that, as he fired, "his face was like a demon," adding, "Brady staggered a minute, then fell down dead." Whatever hope there was of getting to the truth had probably vanished a few weeks earlier when, in June, Stark himself passed away. On his last day on earth, Duncan wrote, "It's politics that forces me to the gallows," and to the end Walter Moran Farmer maintained, "If ever an innocent man was hanged, that man was Duncan."

From his cell, Duncan could hear the sound of the gallows being constructed. He read from the Bible and a prayer book while two Sisters of Mercy from St. John's Convent spent the afternoon with him. Interviewed by reporters, he told them that death was perhaps preferable, for "if he should be spared to again enjoy freedom of action, he might drift back into sinful ways and finally be lost." He selected two hymns—"Nearer, My God, to Thee" and "Shall We Meet beyond the River?"—to be sung at his funeral. Father Dan McErlane, a priest who believed him innocent, remained to console him through the night.

In a last-minute effort to prevent the execution, Walter Farmer had gone to the governor, bringing with him a statement by one of the jurors who indicated he had misunderstood the judge's instructions; but the governor refused to intervene. So at six o'clock on the morning of July 27 the sheriff arrived to take Duncan to the scaffold. The doomed man removed his blue cap. His legs were strapped together. Asked if he wished to make a last statement, he replied: "I haven't got nothing to say." The hood was pulled down over his face. Four hundred onlookers were gathered in the square around the courthouse to witness the execution. And then the trapdoor opened.

The newspapers that day interviewed the county prosecuting attorney, R. Lee Mudd, who said that Duncan should not have been executed, and prominent local attorneys agreed. They believed the judge improperly instructed the jury: the correct charge should have been murder in the second degree, since proof was lacking that Duncan had killed Brady in cold blood. "On the contrary, the testimony proved that Duncan only fired when three policemen were trying to kill him." Mudd did not condone Duncan's crime, even deemed him a "thoroughly bad man," but did not believe he deserved to die. A month after the execution, newspapers would interview a man who claimed he saw Stark, not Duncan, fire the fatal shot, but who did not testify at the trial for fear of angering the police.

Duncan's body, taken to his brother Luther's home, rested in a satin-lined rosewood casket, his hands clasping a crucifix and prayer beads. According to the *St. Louis Post-Dispatch*, more people paid their last respects to Harry Duncan than to any other black person in the city's history. He was buried in the colored section of Friedan's cemetery in North St. Louis. No stone marks his grave.

A poem he wrote in his final days was titled "Harry Duncan's Misfortune." Two of the fifteen verses read:

> My lawyers fought hard to save me,
> And so near did they succeed,
> That everyone knew I was innocent
> Of committing so foul a deed.
>
> Now, friends, I could not be guilty
> Of such a beastly crime,
> And though some may believe me guilty
> The truth will come out in time.

Whether or not the truth will ever come out, people have been singing about Harry Duncan and James Brady for more than a century. They will undoubtedly continue to do so. An early version turned up in 1901, another was collected in 1908, and the song appeared in two books published in 1925: Dorothy Scarborough's *On the Trail of Negro Folk Songs*, and Howard W. Odum and Guy B. Johnson's *The Negro and His Songs*. In 1927, Carl Sandburg included two versions of "Brady" in *The American Songbag*, remarking: "It is a tale of wicked people, a bad man so bad that even after death he went 'struttin' in hell with his Stetson hat." To Sandburg, the lyrics conveyed "the snarl of the underworld, the hazards of those street corners and alleys":

Brady won't come no more!
Brady won't come no more!
Brady won't come no more!
For Duncan shot Brady with a forty-four!

CHAPTER 3

STAGOLEE (1895)

Twas a Christmas evening,
The hour was about ten
When Stagalee shot Billy Lyons,
And landed in the Jefferson pen
O Lordy, po' Stagalee!

On Christmas evening in 1895, a black man named Lee Shelton, known as "Stack Lee," entered the Bill Curtis Saloon in St. Louis. While standing at the bar, he met someone he knew, William Lyons, who was there with a friend, Henry Crump. After a few drinks, Shelton and Lyons got into an argument, apparently about politics, trading blows by striking each other's hats. Shelton mashed Lyons's derby, Lyons asked for seventy-five cents, and when he didn't get it he grabbed Shelton's milk-white Stetson hat. Shelton demanded it back, whipped out his .44 caliber Smith & Wesson pistol, and smacked Lyons on the head with it. When Lyons reached for his knife, Shelton backed away and fired at him, saying, "I told you to give me my hat." Then he went home and went to bed. Lyons died later that night in the hospital. Shelton was arrested, tried, found guilty, and sent to the penitentiary. Released in 1911, he then assaulted another man, was recommitted, and died in the prison hospital in 1912. Even during his lifetime songs were being sung about him, and eventually more than 450 versions would be recorded.

Lee Shelton was born in Texas on March 15, 1865, just a few weeks before the Civil War ended. Not over five-foot-seven, he was a slender man of "mulatto complexion," weighing less than 120 pounds, with black eyes, black hair, and scars on his head, cheek, and shoulder. "His only claim to bulk," it was said, "was a size eleven shoe." His left eye was crossed, the first finger of his left hand was stiff, and he was a heavy drinker. He worked as a carriage driver, sometimes as a laborer, and he may have been a pimp. Known for his involvement in

Democratic Party politics, he also belonged to the Four Hundred Club, a society devoted to "the moral and physical culture of young colored men." He resided at 911 North Twelfth Street, and his moniker, "Stack Lee," apparently was derived from a riverboat on the Mississippi (or possibly from the name of the boat's captain).

Billy Lyons, thirty-one, was born in Missouri and resided in St. Louis for a number of years, where he worked as a levee hand, laborer, and watchman. Although unmarried, he had three small children: Florence, Marie, and Buddy. He resided with his stepbrother on Gay Street. His sister, Elizabeth, was married to Henry Bridgewater, a prominent saloon-owner. Dr. Otto Sutter, the physician who examined Lyons at the hospital—there were seven other homicides that evening, and the staff was working overtime—found that the bullet had entered his abdomen, perforated the transverse colon, fractured a rib, and passed through the left kidney, leaving little hope of recovery. He died at four in the morning.

> Billy Lyons told Stagolee,
> Please don't take my life
> I got three children
> And a dear little lovin' wife

Lyons's relatives—his sister, stepmother, and brother-in-law—were surely pleased that Campbell Orrick Bishop, a prominent attorney (later named to the circuit court bench) would prosecute Shelton.

On the night of the lethal argument, police officers Flanigan and Falvey were sent to the Bill Curtis Saloon. They found Lyons, partially conscious, about to be taken to the hospital. They tracked Shelton to his girlfriend's house on South Sixth Street and, finding him in a second-floor room, arrested him without resistance, took him to the Chestnut Street station, and locked him up. Then they returned to the house and asked the owner if she knew where the revolver was; she said it was in a drawer. "I went to the bureau drawer and took out a .44 Smith & Wesson, fully loaded, every chamber was full," the officer said. Shelton was held for trial pending the outcome of the coroner's inquest.

The inquest was held on December 27. A rowdy crowd of several hundred black men gathered outside, some blocking the hallway, others pushing into the coroner's office, threatening to lynch Shelton and requiring police reinforcements to protect him. Eyewitnesses who had been in the saloon described overhearing the argument between the two men, with Lyons asking "six bits" for his crushed hat and Shelton refusing while demanding that his own hat be returned: "Give me my hat," Shelton said; "If you don't give me my hat, I'll blow your brains out." "I ain't going to give you the hat, you can kill me," said Lyons, approaching Shelton and shouting: "You cock-eyed son-of-a-bitch, I am going to make you kill me." As most people in the saloon cleared out, Shelton fired at Lyons, then calmly picked up his hat and walked out the door, or so the witnesses claimed. The crowd in the coroner's office finally dispersed only when Shelton was charged with homicide.

Taken to the city jail to await trial, Shelton soon retained Nathaniel C. Dryden as counsel. A graduate of Amherst College who had practiced law in Missouri for twenty-five years, Dryden was known for his eloquence. His "very considerable power of rhetoric and pathetic and emotional appeal" had certainly been on display when he once described a little-known Democratic vice-presidential candidate as "a warrior greater than Hector and mightier than Ajax." But Dryden was equally well known for his addiction to morphine and alcohol, habits that gave him a reputation as "the wickedest man in Missouri." It was perhaps a mark of his skill as a lawyer that, notwithstanding his habit, he successfully convicted the first white man who was ever hanged for killing a black man in Missouri.

Shelton's trial did not begin until July 1896, but he did not remain in prison all that time. Once he was permitted to visit his mother when she was fatally ill, and later he attended her funeral. Although he was kept under guard, newspapers complained that he took advantage of his situation, that he "drank as often as he saw fit and spent some hours with his mistress." In January 1896 Shelton came up with $4,000 bail and was released pending the trial (later he would again be required to come up with bail). The newspapers reported that the large

Billy Lyons's death certificate, December 27, 1895.

sums Shelton somehow managed to raise caused heads to turn, since he was obliged to pay the bondsman for assuming the risk.

On July 13, 1896, Judge Thomas B. Harvey impaneled a jury in the criminal court of St. Louis. The testimony began on July 15 and took three days, with Dryden conceding that his client had shot Lyons but maintaining that he had done so in self-defense. The prosecutor, Campbell Orrick Bishop, was a well-known lawyer and author of a book on criminal evidence, of whom it was said "as an orator he has no superior in the courts of Missouri." Yet after deliberating for twenty-two hours, the jury returned with a split verdict: seven members favored second-degree murder, two voted for manslaughter, and three held out for acquittal. Shelton and Dryden may well have been pleased with the result. The judge discharged the jury and ordered a retrial.

But by October 1897, when the new trial was held, Shelton needed to find a new lawyer. Dryden's heavy drinking had damaged his health, and he died that August at age forty-six—after going on another drinking spree. So Shelton retained Charles P. Johnson, who had once served as the state's lieutenant governor, while Bishop again made the prosecution's case. The trial took place before James E. Withrow, a Civil War veteran, a circuit judge since 1888, who, according to a friendly biographer, was known for his "patient investigation of causes, his painstaking research, his fairness and courtesy." The jurors included a clerk, a carpenter, a janitor, a painter, and several woodworkers; the foreman was a contracting agent for a railroad company.

Bishop called Henry Crump—who had been with Lyons in the saloon—as a witness, but Crump testified that Lyons had drawn his knife before he was shot. Bishop quickly objected, claiming that Crump's testimony conflicted with an earlier statement. Shelton's lawyer replied that the earlier statement had not been made under oath: "When it is possible for sneaking detectives to pry around and obtain statements by fraud it is time for men to be careful." As he said this he folded a newspaper and shook it at Bishop, who, in response, advanced toward him, shouting, "What do you mean by your insulting insinuation?" Johnson coolly responded: "There is a sneaking, cowardly way of 'sweating' or examining prisoners and witnesses outside of courts. It is this system that I am complaining about." Bishop replied that the "insinuation is a dishonorable one" and then struck Johnson, who in turn grabbed Bishop, exclaiming, "There was nothing personal in my remark, but if you are looking for a personal encounter, I will give it to you." The judge called for order and reminded the defense attorney that "a man should tell the truth under any circumstances."

It took the jury only two hours (and three votes) to reach a guilty verdict. The judge sentenced "Stack Lee" Shelton to twenty-five years in the penitentiary, and he began serving his time on October 7, 1897.

> They had to try him twice,
> Because the jury could not agree
> Fin'ly he got twenty-five years,
> In the Penitentiary

Shelton was sent to the Missouri State Penitentiary, where, with time off for good behavior, he would remain for the next fourteen years.

Located in Jefferson City, 135 miles west of St. Louis, the penitentiary had opened in the 1830s and became the largest state prison in the country, with more than twenty-two hundred inmates, of whom about one-fourth were African Americans. Shelton was placed in a cell, probably built shortly after the Civil War, with windows "so narrow that they are hardly more than perpendicular slits in the walls. The cells measure 9 x 13 and 8 feet high and are equipped with very narrow double-deck bunks, straw ticks for mattresses, and blankets. . . . As the cell house has no plumbing, buckets are used for toilet purposes. In 146 cells over 800 men are housed which means five or six men to a cell. This cell house is used for negroes." A steel turret with loopholes for guns overlooked the mess hall. A report later condemned the institution for overcrowding, unsanitary standards, poor working conditions, inadequate hospital facilities, and the lack of an educational program.

Prisoners were put to work—making shoes, for example, or clothing or saddle trees—for private companies that provided the equipment inside the prison. The factory producing saddle trees—the bases on which saddles were built—was one of the largest in the world. Lee Shelton was one of the 250 convicts who worked for the A. Preismeyer Shoe Company. Since the prison charged companies only fifty cents a day per worker, businessmen made sizable profits by using convict labor and did so until 1917 when the state legislature discontinued the system because labor unions objected. Meanwhile, the prison spent next to nothing to sustain the inmates: when Shelton entered the penitentiary, it cost eleven cents a day to feed and house each convict. Inmates found the food disgusting: "The oatmeal and fruit were infested with worms, the macaroni filled with bugs, the beans inhabited by weevils, and the corn meal supported a thriving population of meal-worms."

Prisoners who broke the rules—by speaking in their cells, while working, or when eating—or who failed to complete their daily allotted work would be punished by "whipping with a common riding cowhide" or by being confined in a pitch-black cell and given only bread and water. Although floggings had supposedly been done away with by the warden, James I. Pace, in 1894, Shelton, like other prisoners, was nevertheless whipped on several occasions: he was given five stripes—that is, lashes—for loafing in the yard in March 1899; eight stripes for shooting craps in June 1899; and ten stripes for stealing a ham from the kitchen in July 1902. In September 1905 he was placed in solitary confinement for being out of his cell and for playing dice at night.

Within two years of his incarceration, 139 St. Louis residents, some of them probably Shelton's friends or acquaintances, petitioned the governor to pardon or parole him. They argued that Lyons had been a dangerous fellow, that Shelton had acted in self-defense, and that he had been punished enough. Another petition for clemency came from twenty-nine prominent citizens, among them several attorneys and ten of the twelve jurors who had found Shelton guilty at the second trial. In 1899 even the jury foreman, Andrew J. Bromwell, wrote to the governor: "I never have believed the verdict a just one,—did not think so at the time, and still of the opinion that a verdict of acquittal should have been given instead. Lyons the man who was killed was proven to be a very bad negro and was going at Shelton with his hand in his pockets in a threatening manner when the shot was fired. . . . I firmly believe that Shelton was fully justified for shooting Lyons under the circumstances, and it has been a question in my mind ever since the trial as to whether Lyons died from the effects of the shot, or from the operation by unskilled surgeons at the hospital."

There were others, however, who wanted to see Shelton remain behind bars—including Henry Bridgewater, and Billy Lyons's mother and sister, Elizabeth—and they wrote to the governor urging him to ignore the clemency petitions. "I am the sister of William Lyons who was so brutally murdered by Lee Shelton, alias Stack Lee, and having heard that steps have been taken to have him pardoned . . . hope and pray that you will never agree to let a man who never worked a day or earned an honest dollar be turned out to meet us face to face. . . . If justice had been done he would have been hung. Just think he has not served half his term." The governor did not grant a pardon, and in 1901, when it again seemed one might be in the offing, Lyons's sister wrote yet another letter to the governor: "My brother had nothing to protect himself with, and this man shot him in cold blood."

Ultimately even Judge James E. Withrow, who had presided at Shelton's trial, joined the chorus of those favoring clemency. In June 1901, noting that Crump's testimony at the trial had been inconsistent, the judge pointed out that Shelton had already been incarcerated for several years: "Under the circumstances I most respectfully join with numerous others, in recommending at least a commutation of his sentence. It seems to me that an actual imprisonment of seven or eight years in this case would satisfy the ends of justice." Governor Dockery also received a petition signed by ten Missouri senators and representatives urging a pardon, claiming that Shelton had acted in self-defense, and branding Lyons a "desperate character." The petition was devised by John W. Crabelle, an attorney, who in 1902 also urged the governor—unsuccessfully—to meet with Nat Shelton, Lee's father.

As the years went by, the opposition to clemency began to wane, especially after the death of Henry Bridgewater in April 1904. Pleas for leniency continued to be sent to the governor, including one, on December 28, 1905, from James L. Dawson, the city jailer of St. Louis, who claimed that it was not Shelton but Lyons—a "quarrelsome and at times dangerous" fellow when he was intoxicated—who had provoked the fight. The area in which the crime was committed, Dawson said, "was by no means a desirable location for even half decent people to live in and was the hang out of a low order of bawds, colored and white, also many crap shooters. . . . Their ivironments [sic] and avocation was bad indeed and their morals if possible were worse."

Even as appeals on Shelton's behalf were being made, songs about him had begun to circulate. As early as 1897 a song titled "Stack-a-Lee" was performed in Kansas City, and another version was collected in Cripple Creek, Colorado, a few years later. In 1903 a version heard in Memphis contained the lines

> When Stackerlee and Billy Lyons
> Sat down to that game of cards,
> If Billy'd known like bad Stack,
> He'd have made it up with his God
> Cause he laid poor Billy's body down, bad Stackerlee

The song described how, as news of the shooting spread, "all the gang came to see / what cop would have the nerve to pinch bad Stackerlee." John Lomax in 1910 and Howard Odum in 1911 also published lyrics that they had either heard or been sent. A woman in Texas sent Lomax a version in which Stagalee declared:

> "Jailer, O Jailer, I jest can't sleep,
> For the ghost of Billy Lyons
> Round my bed does mourn and weep"
> O Lordy, po' Stagalee!

Whether Lee Shelton heard any of these early versions of the song remains unknown. In any event, his circumstances were deteriorating. In April 1909 he was diagnosed with tuberculosis, and efforts were made to obtain a pardon from the newly elected Republican governor, Herbert S. Hadley. A sympathetic African American politician offered to help Shelton land a job in the railroad yards, and obtained a recommendation from the Preismeyer Shoe Company stating that he had aided the prison authorities "in detecting systematic theft." Even his old foe, Campbell Orrick Bishop, wrote to the governor stating he would have liked to see Shelton sentenced to ten, not twenty-five years, noting, for good measure, that he had recently visited Shelton in prison and "he impressed me pleasantly." On November 25, 1909, to mark Thanksgiving, Hadley granted Shelton a pardon on condition that he obey the law and find work "at some honorable employment."

But that was more easily said than done. In January 1911 Shelton was arrested for breaking into a man's home, beating him with a revolver, fracturing his skull, and stealing $140. Since he was on parole, no trial was held. Instead he was returned to the penitentiary early in May to complete his original sentence. By January 1912, however, his tuberculosis had worsened, so much so that the prison physician reported that he "is getting pretty low and I fear he cannot live much longer. Is bedfast practically all the time now, and extremely emaciated. Is in the last stages, one lung is solid and useless." As the illness progressed, Shelton wasted away, and finally, in February 1912, he obtained a parole based on his terminal condition. He was supposed to return to St. Louis, but he never got there. He died in the prison hospital on March 11, 1912, and was buried a week later in St. Louis.

Although a few songs had been written about Shelton during his lifetime, the wide use of phonographs in the 1920s inspired many more recordings about him. Some of the versions—by Fred Waring's Pennsylvanians (1923) and Duke Ellington's Washingtonians (1927)—were instrumentals. Others, like Ma Rainey's (1926), were generic blues having little or no relationship to the actual events. But Little Harvey Hull and Long Cleve Reed made one of the earliest recordings based on the murder of Billy Lyons. Known as the "Down Home Boys"—Hull came from Mississippi, Reed from Alabama—they cut "Original Stack O'Lee Blues" in 1927:

> Standing on the corner,
> Well I didn't mean no harm
> Well a policeman caught me,
> Well he grabbed me by my arm
> And it's old Stack O'Lee

In their version, however, the murder took place in Chicago, and Lyons was a policeman, presumably white, who tried to arrest Stack O'Lee on a trumped-up charge.

In 1928 Mississippi John Hurt recorded his classic and often-imitated version of the song. It began

> Police, officers, how can it be
> You can arrest everybody
> But cruel Stagolee
> That bad man! O, cruel Stagolee!

Mississippi John Hurt.

As Cecil Brown points out in *Stagolee Shot Billy*, "The image of a white police-man afraid of arresting this black man gives power to the hero, making him bigger and bolder than he was in reality."

> Standing on the gallows, head way up high
> Twelve o'clock they killed him
> They were all glad to see him die
> Oh that bad man, O cruel Stagolee.

The song, Brown says, paints "an indelible image of a man meeting his end with dignity."

Like other men who did wrong, Lee Shelton—"Stagolee"—lived on, and will certainly always live on, in song. True, he is usually portrayed as a "bad man," as a murderer, a gambler, and a pimp. But with time the image of Stagolee was subtly altered. Despite his wrongdoing, for many he came to symbolize strength, a rebellious spirit, and even racial pride. As George M. Eberhart said, "he was transformed into the archetypal bad man, a figure to be feared as well as respected, an antihero whose deeds are cheered vicariously but who ultimately is brought down by the iron fist of the law." Even in death, at least in the popular imagination, he was never wholly vanquished:

> Stagolee he went down to the devil
> And he leaned up on his shelf
> He said, "Come out of here, Mr. Devil
> I'm gonna rule hell by myself."

CHAPTER 4

FRANKIE AND JOHNNY (1899)

Frankie and Johnny were lovers,
Oh lordy, how they could love
Swore to be true to each other,
Just as true as the stars above
He was her man, but he done her wrong

At three o'clock in the morning of October 15, 1899, Frankie Baker got into an argument with her boyfriend, Allen Britt. She was twenty-three, and he was seventeen. He threw a lamp at her, took out his knife, and, she later said, "started to cut me." She was in bed, but she reached for her pistol and shot him. Mortally wounded, he somehow managed to get to his mother's apartment a short distance away and was taken to the city hospital, where he later died. Accused of murder, Frankie stood trial in St. Louis but pleaded self-defense and was acquitted. Soon thereafter, a song was written about the event, and over the years Allen's name was turned into "Johnny." "Frankie and Johnny" became a popular song, and countless versions were eventually recorded. The incident would also find its way into books, plays, radio dramas, and motion pictures.

Frankie was born in St. Louis on May 30, 1876, the only daughter of Cedric and Margaret Baker, who also had three sons, Charles, Arthur, and James. A slender girl, she was just over five feet. When she was old enough to be on her own, she moved to Targee Street, a neighborhood known for its "quiet, respectable homes of substantial Negro folks." A friend described her as a "nice, Christian woman . . . a clean girl who worked at . . . scrubbing, cleaning, washing and ironing." But once her name made the newspapers, she was said to be "an ebony-hued cakewalker" who draped herself in silks and flashed diamonds "as big as hens' eggs." Later she claimed that when she was sixteen or seventeen, she had been with a man when a "perfumed colored girl broke in on us in the parlor of my home and attacked me" with a knife. Her face was permanently scarred, a "grim reminder of her first experience in the realm of love."

Her boyfriend, Allen (sometimes called "Albert") Britt, was born in Kentucky in 1882 and later moved to St. Louis with his parents. His father, George Britt, who had once been a slave in Tennessee and then became a freight handler on a railroad, moved his family—Allen was his only child—to Targee Street, not far from Frankie Baker. His father said that Allen attended Sunday school at a Baptist church: "Leastwise, he tole me and his mother he did. We was strict with that boy. No, suh, we didn't 'low him to hang 'round no pool halls. He used to stay out all night once in a while. Always said he was a-stayin' with some other schoolboys. He quit school when he was in the sixth grade and went to work." Allen was someone "all the girls looked for," and it appears that Frankie gave him money and clothing—mirror-toed shoes, peg-topped trousers, fancy waistcoats, gaudy neckties—and who knows what else.

> Frankie and Johnnie went walking,
> John in his brand new suit
> Then, "oh good Lawd," says Frankie,
> "Don't my Johnnie look real cute!"
> He was her man, but he done her wrong

Britt played the piano, but he also played the field. He had been to a cakewalk at a dance hall with eighteen-year-old Alice Pryor, and, it appears, they had won a prize. On the night of October 14 he was performing at the Phoenix Hotel, and Frankie went to hear him. Apparently, she also saw him in the hall making love to that same Alice Pryor (who would come to be known in the song as "Nellie Bly"). Frankie and Britt began to argue. She asked him to come home with her, he refused, and so she went home alone. Later, around three o'clock that night, Britt entered Frankie's apartment, and they continued to argue.

Years later, Frankie vividly recalled the night. "I jumped up out of bed and says, 'What's the matter with you, Al?' and he says, 'What the hell are you doing in this bed?'" She replied that she was sick, whereupon Britt cursed and then attacked her. She said, "I'm the boss here. I pay the rent and I have to protect myself." Frankie reported that, as he wielded his knife, "I was standing here. Pillow lays this way. Just run my hand under the pillow and shot him. Didn't shoot but one time, standing by the bed." "The bullet entered Britt's abdomen," the *St. Louis Globe-Democrat* reported, "penetrating the intestines. The woman escaped after the shooting." But Frankie did not remain at large for long. Britt, who had been taken to the hospital, presumably gave her name to the police. She was brought to his room so he could identify her, and then she was arrested. She

Frankie Baker in the 1890s. Courtesy of the *St. Louis Post-Dispatch*.

later explained: "I felt terrible, of course, but I simply had protected myself. I had nothing to cry about. I didn't feel smart about it, either. I didn't go to his funeral because I couldn't. I was in jail."

The jail in which she was held was known as the Four Courts. "A magnificent building," "grand and imposing," it housed the city courts, the grand jury rooms, the city marshal, the sheriff, and the offices of the prosecuting attorneys. Police headquarters were there, too, and so were the police stables, the dead animal contractor's office, the coroner's office, the morgue—and, of course, the jail, which could hold 325 prisoners and was built in a circular form with a large court to afford the prisoners ample room for exercise. There were special rooms of detention for women on the third floor. The gallows were located in an open yard between the jail and the morgue.

Although a coroner's jury found that Frankie had acted in self-defense, and the slaying therefore could be considered justifiable homicide, she nevertheless went to trial on November 13, 1899, in the court of criminal correction. The judge, Willis Henry Clark, was a Republican who had practiced law for ten years before his appointment to the bench. Frankie pleaded self-defense, claiming, truthfully, that Albert had attacked her with a knife. "You know, I was afraid of Albert," she recalled. "He beat me unmercifully a few nights before the big blow-off. My eye was festering and sore from that lacin' when I went before Judge Clark. He noticed it, too." The judge not only acquitted her, but also apparently returned her gun. "Don't know what I did with it," she said. "Guess I pawned it or gave it away. Everybody carried a gun in those days."

Frankie, however, did not remain in St. Louis for long. She left in 1901, she later said, "to get away from the constant annoyance and humiliation." First she went to Omaha, Nebraska, but there, too, "I just couldn't get away from it. . . . It was humiliating and harrying. I just got sick and tired of it. I heard it on the street and I heard it on the phonograph and I heard it on the radio." So, after visiting Portland, Oregon, in 1913, she decided to settle there, "to seek peace and happiness." She had read about the roses in the city, she said, and "somehow they meant peace to me." By the mid-1920s, after some early run-ins with the law, she opened a shoeshine parlor and then began working as a chambermaid at a hotel. Eventually, however, she became ill, required surgery, and by 1935, no longer able to work, lived by herself. Autograph seekers occasionally bothered her, she said, when all she wanted was "an opportunity to live like an ordinary human being. I know I'm black, but even so I have my rights."

By then, many versions of the song had been published and recorded. Within days of Albert's death, it seemed that a St. Louis singer and pianist, Bill Dooley, was performing "Frankie Killed Allen." One of the earliest published versions appeared in 1912, with "Johnny" used in place of "Albert"—probably in deference to Britt's family, or else to avoid copyright infringement issues. The lyrics were attributed to Ren Shields and the music to the Leighton Brothers:

> Frankie and Johnny were sweethearts,
> They had a quarrel one day
> Johnny he vowed that he would leave her,
> Said he was goin' away
> He's never comin' home
> He's goin' away to roam

Recordings also began to appear in the early 1920s, by Al Bernard (who used Shields's lyrics), by Frank Crumit, and by Ernest Thompson. Within a decade, more than twenty-five versions had been issued.

One of them, recorded by Mississippi John Hurt, later became very well known. In February 1928, Okeh Records paid his way from Avalon, Mississippi, to Memphis, where, accompanying himself on the guitar, he recorded "Frankie" along with several other songs, receiving twenty dollars for each. The company pressed seven thousand copies of "Frankie" and released it that spring. (The flip side was "Nobody's Dirty Business.") Hurt's version, like nearly all the others, told of Frankie paying "one hundred dollars for Albert's suit of clothes," hearing from the bartender that Albert had left "with a girl you call Alice Frye," peeking through "one of the keyholes" and spying "Albert in Alice's arm," and shooting him "three or four times." Love, betrayal, murder, and revenge—even, in the end, redemption, were all themes:

> Frankie and the judge walked down on the stand,
> Walked out side to side
> The judge says to Frankie,
> "You're gonna be justified
> For killing a man and he done you wrong"

The judge was telling Frankie that she would be subjected to justice for killing Albert, not that she was justified and would be exonerated.

In 1929, several other singers, some of them black, others white, recorded versions of the song. The Mississippi bluesman Charley Patton offered his rendition of a contrite Frankie:

> Well Frankie went down to the courthouse,
> To hear little Albert tried
> Oh, Albert was convicted,
> Frankie hung her head and cried
> "Say, he was my man but he done me wrong"

> Well Frankie went to the cemetery,
> Fell down on her knees
> "Oh Lord, will you forgive me,
> And give my poor heart ease?
> Say, you was my man but you done me wrong"

Jimmie Rodgers also sang a version, which adopted a very different tone and used a slightly different refrain after each verse, moving from Frankie's belief that "he's my man, he wouldn't do me wrong," to "he was my man but he done me wrong," and, ultimately, to "I shot my man, he was doing me wrong":

> Frankie said to the warden,
> What are they going to do?
> The warden, he said to Frankie,
> It's the electric chair for you
> 'Cause you shot your man, he was doing you wrong

Charley Patton, ca. 1929.

Soon after these recordings appeared, John Huston wrote a marionette play about the story. The son of a well-known actor, Huston had been an amateur boxer, a Mexican cavalryman, a painter, and a journalist before finally deciding on a career as a filmmaker (he later directed *The Maltese Falcon* and *The Treasure of the Sierra Madre*). In 1930, at twenty-four, he published *Frankie and Johnny*, after friends in St. Louis had put him in touch with Frankie Baker herself. In the play—the setting is given correctly, 212 Targee Street in the "colored section" of St. Louis, as is the date, October 15, 1899—Johnny has died from knife wounds, and Frankie is on the scaffold about to be hanged. Asked if she has any last words, she relates what happened, telling how she used her "big forty-four": "Ye ain't ditchin' me, Johnny?" she asked, and Johnny replied; "Aye, I'm a-lightin' out for good." Someone explains: "She's drilled him clean. Ye can see the starlight through him." In an epilogue, Huston offered many variations of the song.

In 1936, Thomas Hart Benton, one of the best-known American artists, depicted the story on a wall of the Missouri State Capitol in Jefferson City as part of *A Social History of the State of Missouri*. The mural scene, set in a barroom, shows Frankie shooting Johnny as he tries to avoid the attack. His hat has fallen to the floor. The other customers are fleeing, as Johnny crashes into a table and chair. Apparently some legislators wanted to paint over the mural, regarding it as too controversial, but their effort was defeated. Benton, a native Missourian, who also used themes from other folk songs, defended his portrayal of Frankie and Johnny, stating: "Anyhow the story is a part of Missouri mythology like the Jesse James and Huck Finn stories."

In June 1938, "Frankie and Johnny" was performed as a ballet in the Great Northern Theater in Chicago, as part of a program sponsored by the Works Progress Administration's Federal Dance Project. Choreographed by Ruth Page and Bentley Stone, it portrayed Frankie as a woman who was wronged, who stood up for herself and was vindicated. Page commissioned twenty-five-year-old Jerome Moross to compose the music and the libretto, and three women acted as a latter-day Greek chorus, commenting on the action and playing tambourine, bass drum, and cymbals. In the production, Frankie tried to hang herself from a lamppost but was saved by Nellie Bly, only in the end to be left alone by Johnny's coffin. Critics hailed the ballet as "arresting" and "vital."

Having made its way onto records, on the stage, on a mural, and as a dance, the story eventually turned up in motion pictures. The actress Mae West had heard the song "Frankie and Johnny," and in 1933 she performed it in the Republic Pictures release *She Done Him Wrong*. In fact, it became one of her trademarks. In the film, she played Lady "Diamond" Lou, a role that added to her reputation for sexual innuendo and double entendres. (West also arranged for a black actress to appear in the film, as part of her effort to combat racial discrimination in the industry.) Singing many of the usual verses to the song, she had Frankie toting her gun and seeing Johnny lying on the floor, where he pleaded,

> "Turn me over, Frankie,
> Turn me over slow
> Turn me over on my right side, Frankie,
> Why did you shoot so low?
> I was your man, and I done you wrong"

In 1936, Republic Pictures tried again, this time with a film entitled *Frankie and Johnnie*, starring Helen Morgan, who had recorded the song years earlier but did not sing it in the movie, and an all-white cast.

It was the movie with Mae West that naturally attracted the largest audience. Frankie Baker had seen it in Portland and believed that it depicted her in a demeaning way—to the extent that even strangers, passing her house, were starting to stare at her. "I'm so tired of it all, I don't even answer any more," she told a reporter. In April 1938 she filed a lawsuit, the first of several, against Republic Pictures, asking for damages amounting to $200,000, contending the character played by Helen Morgan in the 1936 film was based on herself, and that the film depicted her as a "woman of unchaste character, a harlot, an adulteress, a person of lewd character, and a murderess," invaded her privacy, and held her up to "ridicule, scorn and contempt."

The pretrial proceedings began in October 1939. One of Frankie's first witnesses was Richard Clay, a local movie producer, who said that his friend, Albert Britt, had "a roving eye for the girls, but he didn't live up to his song and movie reputation either." Clay testified that Frankie was a good girl, "a woman just like the rest of them," who resided in a decent, respectable neighborhood. Under cross-examination, when asked if Frankie had behaved like a lady, he simply said Frankie was Albert's "main girl." He also said Benton's painting was not accurate, since Frankie had shot Albert in her bedroom, not in a barroom.

The next witness, Tillie Griffin, was an assistant pastor of the Weatherford Christian Spiritual Temple in St. Louis. She testified that Frankie had a good reputation "and lived with her younger brother and another girl friend named Pansy." Britt was a "fine looking, dark-skinned boy," she said, not a drinker, but rather someone "all the girls looked for." The song had become popular shortly after the shooting, but when Britt's family "raised a racket," his name was changed to "Johnny." Frankie, she said, was brokenhearted after the slaying: she "wept over it and grieved about it. I don't think she ever got over it."

Eventually, Allen Britt's aged father, George, took the stand. He testified for an hour, describing his son's childhood and admitting that Frankie was a "right nice-lookin' woman," who, he believed, was thirty or thirty-five years old in 1899—old enough, that is, to be Allen's mother. When asked, "Did Frankie pay $100 for making Albert's clothes?" he replied: "Al never wore no such stuff as that. His mother bought his clothes and they was showed to me. His suits cost about $7 or $8 the size he was." When asked if Allen wore a diamond ring, his father said: "No sir. He didn't even have a brass ring, let alone a diamond one. And he didn't have a walking stick." His son's funeral had been well attended, he said, but there were no "milk-white horses," as the song had it.

The trial itself finally got under way on February 17, 1942, in the Civil Division of the St. Louis Circuit Court. The judge was William H. Killoren, and the jury consisted of "clerks, accountants and factory employees." Joseph McLemore represented Frankie, and Hugo Monnig the film company. (When Frankie arrived, she parried the reporters' questions. "Al was a conceited piano player, not a sporting man," she said. Had she bought him hundred-dollar suits? "Not necessarily." What had happened to Alice Pryor? "I heard she passed out," she said.) McLemore called as an expert witness Nathan Ben Young, a black attorney and newspaper publisher, who testified about the song, saying he was convinced that it was written by Bill Dooley, who also wrote "the topical, gay and ribald songs which emanated from the Negro quarter." The song became popular, he said, after Frankie shot Britt.

On February 20, 1942, Sigmund Spaeth took the stand for the defense. A Princeton-trained musicologist and the author of many books, he had served as the host of a popular radio program, *The Tune Detective*. He testified that he had first heard *Frankie and Johnny* in 1901 when he was a college student. "I'm glad to see Frankie is such a nice woman," he said: "I always thought she should have been punished severely." He testified for nearly two days—although, as Nathan Young saw it, "Spaeth didn't testify, he lectured. He knew everything. . . . Spaeth just took over the trial" and talked "incessantly." One of the jurors, however, later commented that Spaeth seemed "sharp," while Frankie, by contrast, made a poor impression, her memory weak, and unable to recall dates.

Frankie's lawyer decided to have the jury view the 1936 Republic Pictures film, with its white cast, a move that may have backfired by making it difficult for the jurors to identify with a black woman. Other observers believed that the lack of evidence supporting Frankie's claim was key to the jury's verdict. In his summation, Frankie's lawyer, McLemore, called the case "one of the most picturesque in the history of American law suits," and predicted that the jury's verdict would be quoted "a thousand times by authorities and writers." Arguing on behalf of the motion picture company, Hugo Monnig pointed out that the film depicted an earlier time, the 1870s, that all the characters in it were white, and that the setting did not resemble Targee Street. He added: "If you give her a verdict, she will have a claim against everybody who ever sang the song. Send her back to Portland, Oregon, and her shoeshine business; for an honest shine, let her have an honest dime. Don't make her a rich woman because forty years ago she shot a little colored boy here in St. Louis." The ballad, he concluded, had become "the common possession of the people of America."

In the end, Frankie lost the case, and even had to pay $250 in court costs. Although the song "Frankie and Johnny" had become well-known, she felt forgotten. "It's funny," she commented, "but most people think of me as being dead a good many years." She returned to Portland, where she eked out a living, finally having to rely on relief. She became the first lifetime member of the city's Urban League. When interviewed, as she occasionally was, she appeared "a little infirm of tooth and eye, and a little old-fashioned in her ways." She sometimes wandered around with a shopping bag, or, when the weather was bad, sat peering out her window. She usually wore a ragged gray sweater and a cap fashioned from an old stocking. In 1950 she was sent to a hospital at Pendleton, Oregon, where she was examined for mental illness. Then she lost her home, and went to the Multnomah County Home and Farm for the mentally disturbed. Officials reported that she had a persecution complex, was a danger to others, and sometimes "frightened and attacked persons at the farm." Finally she had to be hospitalized. Frankie Baker passed away on January 6, 1952, and was buried in Los Angeles.

"I'm the one they wrote that song about," Frankie once said. "They are all making plenty of money out of that song and nobody ever gave me a nickel." True enough, a great many others—artists and writers, musicians and choreographers, actors and actresses—had profited from a heartbreaking event: a teenage boy's life lost and a young woman's devastated. More than a century has passed since Frankie Baker spied Allen Britt making love to Alice Pryor, began arguing with him, and, fearing for her life, shot him, yet the tragedy still remains compelling:

> Frankie heard a rumbling,
> away down in the ground
> Maybe it was Albert,
> where she had shot him down
> He was her man, but he done her wrong.

Lying Cold on the Ground

CHAPTER 5

OMIE WISE (1807)

I'll tell you a story
About poor Omie Wise
How she was deluded
By John Lewis's lies

In March 1807, during Thomas Jefferson's second term as president, a brutal crime was committed in Randolph County, North Carolina. A young man named Jonathan Lewis murdered Naomi Wise—whom he had gotten pregnant—by drowning her in Deep River in the north central part of the state. A few years later, Mary Woody, who was only a child at the time, wrote a long poem, "A True Account of Nayomy Wise," which described the crime. A much longer account, "Life of Naomi Wise: True Story of a Beautiful Girl," was written in 1851 by Braxton Craven, a twenty-nine-year-old Methodist minister who later became president of Trinity College. "Omie Wise," a song written about the slaying, is one of the oldest American murder ballads.

Woody's poem, nearly two hundred lines long, provided a reasonably accurate if somewhat embellished version of the event on that early spring evening. She correctly observed that Naomi Wise had already borne two children out of wedlock before becoming "defiled" by Jonathan Lewis, a man who "held himself of high degree / But too fond of Carnality." She said Naomi was pleased to have again become pregnant, and far from keeping her condition secret boasted of it to friends, which, of course, "inraged Lewis." So he threatened her:

He told her then he thought he might
Apoint to meet next Sunday night
And Charged her that She might conceal
The matter unto none reveal

"Where Naomi Wise was drowned," Naomi Falls, North Carolina. Randolph County Historical Photographs, Randolph County Public Library, Randolph Room.

But she disregarded his threat, "Seemd not afraid," and even told a friend about the planned tryst. Although warned that "He out of fury rage and spite / To her some private mischief might," Naomi paid no heed and went to her doom. Neighbors found her body the next day, began a search, soon took Lewis prisoner and "brought him there firmly bound / Unto the place Where She was drownd." Lewis was asked to touch the corpse, "And So he did We understand / With a pale face and a trimbling hand." After a coroner's jury tried Lewis and found him guilty, "Neomy then was Carried by / Said Lewis Who had made her die."

Woody's poem did not come to light until 1952, when it was donated to the UCLA library. Meanwhile, a far longer but less accurate account came from Craven, a native of Randolph County, whose version of the story appeared in the January and February 1851 editions of *Evergreen*, and was later reprinted as a twenty-seven-page pamphlet. To be sure, in telling the tale of the murder, Craven offered some accurate information about the families involved, but most of what he reported—for example, an extended dialogue between Jonathan and Naomi on the day he killed her—is fabrication. Craven made Naomi, whose "young and guileless heart beat with new and higher life," into a paragon of Victorian virtue, and turned Jonathan into "a hyena, skulking about the pathway of life, ready alike to kill the living or to tear the dead from their graves." He placed most of the blame for Lewis's deed on his mother—as Craven put it, "an evil genius crossed the path of Lewis in the shape of his mother"—whose "ambitions and avarice" made her want her son to forsake Naomi and marry instead Hettie Elliott, his employer's sister.

Although Craven described Naomi Wise as "a lovely girl, just blooming in all the attractiveness of nineteen," whatever her age may have been it assuredly was not nineteen. Before she became pregnant in 1807, she had already given birth to two children: a boy named Henry who was four years old, and a daughter, Nancy, who was nine. So even had her daughter been born when Naomi was a teenager, she would have been, at the time of her death, in her mid-to-late twenties, probably older than Jonathan Lewis, who was twenty-four. Although there is no record that she was ever married, "Bastardy Bonds" for Nancy and Henry are on file in the North Carolina State Archives. In accordance with the child-support laws of the time, Naomi had charged each father with "begetting a child on her body," and each posted a bond insuring that the county would never have to pay to support the children.

Braxton Craven, president of Trinity College. Duke University Archives.

Naomi Wise was an orphan, indentured as a child and taken in by William and Mary Adams. She worked around the house, cooking, cleaning, and caring for the children—the Adamses', presumably, as well as her own. It seems that the family treated her well, dressed her nicely, and allowed her the use of a horse so she could ride to church on Sunday. The family made its home in Randolph County, just to the south of Guilford County where Jonathan Lewis resided with his parents, Richard and Lydia, and his brothers. Jonathan, born in 1783, worked as a store clerk in the town of Asheboro. He boarded at the store, owned by Benjamin Elliott, and rode home, a distance of about fifteen miles, to be with his family on weekends. On his journey each week, Jonathan passed the Adams house and so became acquainted with Naomi Wise.

> "So jump you up, Omie,
> And away we will ride
> To yonder fair country
> And I'll make you my bride"

It seems probable, although there is no way to know for sure, that Naomi, pregnant now for a third time, wanted Jonathan to marry her, and that he played along, planning all the while to murder her. So one evening, he arranged to take her to the Adamses' spring, not far from where she lived. Since she did not have a horse, she must have mounted behind him on his, and ridden off together. Exactly what passed between them cannot be known but can readily be imagined. Tradition holds that he first gave her time to "prepare herself to meet her god," before he pulled her long skirts above her head and forced her underwater, holding her there until she stopped breathing. Naomi must have screamed, since Ann Davis, who lived nearby, heard the commotion and sent her sons to see what was happening. They heard a thrashing about in the water and called out, but it was nighttime and too dark to see anything, so they returned home.

> The wretch then did choke her
> As we understand
> And threw her in the river
> Below the mill dam

The next day, Mary Adams, having spent a sleepless night, went with her husband to search for Naomi. They found her empty pail, and footprints, and the horse's hoofprints. So Mr. Adams summoned some farmers, and they followed the tracks to the banks of Deep River, and there they found Naomi's body, soaked, rumpled, half floating on a bed of weeds. There were marks on her neck where she had been strangled, and it was apparent she was pregnant. The coroner was summoned and announced, "Drowning by violence."

The authorities, along with some neighbors, first went to Lewis's home in Guilford County, where he lived with his parents (on Polecat Creek!) but failed to find him there or at Benjamin Elliott's store in Asheboro. According to one version of events, a woman reported that he had come to her door early in the morning. Sheriff Isaac Lane deputized Robert Murdock to find him, and the deputy, after making inquiries, located Lewis, who was described as "reserved, downcast, and restless," brought him to the riverbank where Naomi's body still lay, and placed him under arrest.

> They sent for John Lewis
> To come to that place
> They set her up before him
> So he could see her face

The evidence, although circumstantial, seemed sufficient to take Lewis to Asheboro and lock him up. As Craven reported: "The hoof prints from the stump in the river exactly fitted his horse; hairs upon the skirt on which she rode were found to fit in color; a small piece, torn from Lewis' accouterment, fitted both rent and texture; his absence from Ashboro, and many other minuter circumstances, all conspired to the same point." Fearing that a lynch mob might abduct Lewis, county officials appointed his employer, Elliott, to supervise a unit of men to protect him.

A grand jury in Randolph County indicted Lewis for murder "committed on a certain Omi Wise, found dead in the Deep River." Witnesses were summoned to appear at the trial scheduled for late October. At the pretrial hearing, Mary Adams and several other people came forward to implicate Lewis. Ann Davis testified that she had heard a shrieking sound coming from the river, "as if Some Woman might be dying." Despite the posting of members of the militia to guard the jail, shortly before the trial was to begin, Lewis, who had languished in prison for nearly eight months, managed to break out.

Blame was placed on "a shackley frame jail from which his escape could easily be made, however, considering the heavy guard placed by Col. Elliott it is easy to believe that friends of the accused Lewis aided in his escape." One of those friends was Daniel Dawson, who had been standing guard several weeks but now provided Lewis with "one knife and one Sword to the intent and purpose that . . . [he] should thereby be enabled to make his Escape." In addition, Sheriff Isaac Lane, of all people, and four other men were blamed for aiding the escape but were later granted clemency.

For four years, Jonathan Lewis remained at large. He moved west, to parts unknown, perhaps to Ohio, finally settling in Indiana, where it appears some of his relatives also made their homes. In March 1811 he married Sarah McCain, and the couple later had children, a girl and a boy. In the fall of that year, according to Braxton Craven (who may or may not have gotten the story exactly right), Lewis was present when someone sang the song about Naomi Wise "who was sadly deceived by Lewis's lies." His agitation on hearing it aroused the suspicion of someone who wrote to Sheriff Lane, and a three-member search party, led by Lane, was sent to Indiana to track him down.

They found him one evening attending a dance. As Craven described it: "His hair was long, bushy and matted as if it had never known the virtue of a comb; his eyebrows were dark and heavy; his step was decided and firm; he wore a belted hunting shirt, in the band of which hung a long, double-edged hunting knife, and under its folds were plainly visible two heavy pistols." Although "aware of their peril," the search party tried to seize him; he resisted and would have escaped had the villagers not overpowered him. On the trip back to North Carolina, Lewis appeared so tractable that his bonds were loosened, whereupon he made a run for it, finally being overpowered just before he reached a "dense thicket" that could have enabled him to make his getaway.

In the fall of 1811, Lewis was locked in jail in Randolph County, and he remained there for a year. It was not until October 1812 that friends could come up with the requisite bail of 500 pounds. Lewis finally stood trial in October 1813, but after six years many witnesses were no longer available. He was either acquitted of the murder charge or the charge was dropped—the evidence being considered only circumstantial—but he was convicted of "breaking the Jail & rescuing himself" and was sentenced to serve thirty days and pay a fine of ten pounds. Penniless, he had to spend more than an additional two weeks in his cell. On November 20, 1813, having taken an oath of insolvency—Lewis swore, "I have not the worth of Forty Shillings Sterling money . . . in any worldly substance"—he was relieved of his debt and emerged from jail a free man. Further efforts to convict him of the murder of Naomi Wise proved unavailing. He headed west to rejoin his wife and children, who by then had moved to Kentucky.

Although still a relatively young man, Jonathan Lewis was running out of time. In 1817 he took ill, and if Craven can be believed, "for two days the death rattle had been in his throat, and yet he retained his reason and his speech." In his final moments, according to Craven, Lewis asked family members to leave his room so he could be alone with his father, and he made his deathbed confession: "He declared that while in prison Naomi was ever before him, his sleep was broken by her cries for mercy, and in the dim, twilight hour her shadowy form was ever before him, holding up her imploring hands." And so Jonathan Lewis passed away, not yet thirty-five years of age.

Deep River now runs by the town of Randleman, North Carolina, where one can find streets, bridges, churches, mills, and a factory named for Naomi Wise. There is a Naomi Falls, a Naomi Bridge, a Naomi Ford, a Naomi Street, and there was once a Naomi Methodist Church. A cotton mill built at the Old Ford of the river was named the Naomi Falls Manufacturing Company. At its completion in 1880, the mill was dedicated to the service of God by—of all people!—Reverend Braxton Craven, "and is believed to be the only case in history where such a dedication has taken place." The name Naomi Wise itself became so popular that even West Virginia laid claim to it, erecting a gravestone on top of Pheasant Mountain. The ballad about her found its way into the West Virginia Songbag, and the state's Heritage Encyclopedia lists her as a "bona fide" West Virginian.

A song about Naomi Wise, often called "Omie Wise," was evidently being sung soon after her death, and lyrics to "Poor Naomi" were printed in Braxton Craven's pamphlet. Vernon Dalhart—born in 1883, a year after Craven's death—made the first recording of the song in 1925. Dalhart's name was actually Marion Try Slaughter: "Vernon" and "Dalhart" were simply the names of two towns in his home state of Texas. An opera singer before turning to country music, Dalhart scored his first huge success with "The Wreck of the Old 97," which sold seven million records, and soon thereafter recorded his version of "Naomi Wise," which included the lines

> John Lewis he concluded
> To tell her his mind
> John Lewis he concluded
> To leave her behind

Although more than two centuries have passed since Jonathan Lewis lured Naomi Wise to the banks of Deep River, the song about the crime continues to be sung and can still stir the emotions of those who hear it. Granted, she was not as young, nor perhaps as innocent, as the verses make her out to be. But Lewis will always be remembered for his coldhearted, vicious act of murder. By callously deceiving Naomi Wise, by raising her hopes and then, in a flash, shattering them, he ensured that his name, immortalized in song, would forever be synonymous with duplicity and foul play.

CHAPTER 6

THE BALLAD OF
FRANKIE SILVER (1831)

This awful dark and dismal day
Has swept my glory all away
My sun goes down, my days are past,
And I must leave this world at last

In 1831, three days before Christmas, twenty-one-year-old Frances "Frankie" Silver murdered her nineteen-year-old husband, Charles, at their cabin in the tiny mountain community of Kona, located in the northwestern corner of North Carolina, about forty-five miles from Asheville. The couple had a thirteen-month-old daughter, Nancy. It seems that Charles drank too much and abused his wife, and she suspected him of infidelity. When he fell asleep on the floor (the likeliest scenario, although he may possibly have been awake), Frankie took Nancy from him and smashed him in the head with an ax, later claiming he had earlier threatened to shoot both her and the child. While Charles rose and thrashed about, Frankie hid, and when she heard his body fall to the floor, she struck again, this time severing his head from his torso. Then she brought her mother and her brother to the scene to help dispose of the body.

Soon, however, a search of the house revealed Charles's dog, Drum, who was known never to leave his master, and then, under the floorboards, pieces of bone, charred flesh, a pool of dried blood, and shreds of clothing. Frankie was arrested, as were her mother and brother. She alone was charged with murder, then tried, convicted, and sentenced to death. An appeal to the state supreme court failed, but she managed to escape from jail, disguised herself as a boy, and headed off to Tennessee with her father and her uncle. She was soon apprehended and locked up in Morganton, North Carolina. Although public sentiment swung in her favor—seven of the jurors later asked that she be pardoned—the governor let the execution proceed. Frankie Silver went to the gallows on July 12, 1833, wearing a white dress, a gift from the ladies of the town.

Charles and Frankie Silver had been married in 1829 when they were both in their teens. They resided with their daughter near Morgantown, the county seat named for the Revolutionary War general Daniel Morgan. Someone who knew Frankie said she "was a mighty likely little woman. She had fair skin, bright eyes, and was counted very pretty. She had charms. I never saw a smarter little woman. She could card and spin her three yards of cotton a day on a big wheel." By contrast, Charles was described as "a man of rather vagrant and intemperate habits" who subjected his wife to "ill grounded abuse." Further, those who later spoke in Frankie's defense claimed that Charles "was one of that cast of mankind who are wholly dissolute of any of the feeling that is necessary to make a good Husband or parent. . . . He treated her with personal violence." He did not provide well for his family, and even his relatives said he was "a lazy trifling man."

There are conflicting accounts of what transpired on the night of the murder. One resident of Morganton later said "Silvers was loading his gun to kill her and she took the ax and struck him on the head and knocked him down, and he seemed to suffer so awfully that she thought it would be mercy of her to kill him." Another man claimed that Charles was drunk, had started beating Frankie with a stick, "and she struck back and killed him, not intentionally but just to keep him from beating her." Others thought that Charles had fallen asleep on the floor, and that Frankie had hit him with the ax because he had threatened to shoot both her and the child. What is certain, however, is that Frankie had used the ax to make "one mortal wound of the length of three inches and the depth of one inch."

After committing the murder, Frankie went to fetch her mother, Barbara, and her younger brother, Blackstone, who was only fourteen. It appears that they attempted to conceal the crime by dismembering the corpse, burning the body parts in the fireplace, and then hiding the remains under the wooden floor of the cabin and perhaps in a hollow tree outside. They even did their best to wash away the bloodstains, hoping to make it appear that Charles had simply left the house and not returned.

> And on a dark and doleful night
> I put his body out of sight
> With flames I tried to consume
> But time would not admit it done

According to Alfred Silver, Charles's younger half-brother, Frankie not only helped dispose of the body but also later "confessed as much" to someone she knew.

The cover-up was probably doomed from the start. One of the neighbors slipped into the house the next day—Frankie, for obvious reasons, had decided to stay at her parents' home, less than a mile away—and noticed telltale signs: bits of charred body parts, greasy remains in the fireplace, a large amount of blood. She reported what she had seen to the authorities, and a search was undertaken in the woods, along the river, and inside the house. A heel iron of the kind that Charles wore turned up. Then "a circle of blood as large as a dog's liver" was found under the floorboards, as well as a skull and bones in the ashes of the fireplace, "and in a bench was a deep gash made with an axe, together with blood, where to appearance the head of the victim had been chopped off." Then, human remains were found buried some distance from the house. Even two or three miles away neighbors "perceived a very strange and offensive odor in the air, at the time the body is supposed to have been burning."

On January 9, 1832, arrest warrants were issued, and the next day Frankie, her mother, and her brother were taken to the county jail in Morganton. An inquiry was held, and a true bill returned, but only against Frankie: Barbara and Blackstone, originally charged with aiding and abetting her, were released after a week, "there appearing no evidence on behalf of the state against them." The grand jury formally indicted Frankie late in March. She pleaded not guilty, and a jury was quickly chosen. Her lawyer, Thomas Worth Wilson, forty years old, had recently established a practice in Morganton, while the prosecutor was William Julius Alexander, a graduate of the University of North Carolina. The case was heard before Superior Court Judge John Robert Donnell. Born in Scotland, he had immigrated to the United States at the age of ten, and through marriage and inheritance had gone on to acquire a fortune estimated at half a million dollars. He was described as "an able, quiet, unobtrusive, upright gentleman."

The victim's father, sister, and two of his uncles testified for the prosecution, as did others who likely had observed the scene of the crime. The prosecutor placed in evidence Charles's heel iron found in the ashes, and presumably other items as well. The defense called three witnesses, none of whom, however, had any firsthand knowledge of the murder. It took only one day for all the testimony to be heard, for the lawyers to make their closing arguments, and for the judge to charge the jury. The next day, the jurors asked to hear additional testimony from some witnesses. One person who never testified, however, was Frankie Silver. Courts in North Carolina still followed the English common law under which "the accused was deemed an incompetent witness and could not take the stand in his or her own defense." The state's criminal code would be revised in 1835, but not until 1857 was it possible for accused persons to testify if they wished to do so.

In the end, Frankie's attorney made what was almost certainly an unwise decision: to argue she had not murdered her husband, rather than to claim justifiable self-defense. Although at first members of the jury seemingly stood nine to three for acquittal, after they heard the additional testimony the vote to convict was unanimous. Nor was there was any opportunity for the defense to rebut that testimony. As her attorney later said in a petition to the governor: "She was precluded by the rule adopted by the court—that no new witness should be examined at that stage of the trial nor remarks of counsel heard." On April 2, 1832, the verdict having been handed down, the judge sentenced Frankie to hang.

> But oh! That Dreadful Judge I fear
> Shall I that awful sentence hear:
> "Depart ye cursed down to hell
> And forever there to dwell"?

So Wilson turned to Governor Swain, pleading for Frankie's life and arguing that her conviction rested "on Circumstantial evidence alone"—which, in fact, it did. As he explained to the governor: "NO one knows but your petitioner the circumstances and the truth of the facts under which the act was committed—Being a woman and entirely ignorant of the laws of the country she felt a repugnance to making any confession from a fear of involving herself in still greater difficulties." Later still, he would write to Swain: "It was clearly a case of manslaughter if not Justifiable Homicide." Wilson was not alone in calling for mercy: seven members of the jury also signed a petition asking the governor to spare Frankie's life, as did the attorney who served as clerk of the court.

Her last remaining hope was the North Carolina Supreme Court, which heard her appeal in May 1832. But in June the justices denied it. The court decided that the appeal "was based solely on the fact that the witnesses, who had been sequestered before their testimony, had been dismissed and allowed to mingle and confer before they were called back for new questioning by the jury." Chief Justice Thomas Ruffin, who wrote the court's opinion, held that it was impossible to keep witnesses from speaking with each other, that cross-examination provided "the great safeguard" against collusion, and that the law required not that witnesses be kept apart but only that they not "be examined together." In Ruffin's view, "The expectation is not to prevent the fabrication of false stories, but by separate cross-examination to detect them."

Frankie Silver's fate, however, hung in abeyance for nearly a year. Although she was to be formally sentenced in the fall of 1832, in September, one of the judges, David Lowry Swain, suffered a serious injury in a carriage accident,

Jacob Silver, Frankie's father.

fracturing his arm and dislocating his shoulder, and the court canceled its session. Then, Swain decided to run for governor; in November 1832 he was elected, succeeding Montfort Stokes, and gave up his judgeship. The court did not reconvene until the spring of 1833, when a date for execution—by hanging—was set for June.

Meanwhile, numerous last-minute pleas for clemency poured into the governor's office. One such petition was signed by 113 men, and another by 40 men, both claiming that Silver's conviction was based on circumstantial evidence and citing such mitigating circumstances as her relative youth, her humble parents, and her young child. The pleas also noted that she had "suffered greatly in health since her confinement and is now laboring under disease," and that she was "a poor woman whose very name 'tis frailty for example's sake." Some attempted to defend, if not justify, her act, which they said was caused by the "brutal conduct of the husband toward the wife." The execution of a woman occurred infrequently, her supporters declared, and "would reflect indictable disgrace on the Community."

If her sympathizers were reluctant to see Frankie Silver go to the gallows, members of her family took action to prevent it. On the night of May 18 she disguised herself, cutting her hair and dressing as a boy, and, with the help of her father and her uncle Jessee Barnett, escaped from prison. John Maguire, the jailer who had signed two of her petitions for a pardon, may have aided her; or, as the newspapers reported, someone "who entered the jail by one of the basement story windows, and opened the doors leading to the prisoner's apartment by the aid of false keys," may have assisted. She eluded the law for a week, but her escape was hampered by flooded roads, and on May 26, as she was traveling with her father and her uncle in the southeastern part of the state, a sheriff appeared. Her uncle inadvertently gave her away by saying that "her" name was Tommy, and she was taken into custody. Her relatives were also jailed as accessories, but as her lawyer said, "I do not believe they can be convicted without her testimony," and they were eventually released. Frankie, however, was not so fortunate.

In June, Swain, now governor, granted a two-week reprieve, and set a new execution date for July 12, 1833. By then, back in the prison where she had been held for eighteen months, often chained to the floor of her dungeon, Frankie made a confession, first to her friends, and later to her lawyer, who said that he "heard her statement in her own language" and was convinced she was telling the truth. From the time she had been recaptured, he said, "she lost all hope. Under the impending responsibility of passing from time into eternity she made a free and full disclosure of all the facts and circumstances attending this unhappy occurrence."

Yet even as the execution neared, petitions urging clemency continued to arrive at the governor's office. One, signed by thirty-five women, many of them socially prominent, spoke of the abuse and "indecorous and insupportable treatment" that Frankie had endured, and said that her husband was "one of that cast of mankind who are wholly dissolute of any of the feeling that is necessary to make a good Husband or parent—the neighborhood people are convinced that his treatment to her was both unbecoming and cruel very often and at the time too when female Delicacy would most forbid it." The petition went on to say that her husband had been violent, and was known "to have been a man who never made use of any exertions to Support either his wife or child which terminated as is frequently the case that those dutys Nature ordered and intended the husband to perform were thrown to her. His own relatives admit of his having been a lazy trifling man. It is also admitted by them also that she was an industrious woman. But for the want of Grace Religion and Refinement she has committed an act that she herself would have given a world to have been able to call back." The petitioners noted that Frankie's child needed a mother's protection, and said that a pardon would "wipe from the character of the female in this community the Stigma of a woman's being hung under the gallows." Many others also wrote to urge clemency.

But it was all to no avail: Governor Swain rejected these and other appeals, and on July 12, 1833, Frankie Silver was led to the gallows. Although a wooden wall was constructed around the area so spectators could not observe the execution, there were those who found ways to see it anyway. The sheriff who performed the hanging had tears in his eyes. The day's oppressive heat and humidity caused her father to bury her quickly, in an unmarked grave, rather than closer to home. More than a hundred years later, in 1952, the publisher of a local newspaper erected a marker with a marble tombstone a few miles north of Morganton. In time, Frankie's daughter, Nancy, was married, twice—her first husband died in the Civil War—and she would name her son, Charles, after her father.

In 1885 a North Carolina newspaper published a poem, thirteen verses long, titled "Francis Silvers's Confession"—an earlier written version dates from 1865—remarking that "some of our readers will remember the facts in the case." One of the verses read

> There shall I meet that mournful face
> Whose blood I spilled upon this place
> With flaming eyes to me he'll say
> "Why did you take my life away?"

The author, only seventeen, was Thomas W. Scott, who based the song on "Beacham's Address" or "Beauchamp's Confession," a ballad about an execution that had taken place in Kentucky. Eventually, journalists even got around to interviewing Alfred Silver, the victim's half brother. In 1903, at the age of eighty-eight, he told a writer for a Charlotte, North Carolina, newspaper that the years had not shaken his conviction that Frankie had murdered Charles with malicious intent.

A few recordings of "Frankie Silvers" were eventually made in the early 1930s, several by Clarence Ashley, who was sometimes accompanied by Byrd Moore and His Hot Shots, or by Tex Isley. In Ashley's version, Judge Donnell was rendered as "Judge Daniels," but in many respects he accurately presented Frankie's perspective:

> Judge Daniels has my sentence passed
> These prison walls I'll leave at last
> Nothing to cheer my drooping head
> Until I'm numbered with the dead

Thirty years later, in 1962, the New Lost City Ramblers recorded a similar version, and in 1966 the folksinger Hedy West included a verse in which Frankie explains

> For weeks and days I spent my time
> A-planning out this awful crime
> 'Twas on that dark and awful night
> I put his body out of sight

Byrd Moore and His Hot Shots, ca. 1929. *Left to right*: Byrd Moore, Clarence Greene, Clarence "Tom" Ashley.

More recently, the story of Frankie Silver has become the subject not only of books and articles, but also of a motion picture, a film, a play, a ballet, and a novel, even a YouTube documentary. In some recent treatments, the "poor miserable retch [*sic*]," as her lawyer described her, has begun to have her say, appearing less the cruel, sadistic woman than a victim: one who—notwithstanding the brutality of her act—was driven to it by her husband's threatening behavior. There is no way of knowing how much remorse Frankie Silver truly felt, or, indeed, whether she felt any—although, as one might expect, the song written about her assumed she regretted what she had done:

> Farewell, good people, you all now see
> What my bad conduct's brought on me
> To die of shame and disgrace
> Before the world of human race.

CHAPTER 7

TOM DOOLEY (1866)

Hang down your head Tom Dooley
Hang down your head and cry
Killed poor Laura Foster
Poor boy, you're bound to die

In June 1958, the Kingston Trio—Dave Guard, Bob Shane, and Nick Reynolds—recorded "Tom Dooley" on their inaugural album. Their arrangement used only two chords, with Shane observing it was "very easy to do." Released as a single in August, the song sold a million copies within only months. Eventually it sold three million copies, and the group received a Grammy Award for the Best Country and Western Recording. "Tom Dooley" had first been recorded in 1929, and several other recordings had appeared in the early and mid-1950s, but the Kingston Trio's version became the most widely known. The song eventually became so popular that versions appeared in French, German, Italian, and Danish. Most people who heard the song, though, and even most who sang it, did not know that Tom Dooley had fought for the Confederacy during the Civil War—or that he had murdered Laura Foster shortly afterward, because he believed that he had contracted syphilis from her.

His name was not, in fact, Dooley, but Thomas Caleb Dula. He was born in 1844, in the Yadkin River Valley, in the western foothills of North Carolina, the youngest of six children, three boys and three girls. His father died when Tom was only ten. In April 1862, nearly a year after North Carolina had seceded, he enlisted in the Confederate army, as did his brothers, both of whom later perished in the war, one from pneumonia and the other possibly from typhoid fever. Tom was only seventeen, but he lied about his age, joined an infantry regiment as a private, and served until he was captured in March 1865 at the battle of Wyse's Fork. He spent the next few months at a prisoner-of-war camp in Maryland, and was released on June 15, 1865, after having taken an oath of

Tom Dula, ca. 1860s.

allegiance to the Union. So, at twenty-one, he returned to Wilkes County, North Carolina, where times were hard and food was scarce.

Somewhat taller than average in height, Dula was described as "not hand-some" but "good-looking," and it was only a matter of time before he became involved with several young women. One of them was Ann Foster, whom Tom had known before the war, but who in 1859, as a teenager, had married twenty-one-year-old James Gabriel Melton. Tom resided with them, and, a witness later claimed, he would often crawl into bed with Ann after her husband was asleep. But beginning in March 1866, Tom also had sexual relations with one of Ann's distant cousins—Pauline Foster—who had come to reside with the Melton family. And Pauline had a cousin, Laura Foster. By March Tom had begun courting her, too, if courting is the right word, since Laura's father claimed that he had found them in bed together on more than one occasion.

In March, Pauline visited Dr. George N. Carter, one of the few physicians in the vicinity, seeking treatment for syphilis. By early April, Tom Dula also began to exhibit symptoms of the illness, and so did Ann Foster Melton. (Carter prescribed the only treatment available at the time, an ineffectual combination of blue stone or copper sulfate—one-third of which consisted of a poison, mercury—and caustic soda.) There was surely blame enough to go around: Tom believed Laura had infected him, and Ann believed that Tom had infected her (and as a result her husband, James). And soon there were threats enough to go around. Ann Foster Melton, described as "possessing almost all the faults one woman could have," said she meant to murder Laura, and warned Pauline that if she told anyone she'd kill her, too. Tom Dula, believing for whatever reason that Laura was responsible for his illness, paid her two visits, on May 20 and 23. Then he borrowed a mattock, a heavy two-bladed pickax-like tool used to break up hard soil and slice through thick roots. Laura Foster was never seen alive again—murdered a day or two later, probably on Friday, May 25.

> You met her on the hilltop
> You said she'd be your wife
> You met her on the hillside
> And there you took her life

When her friends and relatives realized that Laura was nowhere to be found, searches were conducted over many days. But all that turned up was a piece of rope that had been used to tie her horse. Tom Dula did not participate in the search but took off for neighboring Watauga County, and on June 28 a warrant was issued for his arrest, based on a complaint by Laura's father, Wilson Foster, who said his daughter "had mysteriously disappeared from her home under circumstances as to induce him to believe that she had been murdered or otherwise foully dealt with by certain persons under suspicion." Meanwhile, Tom had left the state and was fifteen miles away in Tennessee, where, early in July, he turned up at a farm owned by Lieutenant Colonel James W. M. Grayson, who had fought for the Union during the war.

Tom worked for Grayson as a field hand for about a week and bought himself a new pair of boots but was long gone by the time a posse arrived at Grayson's farm to track him down. The very next day Grayson and two deputies began to search for him. They found Dula in Pandora, nine miles away, soaking his feet in a creek because his boots hurt so much. After locking him in a corn-crib overnight to ensure he did not escape, Grayson, with Dula in tow, his hands and feet securely bound, returned him to Wilkes County. On July 11 he was thrown into jail.

Lieutenant Colonel James
W. M. Grayson.

It was not until September 1, however, that Laura Foster's body was discovered, quite by accident, when a horse startled and began to snort near the place where she was buried. A makeshift grave was discovered and opened. Dr. Carter was summoned, examined the corpse, and testified to finding a knife wound that might well have proven fatal (although "the body was in so decomposed a condition that I could not ascertain whether the knife had cut the heart or not. The clothing around the heart was in a rotten condition"). Laura's father was able to identify the remains, and so was Pauline Foster. Ann Foster Melton was then taken into custody and placed in a cell next to Dula's in the Wilkesboro jail.

On October 1, 1866, a grand jury indicted Tom Dula for murder—or, in the parlance of the day, for "not having the fear of God before his eyes, but being moved and seduced by the instigation of the Devil"—and also indicted Ann Melton as an accomplice. Bail was not granted. The trial was moved to neighboring Iredell County, and the defendants were transferred to the county jail in Statesville, where eight men took turns standing guard, even though Dula was in manacles and leg irons. The presiding judge was Ralph B. Buxton, and the prosecutor was District Attorney Walter Pharr Caldwell. Tom's lawyer, Zebulon Baird Vance, was a conservative Democrat who had led a Confederate regiment, a former governor—and a future United States senator—well-known for his opposition to granting equality to freed slaves. He was practicing law in Charlotte

Zebulon B. Vance, ca. 1870s.
Courtesy of the Library of Congress.

when someone, it is not known who, asked him to take on the defense of Tom (whose case had been severed from that of Ann Melton, who would be tried separately).

The trial began on Friday, October 19, 1866, and lasted only two days. Witnesses for the prosecution, among them Dr. Carter, Wilson Foster, and Pauline Foster, described finding the partially decomposed corpse of Laura Foster, who had been stabbed through the heart. They also noticed a "discolored spot of ground" and saw a rope indicating that a horse had been hitched to a dogwood tree. Laura's body had been buried more than half a mile from where she was murdered. Dr. Carter testified that Dula had asked him for medication to treat syphilis: "He had the syphilis—told me he caught it from Laura Foster." Pauline reported that when she told Dula she thought that he would run off with Laura, "he laughed & said, 'I have no use for Laura Foster.'" She added that when it was rumored about that Dula had murdered Laura, "Dula laughed and said, 'They would have it to prove and perhaps take a beating besides.'" Another witness, Rufus D. Hall—Tom's second cousin—said he encountered Dula, who "said to me that he was diseased, and he was going to put them through, who diseased him. I replied, Tom, I would not do that."

The evidence linking Dula to the crime was reasonably strong, although by no means conclusive. It appears that only five witnesses testified on his behalf, but they had little information to offer, and certainly could not provide an alibi. His mother, Mary Dula, admitted her son was not at home on the Friday in question. She said he returned for dinner but had no appetite. That night she heard him moaning, complaining he had the chills: "He was my sole remaining boy—I had lost two in the War. I leaned my face down and kissed him." She did not hear him leave during the night, and he appeared for breakfast the next morning. The other witnesses for the defense merely testified to Dula's good character.

> You dug the grave four feet long
> And you dug it three feet deep
> You rolled the cold clay over her
> And tromped it with your feet

The trial ended on a Saturday, and the jury returned the next morning with a guilty verdict. Judge Buxton sentenced Tom to death by hanging and set the execution date for November 9, 1866. But his attorney appealed to the North Carolina Supreme Court, which found that certain incriminating evidence had been admitted improperly: in particular, a conversation between Pauline Foster and her friend, Betsy Scott, which "was entirely accidental, and consisted simply of answers to inquiries which the curiosity of Mrs. Scott induced her to make. These answers may have been true, or they may have been false, but they were not verified by 'the tests' which the law of evidence requires, and it was error to admit them as evidence against the prisoner." The court ordered a new trial. It was scheduled for October 1867 but postponed at the prosecution's request because several witnesses—including James Grayson, now a member of the Tennessee legislature—were unable to be present.

The second trial was finally held in January 1868 before a special Court of Oyer and Terminer ("to hear and decide"). The judge, William M. Shipp, had been a delegate to North Carolina's secession convention, had signed the secession ordinance, and had served briefly in the Confederate army. Much the same evidence was presented as had been offered at Tom's first trial. Vance's summation to the jury, one observer said, "was ingenious, eloquent, and distinguished for legal lore of the highest grade; but failed to inspire the minds of the Jury with a reasonable doubt." Dula was again found guilty and again sentenced to be hanged. A date was set in February, but another appeal to the state supreme court delayed matters. In April, that court upheld the verdict, and Judge Anderson Mitchell (who, like Shipp, had attended the secession convention but, unlike him, had voted not to secede) set the execution date for the afternoon of May 1, 1868.

Tom Dula remained in prison in Statesville, in Iredell County, evidently spending some of his time trying to loosen his shackles with a piece of glass. He was visited by one of his attorneys, and had himself baptized by a Methodist minister. The sheriff, William Franklin Wasson, had a gallows erected near a railway depot just outside town. On the appointed day, a large crowd, numbering perhaps three thousand, showed up to view the execution. Taking no chances, the sheriff ordered the barrooms closed in order to avoid drunken brawls. Dula rode in a cart, accompanied by his sister, Eliza, and his brother-in-law. "He looked cheerful and spoke continually to his sister of the Scriptures, assuring her he had repented and that his peace was made with God." The coffin was also in the cart. Asked if he had any last words, he said: "Gentlemen, do you see this hand? Do you see it tremble? Do you see it shake? I never hurt a hair on the girl's head." When the noose was fastened, he joked: "I would have washed my neck if I had known you were using such a nice clean new rope."

Since he was entitled to address the crowd, Dula, according to a reporter for the *New York Herald*, spoke for an hour in a voice "that rang back from the woods as if a demon there was mocking the tone and spirit of a wretch who well knew he was going into eternity with an unconfessed murder upon his mind and falsehood on his lips." He talked of his childhood, his military service, the political situation, and, while stubbornly maintaining his innocence, claimed that some of the witnesses who testified against him at the trial had lied. The reporter, however, believed that "the opinion of all was that he was a terrible, desperate character," adding: "Few there were who pitied him, dying, as they believed him guilty without a confession, and none sympathized with him."

At 2:24 in the afternoon, the cart on which Tom was standing was pulled away. He dropped about two feet, but his neck was not broken, and he continued to breathe for several minutes, while still swinging from the rope. After about ten minutes, his heart stopped beating, and a local physician pronounced him dead. His body was taken down, placed in the coffin, and turned over to family members. He was buried on a farm owned by his cousin, near Elkville, North Carolina. On the day before he died, he had given one of his attorneys a note saying, "I declare that I am the only person that had any hand to the murder of Laura Foster."

> At this time tomorrow
> Where do you reckon I'll be?
> Down in some lonesome valley
> Hanging on a white oak tree

Several months later, in the fall of 1868, Ann Melton stood trial in Wilkes-boro. She was also represented by Zebulon Vance, but Tom Dula's death-house note meant that the case against her as an accessory to murder was bound to collapse, as indeed it did. The local newspaper reported: "The unfortunate woman has suffered about two years imprisonment, and if guilty, she has been severely punished, and the gallows would have added little to her punishment. Thus ends this woeful tragedy." She returned to her husband, James Melton, and her child, and in 1871 gave birth to another daughter. She died within a few years, however, either as the result of an accident or because of complications from syphilis.

A song about Tom Dula and Laura Foster was being sung as early as 1867, it appears, even as the case was still working its way through the courts. The folklore scholar Frank C. Brown, who taught at the University of North Carolina—it was said of him that "his principle was to collect everything of possible value"—came across three versions of the song over a period of thirty years. One was given to him in 1921 by Maude Sutton, a resident of Caldwell County, who claimed she had gotten the verses from a man who, in the 1860s, had resided in the same vicinity as Laura Foster. One of Brown's informants said that the song had "been sung and played for many years (probably for over forty) in Watauga [County]. . . . There is hardly a fiddler or banjo picker in our county who cannot play 'Tom Dooley.'"

Appropriately, Gilliam Banmon Grayson, the nephew of Colonel James W. M. Grayson, the man who had captured Dula in Tennessee, made the first recording of "Tom Dooley." Grayson, who was born in North Carolina but spent most of his life in Tennessee, claimed he had learned the song from family members. He recorded it in Memphis with Henry Whitter in 1929. The record did well, selling about four thousand copies. (Grayson died in a car accident only a year later.)

> This world and one more
> Then where you reckon I'll be?
> Hadn't a-been for Grayson
> I'd a-been in Tennessee
>
> Took her on the hillside
> To make her your wife
> Took her on the hillside
> Where there you took her life

In 1938, the folklorists Anne and Frank Warner were in North Carolina, where, in Watauga County, they met Frank Proffitt, a twenty-five-year-old carpenter and tobacco grower who played several instruments, including the fretless banjo. He sang a version of "Tom Dooley," claiming he remembered hearing his father play it on the banjo. "I got a television set for the kids," he later recalled. "One night I was a-setting looking at some foolishness when three fellers stepped out with guitar and banjer and went to singing Tom Dooly [*sic*] and they clowned and hipswinged. I began to feel sorty sick, like I'd lost a love one." He also said that he had heard the song from an aunt whose parents had lived in Wilkes County and had known both Tom Dula and Laura Foster. The Warners returned in 1940 and recorded his version of the song, one that was quite similar to the arrangement by Grayson and Whitter.

Soon Frank Warner was singing it, too, explaining: "I used 'Tom Dooley' in every lecture and program, telling the story of Tom—and of Frank Proffitt—and singing my own modifications of Frank's version, having taken the essence of the story and reduced it from six stanzas to four, and—over many years—having reshaped the melody line to fit my own feelings about the song." Warner taught the song to Alan Lomax, who included it in *Folk Song: U.S.A.* (1947), and he also recorded it himself in 1952. During the folk revival of the 1950s, a number of musicians also covered Warner's version. Eventually, as one commentator said, it appeared "on collections of Irish folk, songs of the American West, hit parade rock, country & western, and love songs."

Then, in 1958, the Kingston Trio recorded "Tom Dooley" and had a huge hit. Dave Guard said he had learned the song from a 1953 recording by the Folksay Trio, and Bob Shane recalled: "We eventually rewrote it just enough to try and claim it for our own and signed our name to it, got sued and lost because it was in Lomax's collection before that." When the song turned out to be immensely successful, and profitable, a long legal battle over the rights to it resulted. Finally, in 1962, an out-of-court settlement was arranged under which all subsequent royalties were to go to Ludlow Music, which represented John A. Lomax, Alan Lomax, and Frank Warner. Half of Warner's share was to go to Frank Proffitt.

That settlement was reached about a century after Thomas Caleb Dula had enlisted in the Confederate army to fight on behalf of slavery and secession, and then had his rendezvous with Laura Foster. Although "Tom Dooley" would become an enormously popular song, most versions mentioned only a few key elements of the case: the murder, the arrest, and the execution. The song omitted many of the most interesting aspects of the story: Dula's family and his career as a Confederate soldier; the importance of venereal disease as a motive for the slaying; the two years of intricate legal wrangling before the courts; the central role played by Ann Melton in the murder; and Dula's brash behavior in the days leading up to his execution. No one would have been more surprised than Dula himself to learn that National Public Radio would choose "Tom Dooley" as one of the most important songs of the twentieth century.

CHAPTER 8

POOR ELLEN SMITH (1892)

Poor Ellen Smith
How was she found?
Shot through the heart
Lying cold on the ground

In May 1892, the Hotel Zinzendorf, the newest, most elegant structure in Winston-Salem, North Carolina, celebrated its grand opening. It was named for Count Nicolaus Ludwig von Zinzendorf, an eighteenth-century patron of the Moravian Church. Four stories high and the length of a football field, the hotel sat atop the highest knoll in town, its ten towers giving it the aspect of a medieval castle. With elevators, electric lights, and private baths on every floor, it was designed to attract well-to-do guests from around the world. Unfortunately, in November the structure caught fire and burned to the ground. But on the afternoon of July 1 its manicured grounds served as the meeting place for two star-crossed former lovers: Peter DeGraff and Ellen Smith. There, in the garden, Peter shot Ellen through the heart.

Only seventeen or eighteen years old, Ellen was said to be "not bad looking. . . . Her short dark hair tended to curl and she had blue eyes and straight white teeth." Her father, Julius, was a white man who worked as a farm laborer in the town of Forbush, in the easternmost part of Yadkin County, North Carolina; her mother, Julia, was listed in the 1880 census as a mulatto and gave her occupation as "keeping house." Ellen, who was six when the census taker came around, had a younger brother, John, who was four, and a sister, Emma, only two; all the children were listed as mulattos. When Ellen—her name in the returns was spelled "Ellin"—was born, her father was only twenty and her mother, nineteen. Ellen's maternal grandmother, Mary Head, resided with the family, and since she listed her race as "white," Ellen's grandfather was presumably a black man.

75

The fire at the Zinzendorf Hotel, November 1892. Courtesy of the Forsyth County Public Library photograph collection, Winston-Salem, NC.

In 1892 Peter DeGraff was twenty-four. He resided not far from Ellen, in the adjacent county of Forsyth, in the town of South Fork. His father, Anthoney Degraf, was born in France in 1811, so at the time of Ellen's murder he was eighty-one. He worked as a "laborer." His wife, Elen, twenty-six years younger than her husband and a native North Carolinian, also said her occupation was "keeping house." Peter had an older brother, Joseph, an older sister, Mary, and a younger brother, Lee. Young as they were in 1880, fourteen-year-old Joseph and twelve-year-old Peter said they were "laborers."

No one knows for sure why Peter sent Ellen a note asking her to meet him at the hotel, or whether he planned from the outset to murder her. It appears he had gotten her pregnant, she had recently given birth, and the child had died in infancy. Perhaps she now wanted him to marry her, which no doubt was the furthest thing from his mind. He had a reputation as a philanderer who had been involved in several other casual affairs and had gotten other young women "in trouble." Much later he would admit that on the fateful night he had had too much to drink, and that he placed the pistol against Ellen's breast and pulled the trigger: "The only words she said after I shot her were: 'Lord, have mercy on me.'"

Her clothes were all scattered
And thrown on the ground
And blood marks the spot
Where poor Ellen was found

Then he fled, and early the next morning a black woman who worked at the hotel discovered the body in the woods nearby. A postmortem examination "found that the woman had been shot in the left breast the ball passing through the body." There were powder burns on her dress. The examination also revealed that she had recently given birth. The newspapers reported that a note was found "upon the person of the dead girl from DeGraff making an engagement to meet her near the place where the murder was committed." But that note was somehow misplaced and never found.

Search parties were organized to find the murderer, but he fled to places far removed—to Virginia and New Mexico—though eventually he returned to North Carolina, settling in Mount Airy, about thirty-eight miles northwest of Winston-Salem. The sheriff, however, seemed uninterested in tracking him down, so uninterested that a newspaper asked "why persons charged with murder are thus permitted to strut about the country in broad daylight while our officers timidly keep out of their way." His failure to apprehend DeGraff evidently played a role in the sheriff's defeat in the fall election. The newly elected sheriff, R. M. McArthur, a Democrat, pledged during the campaign that if he were elected "no DeGraff could run loose in the county."

Nearly a year went by until the sheriff made good on his promise, and he succeeded only because DeGraff decided to return to Winston-Salem. On June 23, 1893, tipped off that DeGraff was back in town, the sheriff sent his men to search DeGraff's parents' home and other locations, and followed a tip that the fugitive had returned to the scene of the crime, all to no avail. By midnight, Sheriff McArthur and three other officers finally found him at a friend's house two miles west of the city. One of the policemen, seeing DeGraff at a window, called out: "Peter, you had just as well give up; you may get one of us, but we will get you." The officer reported that he entered the house: "I pointed my pistol at the prisoner; prisoner had three heavy pistols and fifty-two rounds of cartridges in a trunk by the bed."

The fugitive's demeanor, he added, was hardly that of a man about to be charged with murder. DeGraff spoke matter-of-factly about having fled to other states before returning to North Carolina. He got dressed, and then "he began to make fun of us for coming after him with little popguns (we had Smith & Wesson's pistols). He even said, 'Let me show you some pistols,' and he showed us these three large pistols." The officers mounted their horses, providing

Sheriff R. M. McArthur. Courtesy of
the Forsyth County Public Library
photograph collection, Winston-
Salem, NC.

one for the prisoner to ride, and escorted him back to town. "He was not fright-
ened, nor was he tied. No threats were made to him, and no promises, and his
statements were voluntary." A few days later, after a preliminary trial before a
justice of the peace, Peter DeGraff was formally charged with the murder of
Ellen Smith.

> They carried me to Winston
> My trial to stand
> To live or to die
> As the law may command

He was arraigned before Judge Robert W. Winston, a graduate of the University of North Carolina and a former member of the state legislature, who,
while only thirty-two years of age, was already a superior court circuit judge.
The trial got under way on August 11, 1893. Two attorneys—Thomas H. Sutton
and Frank D. Baldwin—represented DeGraff. They raised several procedural
objections during the course of the trial, but the North Carolina Supreme
Court, on appeal, would find them to be unconvincing. For example, the defense
moved to quash the indictment on the grounds that one of the grand jurors was
a cousin of the victim and should have been disqualified, but the appeals court

ruled the objection was not timely (as it was made only after the jury was impaneled) and said the matter was properly left to the judge's discretion. The attorneys also claimed two of the jurors were biased and had made statements
"adverse to the prisoner." Again, the court ruled the statements "were based
upon rumors only" and did not preclude the rendering of a fair verdict.

The prosecutors called two handwriting experts who testified that "a letter
found in the bosom of the dead woman . . . was in the handwriting of the prisoner." After comparing that letter with other writing samples from DeGraff,
both experts said the handwriting was identical. Citing an earlier North Carolina precedent regarding the qualifications of expert witnesses, the judge
allowed the testimony. In addition, the inclusion of testimony by one state witness who had "before the trial expressed himself in very bitter terms against the
prisoner stating in effect that he desired his conviction, etc." did not, in the
court's view, prejudice the outcome.

Taking the witness stand in his own behalf, DeGraff surely did himself more
harm than good. On cross-examination, asked why he had returned to the
scene of the crime, he admitted that he shouted: "Ellen, if you are in Heaven,
stay there; if in hell, rise!" He explained that he had heard elderly people say
"that if a murderer would go back where he had killed a person and repeat those
words the person could be seen." As the newspapers reported: "The prisoner
seemed not to realize the web he was weaving about himself until the words had
fallen from his lips."

After four days of testimony, the jury returned a guilty verdict. Judge Winston, turning down DeGraff's request for a new trial, sentenced him to be hanged.
DeGraff appealed to the state supreme court, but in December Chief Justice James
E. Shepherd denied the appeal. He found that DeGraff had confessed not out of
any "actual fear of violence" but only after having received appropriate warnings.
The judge also found nothing wrong with a witness who disparaged Degraff's
character, or with the prosecutor who asked a witness "whether the prisoner told
him where the deceased was at a certain time": "There was abundant evidence . . .
to support the conviction of the prisoner, and . . . the hostility of this witness, if
known to the jury, would very probably have had no influence upon the verdict."
Finally, the claim by DeGraff's lawyers that two jurors "had on several occasions
before the trial expressed the opinion that the prisoner was guilty"—and that the
defense had not been informed of their bias—failed to move the appeals court,
which ruled: "After a patient and careful investigation of the record we have been
unable to discover any error in the rulings of the Court, and, in view of the whole
testimony, we see no reason for disturbing the verdict."

The chief justice, who had no intention of reversing the trial court, declared
"the only remedy to be found in a meritorious case is in the executive department

of government." That meant an appeal to Democratic governor Elias Carr—once described as the last in a "fading tradition of planter governors"—but he had not the least inclination to intervene. Instead, he set February 8, 1894, as the day DeGraff was to die. Locked in his cell, the condemned man told his guard that "he had good training, but failed to heed the advice given him. . . . Evil companions and whisky were his worst enemies."

As he stood on the scaffold, Peter DeGraff finally confessed to the crime. He said he had been drunk when he shot Ellen, and warned the crowd of spectators—newspapers estimated the number at six to ten thousand—not to do as he had done. Speaking rapidly, he declared: "I have washed my blood, and hope those who have enmity against me will forgive me. May God bless you all is my prayer on this side of the bar of God." His demeanor, observers reported, was remarkably calm as he continued: "That thing you call corn liquor, cards, dice and other games of chance, pistols and bad women are the things which have brought me to this place to stand on this scaffold. I have kept back for months what I am going to tell you. God told me to keep it back. . . . Yes, I shot the woman. I was drunk at the time. I put the pistol to her breast and fired it. . . . I stand here today to receive my just reward."

Then he shook hands with his two brothers and gave his Bible to Lee, the youngest. (Later in life, Lee chose the apt profession of tombstone engraver.) The "aged father and mother bad [sic] him farewell at the jail this morning, and at the request of Peter they did not witness his execution. The scene moved many to tears." Two ministers conducted a service and offered prayers. Reporters at the scene provided more of the morbidly excruciating details than were perhaps necessary: "The rope was around the prisoner's neck when he ascended the scaffold. He raised his hat and bowed to the crowd, while the death warrant was read by the sheriff." "Sheriff McArthur sprung the trigger at 12:35, and in an instant the life of the condemned man went out. His neck was broken and death was instantaneous, but the heart's action continued for seven minutes."

> My days in this prison
> Are ending at last
> I'll never be free
> From the sins of my past

The newspapers' description of the execution—meticulous, even ritualized—commented on the condemned man's last-minute confession, the preachers' prayers, the family members' anguish, and the precise time that elapsed from the opening of the trapdoor to the final heartbeat. None could have known at the time that Peter DeGraff would be the last person to be pub-licly hanged in Forsyth County. While six convicted men went to the gallows in North Carolina in 1894, public hangings in the state came to an end in 1897. The gallows were then moved inside the prison walls, and in 1910 the electric chair replaced the hangman's noose.

It is likely that "Poor Ellen Smith" was composed and was being sung soon after these events occurred. The melody derived from a well-known spiritual, "How Firm a Foundation." Josiah Henry Combs, a Kentuckian, first collected the lyrics, after hearing them in 1915 from a man named Dan Gibson. Ten years later, in 1925, Combs included the song in his doctoral thesis, "Folk-Songs du midi des États-Unis," submitted—of all places!—to the University of Paris. (In 1967, the University of Texas Press published the work as *Folk Songs of the Southern United States*.) At roughly the same time, the first recordings of "Ellen Smith" appeared: one version, in 1925, by Henry Whitter, and another in 1927 by the Dykes Magic City Trio (made up of fiddler John Dykes, guitarist Hubert Mahaffey, and autoharp player Myrtle Vermillion). Yet even now, after all this time, the song remains popular, and the tale it relates remains heartrending:

> Some day I'll go home,
> And say when I go
> On poor Ellen's grave
> Pretty flowers I'll sow.

CHAPTER 9

PEARL BRYAN (1896)

Now, ladies, if you'll listen, a story I'll relate,
What happened near Fort Thomas in the old Kentucky state
'Twas late in January this awful deed was done,
By Jackson and by Walling; how cold their blood did run!

In the early morning hours of February 1, 1896, a teenage boy was walking in the woods on his way to work near Fort Thomas, Kentucky, a town not far from Cincinnati, when he spied what looked like a woman's body on the ground. He informed his employer, who in turn told the police and also the commander of the United States infantry regiment stationed at the fort. The sheriff soon arrived, along with the coroner, where they found, to their horror, the body of a decapitated woman, her clothing disheveled and a pool of blood near her neck. They also turned up a glove, a scrap of a dress, and blood-splattered leaves on nearby trees. Two investigators were called to the scene, John McDermott and Cal Crim, but their efforts were hampered by curious onlookers who swarmed over the terrain, arriving on foot, on horseback, by streetcar, and in carriages. The doctor who performed the autopsy said the woman was in her early twenties, had been alive when her head was severed, and was nearly five months pregnant. He added: "The stomach content also revealed a large quantity of cocaine."

The police were able to trace the victim's shoes to the manufacturer, then to the store in Greencastle, Indiana, that had sold them, and then, since only two pairs had been purchased, to the person who had bought them: Pearl Bryan, who had gotten them a few years earlier for her high school graduation. The officers questioned her sister and brother, showing them some of the victim's clothing, and they identified the garments as Pearl's. Then the police went to see her mother, Jane, who further confirmed the victim's identity on the basis of her clothing and certain physical characteristics. Pearl, the youngest of her children, born in October 1872, was described as "a Sunday school and church worker, sprightly and vivacious, and a social favourite in her home."

The trail grew considerably warmer when the officers interviewed Will Wood, who had recently dropped out of DePauw University in Greencastle, and was visiting a relative in South Bend. He was a second cousin of Pearl Bryan, and when tracked down he acknowledged that he had introduced her to his friend Scott Jackson, in the spring of 1895. Jackson, twenty-six years old, had barely managed to keep himself one step ahead of the law. As a teenager, he had been involved in an embezzlement scheme with his employer but had testified for the state and avoided conviction. Afterward, he moved to Indiana, where, a friend said, "he was abstemious when it was to his advantage, but could drink heavily when he so desired." He met Pearl in the spring, and by September he had gotten her pregnant. That fall he became a dental student in Cincinnati, and he told Wood he was trying to find a way to end the pregnancy. Jackson, Wood informed the police, had arranged for Pearl to go to Cincinnati to have an illegal abortion, telling her parents she was going to Indianapolis.

Pearl Bryan, ca. 1895. Courtesy of the
Putnam County Public Library.

In fact, late in January 1896, Jackson, who had no intention of helping Pearl, found her a room in Cincinnati. He also took Alonzo Walling, his friend and roommate, whom he had recently met at school, into his confidence. Walling hired an African American cab driver named George Jackson on January 30, and the next night the two men met Pearl at a tavern. Having already given Pearl several abortifacients, none of which had terminated her pregnancy, Scott Jackson prepared a solution of cocaine mixed with water, which he gave her to drink, and by seven in the evening, feeling woozy, she got into the cab with both men. The taxi took them across a bridge into Newport, and after a four-hour drive stopped by a deserted orchard. While Walling waited, Jackson and Pearl walked across a field, but then, for some reason, she tried to return to the cab. Jackson caught her, tried to strangle her, and, as she struggled, scratching his arm as she did, he stabbed her with a knife. Then he cut her throat and decapitated her, wrapping her head in his coat. He returned to the carriage—by then, the driver had already left—and he and Walling drove back to Cincinnati, arriving at their room at about three in the morning.

> Yes, they drove far from the city,
> To a place so far from home
> There they left her body lying,
> Headless and all stained with blood

Using the tip provided by Will Wood, the police staked out the boarding-house, found Jackson nearby, and took him into custody. Although he admitted that he knew Pearl Bryan, he denied having seen her recently. He tried to account for the scratches on his body by saying they were caused by insect bites, but had a harder time explaining the dried blood on his undershirt. After a time, he asked one of the guards, "Hasn't Walling been arrested yet?" That was all the police needed to begin looking for Alonzo Walling. Meanwhile, witnesses who had read newspaper accounts of Jackson's arrest began to come forward: a saloon keeper said that he had the valise Jackson had left in the bar on the night following the murder, and it was found to have a blood-stained lining. Handed the valise and told to open it, Jackson admitted: "It looks like blood. . . . Yes. That is blood." "Isn't that the valise in which you carried the head?" "I guess it is, but I did not carry it." "Well, who did?" Jackson replied: "Walling."

So by early Thursday morning Walling, too, had been taken into custody. Informed that Jackson said that he had committed the murder, he offered his own version of events, self-serving, to be sure, but one that the police found generally credible. He claimed that it was Jackson who had poisoned Pearl, had walked into the woods with her, and had finally murdered her. "Yes, I am almost sure that was the way he killed her," he said. Walling also directed the police to the sewer where he had disposed of Jackson's bloodstained jacket, which was found to contain bloody handkerchiefs inside the pockets. Then, searching the men's personal lockers, the police found additional evidence: a pair of Jackson's trousers, muddy and flecked with blood.

The police questioned other witnesses as well, including George Jackson, the cab driver, who came forward to say he had driven the men and the woman on that night. "I heard a woman groan in the cab, like she was in awful pain. I got scared and wanted to leave," he said, but one of the men threatened to kill him if he did. Then the driver told the police what happened next: "The two of them dragged a woman out of the cab, and hauled her off the road. She moaned as they took her out and then I heard her moan some more after they took her into the bushes." Then he heard a scream: "I got scared, and jumped down off that cab. . . . I started to run, and I never stopped till I got back to Cincinnati." He picked Jackson and Walling out of a police lineup, placing both men at the murder scene. The police had him retrace the route he had taken, and he said that when he had heard the woman moaning and tried to leave the cab, Walling threatened him with a revolver, shouting: "You black bastard, if you try to jump out here, I'll send you to hell!"

Both suspects, now under lock and key, were subjected to a photographic examination that precisely measured the length and breadth of their heads, and the lengths of their middle fingers, their left feet, and their forearms. This commonly used procedure of the time was based on the work of the French criminologist Alphonse Bertillon. His method had recently been introduced in the United States (in the Illinois State Penitentiary) and became the most widely used form of criminal identification until it was replaced early in the twentieth century by fingerprinting. On the basis of the photographs alone, a police sergeant concluded Jackson was "a natural monster" ("he has a head such as Napoleon would have") and that Walling was "supremely indifferent to the consequences and to the crime committed."

Fearing for the safety of the two prisoners, the authorities transferred them on February 11 to the Hamilton County jail on the outskirts of Cincinnati. From there they were taken to the funeral parlor to confront Pearl's sister, Mabel, and brother, Fred, who positioned themselves next to the open casket. Even in those distressing surroundings, however, when asked who had committed the murder, each man coldly blamed the other. Mabel pleaded with Jackson in vain: "For the love of heaven, tell me what you have done with poor Baby's head. Think of her mother if nothing else!"

Pearl Bryan, Scott Jackson, Alonzo Walling, February 1896.

> In came Pearl Bryan's sister,
> And falling to her knees
> Begging to Scott Jackson,
> "My sister's head, O please!"

But Jackson had nothing to say, nor did Walling.

Neither man, however, would remain in Ohio for long. On March 7 a hearing was held to decide where the trial would be held: in Ohio, or in Kentucky where the crime had occurred. The judge who would make the decision, Morris Lyon Buchwalter, a graduate of Cornell University, class of 1869, and the Cincinnati Law School, had an enviable civil rights record. He had recently refused to authorize the extradition of a black man from Ohio to Kentucky until he had received assurances from the governor and sheriff that the man would be safe from mob violence. Much to the defendants' dismay, however, Buchwalter ruled in favor of Kentucky, and on March 17, after a higher court had backed his decision, a horse-drawn patrol wagon took the prisoners on "a wild drive" across the Ohio River, a journey of about two miles that took scarcely twenty minutes. On March 23 they were formally arraigned at the Campbell County Circuit Court in Newport, Kentucky.

The trial got under way on April 21 before Judge Charles J. Helm, a prominent Democrat, who had earlier served as the city's attorney and the county's attorney general, and in 1892 had been appointed a circuit court judge. The prosecutor, Marquis Richardson Lockhart—described as "able, profound and logical; before the jury, eloquent and convincing"—had fought for the Confederacy and been wounded in November 1864 at the battle of Bull's Gap in East Tennessee. After having taught school, he read law, was admitted to the bar, and in 1891 became Campbell County attorney. Jackson, the first to be tried, hired Leonard J. Crawford as his lawyer. Born and raised in Newport, Crawford had attended Cincinnati Law School and was said to be "passionately devoted to the principles of the Republican Party." Colonel George Washington represented Walling.

"We will show that this man has been a veritable Dr. Jekyll and Mr. Hyde," Lockhart began, claiming that Jackson, a "monster," "a heartless butcher," had "led a double life." Jackson, he continued, had "deliberately enticed her from her safe country home, and forced her to Fort Thomas, where he took her head, and took her life!" The boy who found the body, and then the bartender and the cab driver, related their stories, and the coroner declared Pearl had been alive when her neck was cut. The prosecution attempted to introduce a headless dummy dressed in Pearl's bloody clothes; when the defense objected, the judge ordered it removed, but he permitted the bloodstained valise to remain in evidence, as well as Pearl's clothing itself, which her mother identified. Cal Crim, one of the detectives, described the trail he had followed. Will Wood stated that Jackson "had illicit relations with Pearl on three different occasions during the late summer" and had told him that an abortion was the only solution.

When the defense's turn came, Jackson took the stand on his own behalf, denying that he had any knowledge about Pearl's death. "He acted the innocent man to perfection," an observer remarked, and held to his story that Walling alone was guilty. But the witnesses called in Jackson's behalf were ineffectual, and they could not provide anything remotely resembling an alibi. So on May 14, after having listened to three weeks of testimony and hearing the prosecutor declare that Jackson was guilty "of seduction, of murder, of mutilating a dead body, and of killing his unborn child"—and hearing him insist that "nothing less than hanging by the neck until he is dead will do!"—the members of the jury took only two hours to return a guilty verdict.

Walling's trial got under way on May 26, 1896, and lasted little more than two weeks. In the end, the jury found him guilty on the basis of much of the same evidence as had been produced at Jackson's trial. A reporter said that Walling "smiled and, when asked if he had anything to say, replied with an oath." An execution date of August 7 was fixed for both men, but their lawyers took the cases to the Kentucky Court of Appeals, and it took several months, until December, for the justices to reject the appeals. Once the rulings had been made, Governor William O'Connell Bradley ordered the men to be hanged on the morning of March 21, 1897. The mothers of the condemned men were granted a final meeting with their sons, but appeals to Pearl Bryan's parents, asking for mercy, failed.

The hangings would be the first in the area in twelve years, and while several thousand people arrived to view the spectacle, there was room in the yard for only a few hundred observers. As morning broke, however, and as the condemned men were being led to the gallows, Jackson suddenly declared that Walling was not guilty. So the prisoners were returned to their cells, and an urgent message was telegraphed to Governor Bradley. He replied that if Jackson were to make a full confession, Walling's life would be spared. But Jackson refused, and at 11:30 the march to the scaffold resumed. The sheriff had a mechanism built that would spring both trapdoors with a single pull of a lever. Walling said, "I die an innocent man," while Jackson lifted his voice in song: "In the sweet by and by / We shall meet on that beautiful shore."

> We shall sing on that beautiful shore
> The melodious songs of the blessed
> And our spirits shall sorrow no more
> Not a sigh for the blessing of rest

Then the sheriff read the death warrants, and at 11:40, as a minister stepped forward to recite a prayer, the trapdoors opened. But death did not come easily: Walling was pronounced dead after seventeen minutes, and Jackson after fourteen.

The story of Pearl Bryan, appalling in every respect, eventually made its way into ballads that were first collected, then published—for example, in the *Journal of American Folklore*—and finally recorded. Most versions named not only the victim but also the villains. A version from West Virginia, in 1924, included the lines: "One night when the moon was shining, / The stars were shining too, / Softly to her dwelling / Walling and Jackson drew." The first phonograph recording was made in 1926 by Vernon Dalhart (born Marion Try Slaughter in Texas in 1883) and released the following year. Dalhart recorded for different labels, and his version included the verse "We know her dear old parents / Their fortune they would give / If Pearl could just return home / A happy life to live."

At about the same time, the duo of Richard Burnett and Leonard Rutherford put out their own version:

> Down on her knees before him
> A pleading for her life
> "What have I done Scott Jackson
> That you should take my life?"

In 1927, Bradley Kincaid—born, fittingly, in Kentucky in 1895—recorded a startling version of the song. His "Pearl Bryan" begins with a plaintive cry: "What have I done, Scott Jackson / That you should take my life? / You know I've always been good to you / And promised to be your wife." But Jackson is without remorse: "You have not the wings of an eagle / Nor from me can you fly / No human hands can aid you / You instantly must die." In disbelief, Pearl renews her plea: "Scott Jackson I am tired / Of wandering here so long / The way is cold and dreary / I pray you take me home." But in the song, as in life, Jackson is pitiless: "Down on her knees before him / She pleaded for her life / Into that snowy bosom / He plunged a gleaming knife."

Although "Pearl Bryan" has been recorded infrequently, in 2001 the Crooked Jades, an old-time band from San Francisco, added the song to their repertoire. A few videos also appeared online that told the story—"Ghost Hunting Headless Corpse Pearl Bryan Still Haunts"—and included the lyrics. But the song has not been performed nearly as often as other nineteenth-century murder ballads, and probably never will be. Perhaps it was the coldly methodical preparation made by the murderers. Perhaps it was the ghastly nature of the deed. Or, possibly, the carnage involved in the beheading. Whatever the reason may be, "Pearl Bryan" can leave a listener with feelings of melancholy deeper even than the songs about Omie Wise, Frankie Silver, Ellen Smith, or Delia Green.

> Pearl died away from home and friends
> Out in that lonely spot
> Take heed, take heed, believe this, girls
> Don't let this be your lot.

CHAPTER 10

DELIA'S GONE (1900)

Delia, Delia,
Why didn't you run
See that desperado,
Had a forty fo' smokeless gun
Cryin' all I had done gone

In the year 1900, Savannah, Georgia, was a relatively small but thriving city, home to fifty-four thousand people, slightly more than half of them African Americans. Someone called it a town that "preserved an old-world charm which more aggressive centers do not possess." Sadly, however, in December it was also the scene of a brutal murder. Late on Christmas Eve, a young black teenager named Moses Houston shot his fourteen-year-old girlfriend, Delia Green, who died the next day. Houston was arrested, tried, quickly convicted, and sentenced to life in the state penitentiary. He was released on parole, though, after serving nearly thirteen years. A song describing the murder, "Delia's Gone," was written soon afterward. Eventually it would be recorded, and many versions would appear.

At the time, Savannah—like other southern cities—was becoming residentially segregated, as whites increasingly moved to the city center and blacks congregated in a northern section known as Yamacraw (taken from the name of a Native American tribe), near the Savannah River. Segregated public schools also had become the norm; predictably, the classrooms for black children were overcrowded and poorly funded. Although the city was a leading exporter of cotton and naval stores—pine timber, rosin, and turpentine—numerous jobs were closed to blacks, many of whom were relegated to domestic or personal service or other menial labor. There were a number of black clergymen and teachers, but few black lawyers and doctors in the city.

The mayor, nevertheless, boasted of the town's achievements: "The time has passed when there could be any doubt as to the future of Savannah. Its continued growth and prosperity are guaranteed, and with all of its citizens manifesting a renewed interest in its welfare and advancement the early years of the coming century must be full of promise." A black resident, writing in 1902, understandably saw matters differently: "In this land of the free, we are burned, tortured, and denied a fair trial, murdered for any imaginary wrong conceived in the brain of the negro-baiting white man."

In any case, Moses Houston could not have known what lay in store for him that December evening. A month shy of his sixteenth birthday and known by the nickname "Cooney," he did not attend school—in fact, he had never learned to read or write—but worked as a day laborer. He lived with his mother, Jane, who was in her forties, his three younger brothers, two younger sisters, and a nephew about his own age. On Christmas Eve, he was attending a party at the home of Willie and Emma West in the Yamacraw neighborhood. Some said the crowd was raucous, even disorderly, while others claimed that everyone was well-behaved, and the main activity was singing "Rock of Ages" while someone played it on the organ. In any event, West had asked Houston to pick up a pistol from a repair shop, and so Moses got the gun, brought it to the house, and there it was, on the table under a napkin.

Delia Green, who worked as a "scrub girl" for the Wests, was also at the party. Although she and Moses had been "more or less intimate" for some months, she evidently took offense that evening when he called her "his girl." Moses then said: "My little wife is mad with me tonight, she does not hear me. She is not saying anything to me," adding, "You don't know how I love you." Delia replied sarcastically: "You son of a bitch. You have been going with me for four months. You know I am a lady." Moses: "That is a damn lie. You know I have had you as many times as I have fingers and toes," adding: "You have been calling me husband." Delia: "You lie!" Someone then told Moses, who was probably drinking, to leave. But as he approached the door, he grabbed the pistol and fired it at Delia, hitting her in the groin. "I am shot," she cried. Delia was taken to her home at 113 Ann Street, was seen by a doctor named J. W. Ward, but died early in the morning of Christmas Day.

> Rubber tired buggy, two-seated hack
> Took Delia to the graveyard, never brought her back
> She's all I've got, is gone
>
> Cooney lookin' high, Cooney lookin' low
> Shot poor Delia with that hated .44
> She's all I've got, is gone

Willie West chased Houston, who had run into the street, held him while the police were called, and turned him over to patrolman J. T. Williams. Houston said that he shot Delia because she called him a son of a bitch, adding that he would do it again, but also offering to pay for her doctor. He was put in jail, and his trial was scheduled for the following March. The judge who would hear the case, Paul F. Seabrook, in later years would run for mayor and be elected on an independent reform ticket. Houston was represented by Raiford Falligant, a white attorney in his twenties and a recent graduate of the University of Georgia law school. The son of a prominent physician, he described himself as "a practicing lawyer[,] very successful in my profession," and he would, within a short time, become "prominent in the best social circles of the city."

The trial was held in March 1901. Prompted no doubt by his attorney, Houston endeavored to put the best face on what he had done on Christmas Eve. He said that he had gone to the Wests' house at about seven o'clock in the evening, then went home, had dinner, returned "and called for Delia," but she was not there. He was sent to retrieve West's pistol from the gunsmith and was given fifty cents to pay for the repair. Then the other guests, who were "full," sent him on another errand: to obtain beer and whiskey. On his return, he and another boy started to engage in some shenanigans. Cooney maintained that what happened next was an accident: "He got hold of the pistol and in fun we kind of struggled for it. I told him what are you doing with that pistol, and I got it and it went off and struck Delia. It went off when we are funning."

As historian Sean Wilentz has pointed out, Raiford Falligant called attention to Houston's youth, arranging for him to wear short pants at his arraignment, and referring to him as a "mere child." At the trial, he brought to the stand a grocer for whom Houston had worked, who said "his reputation is a peaceable one and he is a peaceable boy so far as my knowledge goes." Further, the attorney tried to convince the jury that Delia Green's murder was accidental: "That upon Christmas Eve night about 11 o'clock in the year 1900, when he was only a boy 14 years of age, he got into bad company in a rough house and got to drinking and tusseling with another boy over a pistol which went off and hit and killed a girl in the house where all of the parties were drinking." His client, Falligant said, "was crazed by drink in boisterous company for the first time in his life and . . . the crowd he was with and in got him drunk."

The prosecution countered with several eyewitnesses, including Willie West, his wife, Emma, guests who were at the party, and the policeman who arrived on the scene. Willie West testified that he chased Houston after he shot Delia: "He snapped the pistol four or five times but it did not go off when I was going after him. I caught him and said he to me, 'Willie, turn me loose for five dollars,' I said, 'I will not turn you loose.'" West's wife, Emma, who was Delia's

The word "alumnus" as used in this letter, refers to any man who has matriculated at the University, whether a graduate or not.

University of Georgia.

DEAR SIR:

As an important part of the celebration of the Centennial of the University, the Board of Trustees has ordered the preparation and publication of a CENTENNIAL ALUMNI CATALOGUE, to contain, as far as possible, a full but concise account of the life and services of all the alumni during the century.

The hearty co-operation of all living alumni, and of the relatives and friends of all deceased, is necessary to the success of the undertaking. Your prompt and careful attention to the inquiries set forth below will be a real service to the University, and will be most cordially appreciated. If you are not able to give the information under any head, please leave the space *blank*, so that it may be filled by others.

The alma mater again extends to all alumni a hearty invitation to join with her in the celebration of the Centennial, June 12th—19th, 1901.

Fraternally yours,

WALTER B. HILL,

Chancellor.

1. Name, in full, (Do not use initials).

    Raiford Falligant.

2. Address; state, county, city, street and number:

    Georgia, Chatham County, Savannah, 111 W. Oglethorpe Ave.

3. Place and time of birth:

    Savannah, Ga., Jan. 12, 1872.

4. Date of entrance, with class entered:

    Sept. 13, 1897, Junior

Rayford Falligant notations, Alumni Catalogue. Courtesy of Hargrett Rare Book and Manuscript Library/University of Georgia Libraries.

cousin, also testified that she saw Houston "with a pistol right after the shooting and the smoke was coming from it. . . . Mose looked as if he had been drinking." Still another witness, who claimed to be only four or five feet away from Delia, said: "Delia touched Mose Houston on the face and cursed him. Cooney told Delia to let him alone and she would not let him alone. He got away a piece and came back again. When he came back he spoke a bad word." They argued, and "he was close to her when he shot and hit her right in the stomach." J. T. Williams, the policeman who was called to the scene, added: "He said that he did it. He said that they had had a little row and they were cursing each other. He said he shot her because she called him a son of a bitch. I got his pistol. Mose told me that he shot the girl and that he would do it again."

After a brief trial, the jury asked Judge Seabrook for a clarification: "What would be the sentence for a murder conviction with a recommendation of mercy?" The judge replied that conviction carried with it, at the very least, life imprisonment. Apparently satisfied that the death penalty was not on the table, the jury returned with a guilty verdict, and the judge sentenced Houston to life at hard labor in the state penitentiary. "In doing so," he said, "I exhort you to be a man, even in confinement, to repent of your past evil deeds and strive to earn the confidence and respect of those placed in authority above you." "Thank you, sir," Houston said. Later, when he was asked to comment on the sentence, he said: "I don't like it at all but I guess I'll have to stand it."

> Cooney said to the judge "What might be my fine?"
> And I told you "Poor boy, you got ninety-nine"
> She's all I've got, is gone

Moses "Cooney" Houston spent the next twelve and a half years behind bars. In all likelihood he began serving his time at the recently opened Georgia State Prison Farm, which housed aged, infirm, and juvenile convicts (the youngest was nine years old!), and later was incarcerated in the State Convict Camp in Commerce. The state prison farm encompassed four thousand acres, one thousand of which were devoted to growing cotton. He undoubtedly did the kind of agricultural or possibly industrial labor that prisoners were required to do. In 1910 the prison had to be rebuilt after a fire destroyed much of the structure. The prison also later housed the state's first electric chair, which was constructed by inmates, who were presumably in a melancholy (or more likely morbid) frame of mind.

After Houston had been imprisoned for a decade, his lawyer petitioned the governor for clemency. He presented supportive affidavits from prison guards and from many of the jury members who now favored clemency, noted that Houston "has been dutiful, faithful and a good convict," and said that he had "an old, infirm and decrepit mother, Jane Houston, 56 years of age, unable to earn a living." Falligant added that "he was just a mere child at the time when he got into bad company and so unfortunately committed the act that he now suffers for." A pardon, he concluded, would allow Houston to be a help "to his poor old mother who is a widow, without home or property and with few charitable friends to help her merely exist in her old age." The prison warden, J. H. McGwier, assured Houston's mother that her son "is in the best of health and makes me a model prisoner. His conduct in every respect is all I could ask and he makes us one of our best hands."

The appeal to the governor failed, however, and so Falligant bided his time, and in March 1912 petitioned the Georgia Prison Commission for a parole. He collected statements from many of the grand jurors and trial jurors, from prison guards and the warden, and even from the state's solicitor general, all of whom now favored Houston's release. Seven grand jurors endorsed the appeal, Falligant said, adding, "One refused because he was opposed to pardons, and one is a railroad man whom I have been unable to catch, and the others are either dead or have gone away." Although Judge Seabrook would not support clemency "because it is his policy not to do so for any one he has sentenced," the solicitor general favored it. If it were possible "for the Board to parole the boy, now a man, if they cannot pardon him," Falligant added, he would be given work in the "Colored Laurel Grove Cemetery," and monthly reports would be submitted as to "the boy's conduct and condition."

The attorney also enclosed an appeal from Houston's mother, who said she cared for two children, "one of whom is crippled in one foot," struggled to make ends meet by selling vegetables at the Savannah market and, having no husband, needed the help of her son, who "was always a good boy and had never been in any trouble . . . and up to that time gave me every cent he earned to help me along, and was of great help to me." She "begs and pleads with the Honorable Pardon Board and the Governor of Georgia, to pardon her boy."

Despite these pleas, one of the governor's aides had his doubts, writing in October 1912: "The only thing advanced in behalf of this man is that he was only fourteen years old when the crime was committed and that no malice was proven. He claims it was an accident. The boy killed a girl on Christmas night, but the trial record does not bear out the claim of accident. It is rather a case of dare-deviltry. He presents a good record as a prisoner." Falligant kept trying, however, pointing out that the man in charge of the cemetery would not only give Houston a job but also report on his progress. The pardon board eventually relented, and on October 15, 1913, Governor John M. Slaton sat down to write: "A negro boy, on Christmas eve night, was in a drinking party with a crowd of negroes, minors and adults. He was fourteen years old and shot a negro girl who cursed him. He has served over twelve years. Prior to the offense, his record was good and his term good in the penitentiary. Parole approved." Moses Houston went free, and four years later, on July 16, 1917, the state prison commission granted him a pardon.

In the fall of 1911, while Houston was still incarcerated, the lyrics to a song about Delia, titled "One Mo' Rounder Gone," were published in the *Journal of American Folklore*. The author of the article, Howard W. Odum, had recently completed two doctoral degrees, one in psychology at Clark University and the other in sociology at Columbia University. He noted that the song "gives a repetition of the burial-scenes and general feeling which was caused by the death of a girl. Its unusual feature lies in the fact that the song applies to a girl."

> Rubber-tired buggy, double-seated hack
> Well, it carried po' Delia to graveyard, failed to bring her back
> Lawdy, one mo' rounder gone
>
> Delia's mother weep, Delia's mother mourn
> She wouldn't have taken it so hard if po' girl had died at home
> Well, one mo' ole rounder gone

Governor John Marshall Slaton and his wife, June 1915. Courtesy of the Library of Congress.

Odum explained that the term "rounder" could apply to women as well as men, and could, in fact, apply to any "worthless and wandering person, who prides himself on being idle."

In 1928, Newman Ivey White published several versions of "Delie" that he had collected over the years in North Carolina, Alabama, and, of course, Georgia. White, a specialist in the works of Percy Bysshe Shelley, taught English literature at Duke University. But he also collected songs, and his book *American Negro Folksongs* included three versions of "Delie" (in which the word "coon" was usually used instead of "Cooney"). One of the songs came from Auburn, Alabama, in 1915–1916, and was "sung by Negro to guitar"; another came from Durham, North Carolina, in 1919—White said he had heard it sung "by old farm Negroes at one of their dancing and singing meetings"—but it bore no relation to the actual event; and in the third version Delia was taken not to a graveyard but to "de bone yard." One of the typical verses:

> Delie, Delie, was a-goin' her last round
> When ol coon came by
> An' shot her to the groun'
> All I had done had done gone

Although several recordings of "Delia" were made during the twenties and thirties, the lyrics had little or nothing to do with the events that had taken place in Savannah in December 1900. In 1924, Reese DuPree recorded the song as "One More Rounder Gone." In his rendition, Houston calls Delia on the telephone to ask: "How can it be? / You said that you loved another man and you don't love me / Well there'll be one more round to go." The verses, however, were quite general:

> I ain't no bully, I don't like to fight
> But there's one thing I'm just crazy about
> A little lovin' every night
> But that rounder's got my gal and gone

In November 1940 John Lomax and his wife, Ruby, while passing through Atlanta, arranged to record Blind Willie McTell in a hotel room. McTell sang "Delia" for them, although he changed "Cooney" to "Curtis" and made Delia a gambler. He also referred to going to the graveyard in a "rubber tired buggy, double-seated hack":

> Curtis' looking high, Curtis' looking low
> Shot poor Delia down with that hateful forty-four
> She's all I've got, is gone

A few years earlier, in the summer of 1935, John Lomax's son, Alan, had come across another version of the song, and it eventually became the one that was most commonly heard. Only nineteen years of age, Lomax was on a folk-song collecting trip for the Library of Congress in the Bahamas and was overwhelmed by the experience: "Here, you see, there is a live, flowing, vital folk culture and the collector lives in a continual state of confusion & exhilaration." One of the groups he recorded was the Nassau String Band, although he substituted "Delia" for the song's original title, "Cooney and Delia." A doctor was called, the band leader sang, and "he did everything that a doctor could, but he couldn't bring Delia back":

> They sent for her mother
> She comes dressed in black
> She cried all day and she cried all night
> But cries wont bring her back
> Delia's gone one more round Delia's gone

The last line would be included in nearly all the later versions of the song.

Is it possible that Moses Houston, who lived until 1927, might have heard the song? There is no way to know for certain, but as the decades went by, many singers, ranging from Pat Boone to Bob Dylan, recorded it. By 1994 Johnny Cash had written entirely new lyrics to "Delia's Gone" and along with Kate

Blind Willie McTell, Atlanta, Georgia, November 1940. Courtesy of the Library of Congress.

Moss had made a video of it. Straying far from the facts of the case, Cash came up with a blood-curdling (and misogynistic) version:

> She was low down and trifling and she was cold and mean
> Kind of evil make me want to grab my sub machine
> Delia's gone, one more round, Delia's gone
>
> So if your woman's devilish, you can let her run
> Or you can bring her down and do her like Delia got done
> Delia's gone, one more round, Delia's gone

Poor Delia Green! Senselessly murdered at a tender age only to be transformed, nearly a century later, into someone she surely never was.

Bold Highwaymen
and Outlaws

CHAPTER 11

COLE YOUNGER (1876)

I am one of a band of highwaymen,
Cole Younger is my name
My crimes and depredations,
Have brought my friends to shame

"**R**ip Van Winkle himself was not so long away," Cole Younger said of the twenty-five years he spent in the Minnesota State Prison, a true enough statement, since Washington Irving's fictional character had slept for only twenty. In September 1876, Younger was arrested along with his younger brothers, Bob and Jim, after they robbed a bank and killed two guards in Northfield, Minnesota. Badly wounded, the brothers pleaded guilty to robbery and murder and received life sentences. In November they entered the prison, generally known as Stillwater. Bob died there, of tuberculosis, in 1889, but Cole and Jim were paroled in 1901. Jim committed suicide a year later. Cole then wrote a memoir, *The Story of Cole Younger by Himself, Being an Autobiography of the Missouri Guerrilla Captain and Outlaw,* in which he told of fighting for the South during the Civil War and discussed his crimes, imprisonment, and eventual release. A song about him was being sung within a few years of his arrest and was published during his lifetime in John A. Lomax's collection of cowboy songs.

Thomas Coleman "Cole" Younger was born in 1844 near Lee's Summit, Missouri, not far from Kansas City. His father was a farmer, a merchant, and a federal mail agent, and the family—there were fourteen children—seemed to be reasonably well off. But with the coming of the Civil War, the life Cole had known fell to pieces. He was seventeen years old, and his father, a Northern sympathizer who believed that slavery should be abolished—although he owned a few slaves!—was killed by Union militiamen in a raid in July 1862. The family's house was burned to the ground. By then, Cole had joined a band of Confederate guerrillas led by William Clarke Quantrill, and three of his brothers also enlisted in the Southern cause. In August 1862 he took part in the battle of Lone Jack in Jackson County, Missouri, and on Christmas Eve, Cole and his comrades attacked a Union outpost in Kansas City, killing six Union soldiers, some of whom, or so he believed, had been responsible for his father's death.

On August 21, 1863, Younger took part in Quantrill's brutal predawn raid on Lawrence, Kansas, that left the town a "smoking funeral pyre." "It was," he confessed, "a day of butchery." Some 150 men and boys were killed, and "a large portion of the town's business and residential districts were in ashes and the faces of those who survived the slaughter bore mute testimony to the tragic scene." Eventually promoted to the rank of captain, Younger led his troops into Louisiana, and later to California, apparently on a recruiting mission, where he remained until the war ended. Then he returned to Missouri—which had not seceded—finding, to his dismay, that Republicans controlled the state government. Those who had advocated secession were excluded from politics, and efforts were under way to enfranchise emancipated African Americans.

Younger left and headed south to Louisiana and Texas, where he made a home for his mother, Bursheba (who would pass away in 1870) and earned a living by driving cattle. By 1866, however, he and three of his brothers had joined forces with Jesse and Frank James and the members of their gang. In February they pulled off a bank robbery, in Liberty, Missouri. In March 1868 they robbed a bank in Russellville, Kentucky, and more holdups followed of banks and stagecoaches in states far and wide: Missouri, Kentucky, West Virginia, Iowa, and Kansas. Over a period of several years, the Younger brothers robbed twelve banks, seven trains, and four stagecoaches. Sometimes the thefts went off without a hitch, but on other occasions they did not. In the course of committing the crimes, the Younger brothers and the Jameses killed at least eleven people.

On July 21, 1873, they pulled off their first train robbery, derailing the Chicago, Rock Island and Pacific Railroad at Adair, Iowa, and looting it. In the crash, the engineer was killed and some passengers were injured. In January 1874, after yet another robbery, this time of the Iron Mountain Railroad at Gad's Hill, Missouri, the Pinkerton National Detective Agency was summoned. In March, two of its agents chanced upon Cole's younger brothers, John and Jim, near Roscoe, Missouri, and a gunfight erupted. One of the detectives was killed, and John, twenty-three years of age, was shot in the neck, mortally wounded. "Poor John," Cole later wrote, "hunted down and shot like a wild beast, and never was a boy more innocent." The robberies, though, continued: in December 1874 of the Kansas Pacific Railroad at Muncie, Kansas; in September 1875 of a bank at Huntington, West Virginia; and in July 1876 of the Missouri Pacific Railroad at Otterville, Missouri. Cole's brother Bob once remarked, with considerable understatement, "We are rough men and are used to rough ways."

> The engineerman and fireman killed
> The conductor escaped alive
> And now their bones lie mouldering
> Beneath Nebraska's skies

Late in the summer of 1876, the gang made its way to Northfield, Minnesota, their target the First National Bank. But this time, some of the townsfolk fought back. In a fierce shootout, members of the gang were killed, as were some residents, and others were wounded. Frank James was among the injured, and so were the Younger brothers: Cole took five bullets, Jim three, and Bob two. Weak and crippled, they managed to escape and headed west, avoiding a sizable posse made up of as many as a thousand men. After a few days, they split up, the James brothers heading in one direction and the Youngers in another, hoping to evade their pursuers. Jesse and Frank James somehow made their way back to Missouri. But the Youngers were eventually surrounded, mired in a boggy swamp. On September 21, a full-blown shootout took place in which the three brothers were more seriously wounded. They surrendered and were taken into custody.

In November they were placed on trial in Faribault, a town about forty miles south of Minneapolis, charged with robbery, assault, murder, and being accessories to murder. The judge was Samuel Lord, and the prosecutor, George N. Baxter. According to Cole, the brothers' defense attorney, Thomas Rutledge, told them their involvement meant they were certain to be convicted. To save their lives, they were advised to plead guilty, since state law provided that "an accused murderer who pleaded guilty was not subject to the death penalty." (The law was designed to avoid the expense of a trial, but shortly thereafter it was changed.) So, one after another, the Youngers did as their lawyer suggested, and on November 30 the judge sentenced them to life imprisonment at hard labor at Stillwater. "I have no words of comfort for you or desire to reproach you or deride you," he said. "While the law leaves you life, all its pleasures, all its hopes, all its joys are gone from you, and all that is left is the empty shell." According to the *St. Paul Pioneer Press*, "an expression of satisfaction and relief swept over their faces."

The Stillwater prison, first constructed in the 1850s, had been rebuilt in the 1870s, made more secure, and enlarged to hold more prisoners, about three hundred in all when the Youngers arrived on November 22, 1876. Cole, Jim, and Bob were assigned numbers 899, 900, and 901. They were given uniforms with penitentiary stripes, and led to cramped, musty cells, five by seven feet, that were infested with bedbugs, were "poorly ventilated, damp and uncomfortable, were overrun with roaches," and emitted a stench that was "almost intolerable." Ventilation was provided by a six-inch hole in the wall. Most of the inmates spent their days in the basement of the prison, man-ufacturing tubs, buckets, and barrels. Cole began in the thresher factory, where he made sieves and belts, but eventually he was assigned to the library and then to the hospital.

> 'Twas there in the Stillwater jail we lay
> A-wearing our lives away
> Two James boys left to tell the tale
> Of the sad and fateful day

Like all inmates, the brothers were subjected to the Bertillon system. Invented in 1879 by Alphonse Bertillon, a French officer, and termed "anthro-pometrics," the method supposedly provided a surefire means of identifica-tion by measuring precisely an individual's physical characteristics: the length and breadth of the head, left middle finger, left foot, left forearm, right ear, and other body parts. The height of prisoners was carefully calculated, as were the dimensions of their extended arms. In Bertillon's view, "every mea-surement slowly reveals the workings of the criminal." First used in the United States in the Illinois State Penitentiary, it quickly spread to other penal institutions and was used until replaced by fingerprinting early in the twentieth century.

Both of Cole's brothers would suffer from acute illnesses in prison, and in Bob's case, a fatal disease. By 1889 he had come down with pulmonary tubercu-losis. As he grew increasingly feeble, many appeals were made to the governor asking "that he may go to his relations before his life ends." One of the letters came from Ignatius Donnelly, recently a Minnesota state senator and author of a book that claimed Shakespeare's plays had been written by Francis Bacon. Bob was "a mere boy," Donnelly said, and should be permitted "to die outside the shadow of the penitentiary, and in the midst of those who love him." His plea, though, and everyone else's, was denied. Bob's sister Retta was allowed to be with him during his final weeks, and his brothers, too, were at his side when, in September 1889, he died at the age of thirty-four.

Jim Younger, too, suffered terribly in prison, chiefly as the result of old gun-shot wounds. A bullet had damaged part of his jaw, and so he could not eat solid food and had to sip his meals through a straw. Another bullet had lodged near his brain, and although an operation in the prison had succeeded in removing

The Youngers: *left to right*, Robert, Henrietta, Cole, and James, September 1889. Courtesy of the Library of Congress.

it, Jim was left badly disfigured, his speech slurred, prone to acute headaches, and nearly unable to swallow. Not surprisingly, he experienced severe episodes of depression, during which, Cole said, "he would give up all hope, and his gloomy spirits would repel the sympathy of those who were disposed to cheer him up."

For Cole and Jim, the years passed slowly, but beginning in the spring of 1888 friends began working for their release, submitting petitions, even on occasion meeting with the governor of Minnesota. They cited the Youngers' good behavior in prison, noted that their "departure from the path of rectitude was unquestionably the direct result of the unfavorable conditions" during and after the Civil War, pointed out "they are now old men," and urged that the law not be "an instrument of torture to satiate revenge." But one governor after another turned down the requests.

In 1896 a glimmer of hope appeared when Colorado adopted a constitutional amendment establishing a board of pardons composed of the governor, the attorney general, and the chief justice of the state supreme court. To grant a pardon required a unanimous vote, and so in June 1897 a letter-writing campaign began, urging the men's release on the ground that, after twenty years of imprisonment, they had been successfully rehabilitated. Even a former warden of the prison now spoke up in their behalf. But the pardon board also heard from those who claimed "these men turned hell loose in our streets," and in the end turned down the application. The "character of this crime renders it one absolutely without extenuating circumstances," the board decided, adding that the brothers had chosen to live as "a notorious band of outlaws."

Finally, in July 1901, the board relented, while also setting several stringent parole conditions: the brothers were to remain in Minnesota, account for any change in their residence, and avoid "evil associations"; nor were they to exhibit themselves "in any dime museum, circus, theater, opera-house, or any other place of public amusement or assembly, where a charge is made for admission." They had to report whether they had been "constantly at work during the last month, and, if not, why not." At the ages of fifty-seven and fifty-three, the two men finally left prison.

They obtained jobs as tombstone salesmen for a granite company, at least temporarily, but Cole's reports to the warden at the Minnesota state prison indicated they did not earn much. "Haven't sold as many stones as I would like to," he reported in August 1901, "the people up here are not in position to buy valuable monuments." In Minnesota, he added, "the people are all new comers and need all this ready money to improve their little homes and leave their dead to wait." Otherwise, Cole generally expressed satisfaction, admitting that he used tobacco, but as for intoxicating beverages, "No. Coffee has been my strongest drink." Naturally, in writing to the warden, he was inclined to put the best face on events, and so his reports often said, "I have been at peace with all of mankind. I am all O.K." or "all is lovely as far as I am concerned."

In Jim's case, however, freedom was not what he imagined. He eventually lost his job and had to make ends meet by working at a cigar stand. By mid-September 1902, a friend remarked, "He gave every evidence of being greatly depressed, and appeared utterly broken down in spirit, in hope and in ambition." Jim told someone, "I reckon a fellow might as well cut his throat and be done with it." Then, an accident caused an old bullet wound to act up, causing him intense discomfort. On October 19, 1902, he took a hotel room and shot himself, leaving a despairing note: "All relatives just stay away from me. No crocodile tears wanted."

Several months later, in February 1903, the pardon board granted Cole Younger a conditional pardon, thereby allowing him to return to Missouri. "I do not want to be received as a hero for I am a hero of nothing," he remarked. Arriving back home at Lee's Summit, he promised not to "exhibit myself as an actor or participant in any public entertainment," but said that he wanted to make "an honest living," and soon became involved in staging Wild West shows, which, he said, were educational, and patronized "by good people." He hooked up with a few entrepreneurs on the make and became a partner with—of all people—Frank James. Younger only worked behind the scenes but nevertheless acted as the general manager. Billed as "The World's Greatest Exhibition," the show included "Russian Cossacks, Bedouin Arabs, American Cowboys, Roosevelt Rough Riders, Indians, Cubans, Western Girls, Mexicans, Broncos, Overland Stage Coach, Emigrant Train, The Siege of Deadwood and the World's Mounted Warriors." Evidently, though, the show was poorly produced, and so it drew small crowds, went into the red, occasionally ran into trouble with rowdies, and closed within months.

In his remaining years, Cole Younger tried his hand at various business ventures—working at carnivals (where patrons could see "The Live Octopus," "The Den of Horrors," and "Cole Younger's Coliseum"), selling oil burners, and promoting an electric trolley—none of which, in the end, panned out. By 1909 he decided to visit cities in the Midwest, the South, and the Southwest, lecturing on "What My Life Has Taught Me." His earnings allowed him to move into a more comfortable house, and as he got older his niece moved in to offer help. He even decided to have himself baptized.

So Cole Younger—who passed away in 1916—may have heard the ballad about him that first appeared in the late 1870s and was later published in John Lomax's *Cowboy Songs and Other Frontier Ballads* in 1910. If so, he surely would have doubted its accuracy, since the lyrics had the brothers robbing a "Union Pacific railway train" and killing the engineer and fireman, when, in fact, the Youngers were not involved in that holdup, which had taken place in the fall of 1877, nearly a year after they were already imprisoned. That robbery, in which no one died, was the work of others. Nevertheless, the lyrics in Lomax's book, folklore scholar Norm Cohen has said, convey a "penitential attitude": "I had my eye on the Northfield bank / When brother Bob did say / 'Now, Cole, if you undertake the job / you will surely curse the day.'"

Mark Williams, a native Texan, made the first recording of a ballad about Cole Younger in November 1930. Known as "the cowboy crooner," Williams had worked as a cowboy before becoming a professional singer. He began recording on the Brunswick label in 1927, at twenty-four, and later recorded for Decca, issuing, in all, thirty-six sides. Later, in the 1930s and 1940s, he performed as "Happy Hank" on a children's radio program in Des Moines, Iowa. He recorded several songs, including "The Dying Ranger" and "The Night Herding Song," at the same session at which he sang "Cole Younger":

Cole Younger, ca. 1915. Courtesy of
the Library of Congress.

We'll ride to avenge our father's death
And try to win the prize
We'll fight those anti-guerrillas
Until the day we die. . . .

Just hand us over your money
And make no further delay
We are the famous Younger boys
We spare no time to play

Less than a year after Williams's version came out, Edward L. Crain recorded
"Bandit Cole Younger." Raised on a ranch outside Longview, Texas, Crain, who
worked driving cattle, played the guitar, fiddle, and mandolin and appeared on
radio programs in Dallas. He learned the song from a ranch hand and recorded
it in 1931 (his version was included more than twenty years later on Harry
Smith's *Anthology of American Folk Music*). He also released another version of
the song much later, while living in Oregon. In the later version, Bob warns Cole
"if you undertake the job / you'll always curse the day":

We run for life, for death was near
Four hundred on our trail
We soon was overtaken
And landed safe in jail

All of these early songs vindicated the brothers, depicting them as brave, fearless men who defended the common people against capitalists and the railroad interests, and even as sensitive souls who were capable of regretting the crimes they had committed.

Since the early 1930s, many other versions of "Cole Younger" have appeared, although not as many as have been recorded about his onetime partner Jesse James. Both men were outlaws—were, in fact, murderers—who had fought on the side of the South during the Civil War, had joined forces on a number of holdups, and for a time had even been friends, but their lives and especially their deaths could hardly have been more dissimilar. Jesse James, who never spent a day in prison and never seemed sorry for the crimes he committed, was gunned down by a traitor, a "dirty little coward," when he was still a relatively young man. By contrast, Cole Younger spent more than a third of his life in the penitentiary, was a model prisoner, then spent many years struggling to make ends meet, and died when he was seventy-two, apparently of old age. If he was not as famous as Jesse or Frank James, Younger's "crimes and depredations" were no less bloody, and no less brutal, than theirs.

CHAPTER 12

JESSE JAMES (1882)

Jesse had a wife to mourn for his life
Three children, they were brave
But that dirty little coward that shot Mister Howard
Has laid Jesse James in his grave

Although other criminals had longer careers than Jesse James, stole more money, and murdered more innocent people, he is arguably the most famous outlaw in American history. More than twenty books and countless articles have been written about him. He has been featured in nearly forty Hollywood films, his character portrayed by the likes of Tyrone Power, Robert Wagner, Robert Duvall, Rob Lowe, and Brad Pitt. More songs have been recorded about him than about any other bandit—more, indeed, than about any other American. Museums devoted to his life's story exist all over Missouri: at the farm on which he grew up in Kearney, at a bank he robbed in Liberty, and at the house in which he was killed in St. Joseph. International arts and film festivals are named for him. Even County Kerry, Ireland, his father's birthplace, has a Jesse James Tavern. More than one hundred years after his death his grave was exhumed and the remains subjected to modern forensic analysis in what proved to be a futile attempt to settle, once and for all, a long-standing debate about whether the corpse was really that of Jesse James.

Jesse Woodson James was born in 1847 in Kearney, Missouri, the son of Robert Sallee James, a twenty-nine-year-old ordained Baptist preacher, and twenty-two-year old Zerelda Cole. Four years earlier, the couple had their first child, Alexander Franklin, who was always known as Frank. A daughter, Susan, was born in November 1850, a few months after Robert had left for California, either to look for gold, get away from his wife, or save more souls. But he soon took sick and died in a mining camp. In 1852, his widow, after experiencing much financial hardship, married a wealthy man, Benjamin A. Simms, but he was killed in a horse accident early in 1854. The following year she married her third husband, Dr. Reuben Samuel, and the couple would have a daughter, Sarah Louisa, born in 1858. "Jesse is light-hearted, reckless, devil-may-care," an acquaintance commented, while Frank by contrast was "sober, sedate. . . . Jesse laughs at everything—Frank at nothing at all."

When the Civil War began in April 1861, Missouri was one of four slave states that did not secede. Nevertheless, Confederate sympathies there ran strong, and many young men backed the Southern cause, among them eighteen-year-old Frank James. He joined William Clarke Quantrill's Raiders and was in Lawrence, Kansas, in August 1863 when Quantrill and his men, numbering in the hundreds, engaged in an orgy of looting and murder. They burned 154 dwellings to the ground and killed 183 boys and men, some as young as fourteen and some as old as ninety, many of the victims being gunned down in view of their families. An eyewitness later said that Quantrill's men "all thirsted for revenge. And they all slaked their thirst in blood. . . . With demoniac yells the scoundrels flew hither and yon, wherever a man was to be seen, shooting him down like a dog. Men were called from their beds and murdered before the eyes of wives and children on their doorsteps. Tears, entreaties, prayers availed nothing. The fiends of hell were among us and . . . they satiated their thirst for blood with fiendish delight." Within the year, by the spring of 1864, Jesse James, only sixteen, was old enough to join his brother in the marauding band.

So they were with Quantrill when he carried out further raids, sometimes murdering people merely because they were Union sympathizers. Jesse himself received a serious gunshot wound in the chest while stealing a saddle. But he remained with the gang until it finally broke up in June 1865 after Quantrill himself was killed during a raid. Even as the raiders dispersed, the James brothers and some of the gang turned to a new line of work: robbing banks. From 1866 through 1869 they pulled off seven such holdups, chiefly in small Missouri towns. The first target, in February 1866, was the Clay County Savings Association in Liberty. While a dozen gang members waited outside, two others entered the bank, forced the cashiers inside a large safe, and stole more than $58,000, government bonds as well as $18,000 in gold and silver coins. As they rode off, one of the robbers shot and killed a bystander. In all likelihood, it was the nation's first daylight bank holdup in peacetime.

That crime, like all the others, was motivated by greed, but occasionally by other considerations—personal hatred, for example. One of the men that Jesse James most despised was Lieutenant Colonel Samuel P. Cox, a Union officer who, back in October 1864, had shot and killed William T. "Bloody Bill" Anderson, a Confederate guerrilla leader whom James idolized. Now, five years later, in December 1869, the James brothers rode into Gallatin, Missouri, meaning to

Jesse James, ca. 1864.

rob the Daviess County Savings Association. Entering the bank, Jesse believed the clerk was that same Samuel P. Cox, and so he shot him through the heart. As it turned out, the victim only resembled Cox; rather, he was John W. Sheets, the principal owner of the bank, who had been a captain in the Union army. The brothers made off with very little cash, yet boasted of their deed afterward, so their purpose all along may have been to take revenge on Cox, whom they mistakenly believed to be there. Then they fled, the law in pursuit, but made their getaway even though Jesse, whose leg caught in his stirrup, was dragged for thirty to forty feet before he could mount his horse. Posses were sent out but failed to find their quarry.

> Jesse and his brother, Frank, they robbed the Gallatin bank
> And carried the money from the town
> It was in that very place that they had a little race
> And they shot Captain Sheets to the ground

It was the first time that the newspapers, reporting a crime, mentioned the name of Jesse James. But it would not be the last. To be sure, the gang lay low for a year and a half following the Gallatin theft. But starting in mid-1871 the James brothers and their followers—one of them Cole Younger—committed a dozen robberies in little more than three years. The crimes took place in an ever-expanding area, starting in Missouri but then branching out to Iowa, Kentucky, Arkansas, Mississippi, and even Texas. At first the gang set its sights on banks, traveling fairs, and stagecoaches, but by the summer of 1873 James decided to go for bigger game—the railroads. The Chicago, Rock Island and Pacific Railroad, wending its way through Iowa, would be the first target. At a certain point on its route where the track curved sharply, the gang derailed the train. The engineer died in the crash, and the train lurched to a standstill, making it easy to board. In a matter of minutes the gang broke into the safe, stole more than $2,300, and then took off for Missouri.

A remarkable feature of Jesse James's robberies was his practice of writing to the newspapers to explain and justify his actions. Some letters he wrote himself, but others were evidently written for him, in whole or in part, by John Newman Edwards, a former Confederate sympathizer and publicist who initially made contact with the gang in the spring of 1870. That June, a letter appeared in a Kansas City newspaper, addressed to the governor and signed by Jesse James, which said that while he was a "peaceable citizen" he knew that "if I was to submit to an arrest, that I would be mobbed and hanged without a trial." Yet another letter published in September 1872 declared: "We are not thieves—we are bold robbers." Like Alexander the Great, Julius Caesar, and Napoleon Bonaparte, James stated, all he did was "rob the rich and give to the poor." Whenever he killed someone, he added, he was acting in self-defense: "But a man who is a d——d enough fool to refuse to open a safe or a vault when he is covered with a pistol ought to die." For good measure, he denounced Republican politicians, saying that if President Ulysses S. Grant was not reelected "then I can make an honest living, and then I will not have to rob, as taxes will not be so heavy."

In April 1874, now twenty-seven, Jesse James decided the time had come to get married. He had known Zerelda Mims since she had cared for him after the gunshot wound he received in 1865. Usually known as "Zee," she was nearly two years older than Jesse, had been named for his mother, and was his first cousin: her mother was Jesse's father's sister. Described as "diminutive, dark-haired and a devout Methodist," she persuaded a minister, who was initially reluctant, given Jesse's notoriety, to perform the ceremony. The couple would have two children, Jesse, born in 1875, and Mary, in 1879. (In 1878 Zee gave birth to twins, who died in infancy.) Two months after Jesse's wedding, his brother Frank eloped with a young woman named Anna Ralston. They were married in June, and the couple had a son.

By 1874, Allan Pinkerton had set out on the trail of the James brothers, a mission that would have unintended, if predictably tragic, consequences.

Founder of the famous private detective agency, whose motto was "We Never Sleep," Pinkerton had emigrated from Scotland to the United States in 1842 and soon entered the crime-busting business. In January 1875, unaware that James was in Nashville, Tennessee (where he had begun using the alias of "John David Howard"), Pinkerton planned an assault on James's mother's home in Kearney, Missouri. He directed his agents: "Above all else destroy the house, wipe it from the face of the earth. . . . Burn the house down." So in the middle of the night, his men surrounded the house, opened fire, and hurled an iron ball, seven and a half inches in diameter, filled with flammable liquid, through a window.

Someone picked up the sphere and threw it in the fireplace, where it exploded, jagged pieces of cast iron flying in all directions. A large fragment hit Jesse's thirteen-year-old half brother, Archie; he died within the hour and would be buried "dressed in a suit of Confederate gray." Another section shattered Jesse's mother Zerelda's right arm, which had to be amputated—it was done without anesthesia—just below the elbow. Other members of the family were also severely injured. Although Pinkerton and some of his men were indicted for the boy's murder, they were never tried. The horrified reaction to the attack on innocent people led the Missouri legislature to pass a bill granting a general amnesty to the James brothers, but it did not receive the required two-thirds majority. Jesse James wrote a letter to the newspapers: "Pinkerton, I hope and pray that our Heavenly father may deliver you into my hands."

Moving to a small town in Tennessee not far from Nashville, James, using his alias and claiming to be a grain buyer, continued to write to the newspapers and blame northern radicals for persecuting the South. He even insisted that the Missouri legislature would grant him "full amnesty." In the meantime, though, he began planning two further holdups, the first of which, in July 1876, went off flawlessly. Along with two of the Younger brothers, the James gang stopped the Missouri Pacific Railroad train two miles east of the Lamine River in Missouri, boarded it, and made off with $18,300. In the course of the robbery, James shouted: "Tell Allan Pinkerton and all his detectives to look for us in hell."

But the second robbery, in September, failed disastrously. The target was the First National Bank in Northfield, Minnesota, chosen because two of its major depositors were a former Union officer, Major General Benjamin Butler, and Adelbert Ames, a northern war hero and an advocate of racial equality who favored a harsh Reconstruction policy. James spent two weeks scouting the area, and on September 7, he and his men entered the bank. Warning that if anyone cried out, "we will blow your God-damned brains out," he ordered a teller: "Now open the safe you God-damned son of a bitch." But the holdup went awry. A cashier refused to open the vault, a bank teller bolted, and townsmen, alerted, advanced toward the bank, opening fire as they did. Climbing onto their saddles amid a hail of bullets, the bandits galloped off, some having suffered serious injuries. A manhunt ensued, and within days Cole Younger and two of his brothers—all had been wounded—were captured. Jesse and Frank James managed to get away when rain erased their horses' tracks, made it safely back to Missouri—a distance of some five hundred miles—and then disappeared from view. One newspaper compared their "bold ride for life" to that of Dick Turpin, the famous eighteenth-century English highwayman.

It was on a Wednesday night
Not a star was in sight
They robbed the Glendale train
The people they did say
For many miles away
It was robbed by Frank and Jesse James

The James brothers had little choice but to lie low. They would not be involved in another holdup for more than three years, and when they finally reappeared, the pickings were slimmer than expected. In October 1879 they hijacked the Chicago & Alton Railroad at Glendale, a station not far from Independence, Missouri. The operation went off smoothly, but the brothers found only $6,000 in cash, not the expected cargo of bullion. The maturing American economic system was becoming less vulnerable to theft than it had been: "The spread of checking to country banks and the emergence of the express companies as financial intermediaries were gradually making the economy less dependent on cross-country shipments of cash, and less vulnerable to robberies."

The gang committed four more holdups in 1880 and 1881, ranging as far as Kentucky and Alabama, but by the spring of 1882 James appeared to be increasingly jittery and ill at ease. His suspicions, however, did not extend to a relative newcomer to his gang, twenty-year-old Robert Ford, or to Ford's brother, Charles, both of whom had been invited to move into the house with Jesse and his wife. Months before, however, in January 1882, Ford had held a secret meeting at a Kansas City hotel with the governor of Missouri, Thomas T. Crittenden, and others who were determined to destroy the James gang. Crittenden offered Robert Ford a reward and a pardon in exchange for murdering Jesse James. The opportunity soon presented itself. On the morning of April 3 Jesse laid his guns on a sofa and climbed on a chair to dust a picture on the wall. Robert Ford shot him in the back of the head, killing him instantly.

> The people held their breath when they heard of Jesse's death
> And wondered how he ever came to die
> It was one of the gang called little Robert Ford
> He shot poor Jesse on the sly

The Ford brothers were indicted for murder, pleaded guilty, and received death sentences; within two hours Governor Crittenden granted them a full pardon. Charles, who suffered from tuberculosis, would commit suicide in 1884; Robert briefly became a city policeman in Las Vegas but in 1892 was gunned down in a saloon in Colorado. Five months after Jesse's death, Frank James turned himself in at the governor's office. He was held in jail for a year awaiting trial for the robberies he had committed in Missouri and Alabama, but juries acquitted him on all counts. He was never extradited to Minnesota for his role in the Northfield raid. He worked for the rest of his life at a variety of jobs, including giving tours of the James's home, and he died in Missouri in 1915, at the age of seventy-two.

The earliest version of a song about Jesse James was published in 1887, in a small book of songs, fifteen years after his death. A few years later, the verses appeared on a New York City broadside. Most of the details in the song were accurate, although its author was said to be "LaShade" rather than "Gashade," the Glendale train became the Danville train, and James's murder, which occurred on a Monday morning, was moved to a Saturday night. In 1910 the song made its first appearance in a book, John A. Lomax's *Cowboy Songs*. Lomax included many stanzas, including those describing Robert Ford as a "dirty little coward" and Jesse James as a latter-day Robin Hood, "a friend to the poor," who "never would see a man suffer pain."

In May 1919, Bentley Ball, a concert-hall singer, made the first recording of "Jesse James." He used the lyrics in Lomax's version, although he thought it prudent to change the phrase "dirty little coward" to the less offensive "mean little coward." Bascom Lamar Lunsford of North Carolina (who was born in 1882, the year of Jesse James's death) made another early recording in March 1924 on a wax cylinder. A year later, Riley Puckett of Georgia, who played the guitar and banjo, also recorded the song. Born in 1894, and blind since childhood, Puckett sang a sad chorus ("Dear old Jesse, poor old Jesse / laid Jesse James in his grave") and verses, no less poignant, about bereavement ("Jesse James had a mother a sister and a brother"); and duplicity ("Robert Ford caught his eye / and he shot him on the sly"); and repentance ("He fell down

Jesse James, shortly after his death, 1882. Courtesy of the Library of Congress.

upon his knees and he handed up the keys / to the bank that he had robbed the day before").

Other recordings made at the time offered equally sympathetic portraits of the outlaw. In 1924, George Reneau, a twenty-one-year-old blind street singer from Tennessee, depicted Jesse James's last moments:

> Jesse said "I'll hang that picture back up there"
> He stooped to pick it up and stood up in a chair
> Ford he aimed a .44 at Jesse's head
> The news went o'er the country; Jesse James was dead

(Sadly, Reneau died in 1933, at only thirty-one years of age, a victim of pneumonia.) Harry McClintock, born, like Lunsford, in 1882, worked as a union organizer in the Texas oil fields in the 1920s. In 1928 he made a recording of the song, which, if anything, turned the outlaw into a still more sympathetic figure, claiming that "he took from the rich and he gave it to the poor," only to be betrayed by Robert Ford, who "came along like a thief in the night and laid poor Jesse in his grave."

But the most benign song about the outlaw—and the least historically accurate—was written by Woody Guthrie in 1939, apparently after hearing about a new film, *Jesse James*, in which Tyrone Power and Henry Fonda portrayed the brothers. Construing them as working-class martyrs, Guthrie wrote in *People's World*: "The Railroad Racketeers hired Hoodlums & Thugs to beat and cheat the farmers out of their farms—and make em sell em for $1 an acre. Frank & Jesse robbed the train to get even. . . . No wonder folks likes to hear songs about the Outlaws—they're wrong allright, but not as 1/2 as dirty and sneakin' as some of our so-called 'higher-ups.'" In Guthrie's rendition, the brothers "never was outlaws at heart"; "the railroad bullies come to chase them off their land"; a "railroad scab" threw a bomb which "killed Mrs. James a-sleeping in her bed"; and Robert Ford, "a bastard and a coward," "made love to Jesse's wife and he took Jesse's life."

There are no signs that interest in Jesse James is on the wane. To the contrary, a controversy rages about whether he actually died on April 3, 1882. Since the mid-1990s, his remains—which had been moved to Mount Olivet Cemetery in Kearney in 1902—have been painstakingly examined. The testing began in 1995 when a judge granted scientists permission to exhume the grave. Using mitochondrial DNA testing—they had two bones and fourteen or fifteen teeth—they compared their results with those of some of James's known relatives, including a great-grandnephew of his sister. Their conclusion, however, was that "none of the remains retrieved from the Mt. Olivet grave were suitable for DNA testing. They were poorly preserved, presumably due to wet and slightly acidic soil conditions."

Largely because the tests had proven inconclusive, additional tests were performed. In 2005, a firearms expert hired by Discovery Channel claimed that bullets fired from Robert Ford's pistol would have left larger exit wounds than were visible in the photo of James's corpse. In 2010, a photo was posted on the "Jesse James Photo Discussion Forum" that claimed to show the outlaw at a 1921 Quantrill Reunion in Missouri. In 2011, a Clay County official, in office at the time of the 1995 exhumation, asserted the DNA results were untrustworthy. In 2012, a handwriting expert claimed that a sample of Jesse James's writing was a perfect match for that of a man in Texas who went by another name, and posted the relevant samples online.

As the years go by, it is likely that new claims regarding Jesse James's demise will be made and that the controversy will continue. Yet focusing on questions concerning his death risks missing what, in life, he represented. He was undeniably a cunning criminal who never hesitated to murder those who stood in his way. But he was more than that: from start to finish, he was a supporter of Southern separatism, an opponent of Radical Reconstruction, an advocate of white supremacy, and an enemy of racial equality. To be sure, he targeted banks, railroads, and stagecoaches, but he also stalked northerners, like Adelbert Ames, who championed the rights of blacks. Perhaps Jesse James will always be seen as a latter-day Robin Hood, but that was never his intent. Rather, as his biographer says, he "was determined to take his place as a warrior against Reconstruction, as a hero of all the South."

CHAPTER 13

JOHN HARDY (1894)

John Hardy was a desperate little man
He carried two guns every day
He shot down a man in the Shawnee camp
You ought to see John Hardy get away, poor boy
You ought to see John Hardy get away

In the southernmost part of West Virginia, just above the Virginia line, lies the town of Eckman, which in the 1890s was still known as Shawnee Camp. Located in "the heart of the nation's coal bin," the town experienced a boom back then, while the population of the surrounding area, McDowell County, grew by more than 150 percent—from 7,300 to 18,750. Many residents in the area worked for the United States Steel Corporation, which maintained huge processing sites, some of the largest operations of their kind in the world. The company had a reliable ally in Democratic governor William Alexander Mac-Corkle, elected in 1892. Young in years, but archaic in outlook, he rarely hesitated to call out the militia to break strikes. As he later wrote in *Recollections of Fifty Years of West Virginia* (1928), "I used troops to put down lawlessness and preserve the peace and dignity of the state." He was, however, exceedingly reluctant to use the power of his office to spare anyone from the gallows.

At the time, executions in West Virginia were carried out by county governments and were public spectacles, attended by hundreds and often thousands of onlookers. Executions—for those convicted of first-degree murder, kidnapping, or rape—were by hanging. (The state did not adopt the electric chair until 1949, and it was the last state to do so.) Over the years, 155 individuals were executed, all of them men. Blacks constituted only a little more than 4 percent of the state's population, but they made up a lopsided 70 percent of those who went to the scaffold. Fully 87 percent of those who were executed were under the age of thirty. Not until 1899 did the state require executions to be carried out in the penitentiary "within an enclosure to be prepared for that purpose . . . so constructed as to exclude public view."

In January 1893, Eckman was the scene of a murder when a black man named John Hardy shot a younger black man named Thomas Drews. Hardy seems to have been born in Virginia, and was about twenty-seven. Other accounts say he was slightly older, in his thirties, but all agree he was quite tall, at least six feet, two inches, "and he was a very black Negro." Drews was said to be only about nineteen. Hardy supposedly shot him because he had lost seventy-five cents (some say only twenty-five cents) in a game of dice. One eyewitness alleged that "this fellow had skinned Hardy, and he went back and started the crap game to get to kill him." Taking every precaution, Hardy had a friend at the scene named Webb Gudger, who "was behind this rock with his Winchester so if Hardy failed he would get him."

Another person at the scene thought the true motive was jealousy: he claimed that Hardy and Drews were both "enamored of the same woman" (in one version of the song her name is Rosella), and when she seemed to prefer Drews, Hardy "seized the pretext of falling out in the game to work vengeance on Drews, who had shown himself equally expert in dice as in love, having won money from Hardy. Hardy drew his pistol, remarking he would kill him unless he refunded the money." Although Drews gave back part of his winnings, "Hardy shot, killing him." But whether the quarrel was over a dice game, a woman's favors, or both, the outcome was the same. Even after Drews returned the money, Hardy said, " 'Don't you know that I won't lie to my gun?' Thereupon he seized his pistol and shot the man dead."

> "I never lied to my forty-four gun
> And hit's never lied to me
> That feller skinned me in craps last week
> We're as even as can be, oh, boy
> We're as even as can be"

More than a quarter of a century after the event, folklorists finally got around to interviewing the officials who arrested Hardy; not surprisingly, their accounts differed in important respects. R. L. Johnson, one of the policemen who helped make the arrest, reported that he and others went looking for Hardy and his accomplice, Gudger, but were only told, "Yonder they go, down the road!" So, Johnson said, the search party boarded a train and followed the trail "to the old bridge below Shawnee and they turned up the hollow, and I says, 'We will follow them up there.' " But someone said, "No, we can't follow them in the woods; they have got a Winchester, as good a gun as we have got." So the men decided instead to watch the train station, and sure enough the wanted man got on board at Grover, "and when they went to handcuff Hardy, Gudger was walking through the coaches, and every one went out to get Gudger, and he made to jerk John off the train; but John held to him till they got the train stopped, and they sent a colored fellow back there to help him, and they put him on the train and brought him back to Keystone," where of course he was put in jail, as was Webb Gudger.

Another eyewitness told a rather different story, claiming it was Sheriff John Effler and his deputy who found Hardy. They heard he had been hiding "around Negro shanties" and in the mountains for several days. When some black residents told them that Hardy could be found in a shanty, they entered while he was asleep, took his shotgun and pistol, woke him, "and put the cuffs on him." Effler handcuffed Hardy to his own wrist, and then boarded the train at Shawnee Camp for Welch. But while going through a tunnel, and moving from one car to another, "Hardy jumped, and took Effler with him." As he fell from the train, the lawman suffered a fractured rib. Hardy tried to wrest the sheriff's pistol from him, but Effler hit him over the head with it "and almost killed him." Then the sheriff uncuffed himself from his prisoner, tied him securely with ropes, and transported him to the jail in Welch.

There he remained until October 1893, when he stood trial in McDowell County Criminal Court. The presiding judge was forty-four-year-old T. L. Henritze, who had formerly represented several large coal corporations. Educated in Virginia, he had read law to prepare for the bar, and in 1886 had moved to West Virginia, where he became active in Democratic Party politics and was soon appointed to the bench by Governor MacCorkle. Hardy was defended by I. C. Herndon, later a state judge, and Walter Taylor, who had recently been admitted to the bar and would go on to become a leading corporation lawyer. Some reports stated Hardy, lacking funds, gave his pistol to Herndon to cover his fee.

The jury quickly found Hardy guilty, and although no record of the trial has survived, the order for his execution does: "At 8 o'clock this morning the jury in the case of the State against John Hardy, colored, for the murder of Thomas Drews, colored, at Eckman, this county, in January last, brought in a verdict of guilty of murder in the first degree. The trouble arose over a game of craps and was a cold blooded crime." Judge Henritze ordered the convicted man to be taken by the sheriff "to some suitable place to be selected by him in this County and there hang the said John Hardy by the neck until he is dead." The execution was set for January 19, 1894. (Hardy's crony, Webb Gudger, was found guilty of voluntary manslaughter; he served eight years in the state penitentiary and soon after perished in a railroad work accident near Elkhorn.)

John Hardy, he was standing in his cell
With tears rolling down his eyes
Been at the death of many poor men
Now I'm ready to die oh boy
Now I'm ready to die

Newspapers reported that Hardy's mother attended her son's trial and was present later at his execution. There is no indication whether she attempted to see the governor to ask for her son's life. But had she done so, her tears would have been in vain. In his memoirs, Governor MacCorkle related that the mother of a doomed man had once made such a plea: "She threw herself at my feet and grasped my knees, and with a terrible gush of anguish and sorrow, made a most heartrending appeal for her son's life." But the governor would have none of it: "I would have forsworn my office had I pardoned him."

From his cell, Hardy could observe the men preparing his scaffold. At first he put on a brave front, telling other prisoners he would never swing from that scaffold, but after a while he began to sing and finally to pray. On the day before his execution, he sent for a white Baptist preacher, Lex Evans; Hardy told him he had made his peace with God and asked to be baptized. "Evans said he would as soon baptize him as he would a white man." So guards took the condemned man to the nearby Tug River, where Evans performed the necessary service. "He had on a new suit of clothes, hat and everything, but he didn't like the looks of his shoes at all," one of the guards said, so Hardy swapped them for a better pair.

"It was a cold, bright morning," said a young woman who attended the execution. "The ground was hard with frost." An estimated three thousand people were present—one of them Hardy's elderly mother, seated in a rocking chair. Most people arrived by horseback, but a special excursion train ran from Cincinnati to Welch, picking up people along the way. Some stood on the tops of train coaches to get a better view. About twenty drunk, disorderly men had to be arrested before the execution could proceed. Standing on the scaffold, Hardy spoke briefly, warning youngsters to avoid alcohol and gambling, expressing sorrow for his misdeeds, as well as hope for an afterlife: "Don't live in sin as I have done, lest you fill your heart with sorrow." He sang a song, and then sailed his hat into the crowd. The *Wheeling Daily Register* reported that the trapdoor was sprung at 2:09 in the afternoon: "His neck was broken and he died in 17½ minutes. He exhibited great nerve, attributed his downfall to whiskey, and said he had made peace with God. His body was cut down at 2:39, placed in a coffin, and given to the proper parties for interment." Several deputy sheriffs who were stationed under the scaffold detected remaining signs of life after the fall, and so "they wrenched his head backward until he was certainly dead." The

John Hardy on the gallows, January 19, 1894. Courtesy of the State of West Virginia Division of Culture and History.

young woman who was there and left an account that day said she did not expect to feel so forlorn.

> They hung John Hardy on the following morn
> They strung him way up in the sky
> The last words that poor John Hardy said,
> "I'll see you in that great bye-and bye, Lord, Lord
> See you in that great bye and bye"

Although a report circulated that Hardy had composed a song about himself while awaiting execution, nothing identifiable as such has survived. Yet many versions of a song—along with many important facts about the case, and recollections by participants—were collected by John Harrington Cox. An early student of American folk song who began teaching English at West Virginia University in 1903, he later helped found the West Virginia Folklore Society and in 1923 received a doctoral degree from Harvard. Cox specialized in Old and Middle English and in medieval literature, but folk music was his true passion. In 1919 he published a lengthy article, "John Hardy," in the *Journal of American Folklore*, and in 1925 Harvard University Press published his doctoral dissertation, *Folk-Songs of the South*, which included many versions of the song.

A man of his times (he was born in 1863), Cox expressed astonishment at "the origin in our day of such a ballad among an illiterate and comparatively primitive people." Putting his prejudices aside, or at least keeping them in check, he accumulated half a dozen different versions of "John Hardy" from a variety of locations. In commenting on the lyrics, he observed that two stanzas from a Child ballad, "The Lass of Roch Royal," had been inserted. Several verses that Cox collected used demeaning terms for African Americans and even Asian Americans. But in one of the songs, John Hardy outwits his captors, escapes the gallows, and makes his getaway:

> "I don't care a damn for the C.&O. Road
> And I don't care a damn what I say
> I don't care a snap for the police"
> But they let John Hardy get away, poor boy!
> They let John Hardy get away

The earliest recordings of "John Hardy" appeared in the 1920s: the first, in 1924, by Eva Davis, a North Carolina fiddle player and singer, accompanied by Samantha Bumgarner, who played the five-string banjo; another by Ernest V. Stoneman; and a third by Buell Kazee, a banjo player from Kentucky. Those versions, while describing John Hardy as a "reckless gambling man" who "carried two guns every day" and who shot a man down (some verses allege that he killed two men, not one), nevertheless portrayed him sympathetically. The lyrics always emphasized his decision to be baptized:

> They took John Hardy to the riverside
> He prayed to be baptized
> The last words I heard John Hardy say
> "I want to go to heaven when I die,
> I want to go heaven when I die."

In Kazee's version, fate itself intervened to spare John Hardy's life, for the very night he was to be hanged, "There came a storm of a hail / And it blew the hanging scaffold down / And they placed John Hardy back in jail."

So the song was known, and was perhaps being widely sung, by the time A. P. Carter, his wife, Sara, and sister-in-law Maybelle Carter (only nineteen years old) recorded it in May 1928. The Carter Family's rendition resembled earlier versions but stressed the sentimental side of the story, most of it fictional. The song included the line about John Hardy's baptism, but then had him walking to the scaffold "with his loving little wife by his side / And the last words she heard poor John-O say / 'I'll meet you in that sweet bye and bye.'" The Carter

Samantha Bumgarner, Asheville, North Carolina, 1937. Courtesy of the Library of Congress.

Family version also said he had two little girls, one of whom followed her father "to his hanging ground / Saying Poppy I been true to you" while the other sobbed, "Poppy, I would rather be dead."

It appears that only white singers recorded the song in the 1920s and even in the 1930s, but in August 1940 Huddie Ledbetter sang a version of "John Hardy" for Alan Lomax at the Library of Congress, and he recorded it again in 1944. Lead Belly's lyrics differ only slightly from earlier ones, but the differences are still striking. Although the song has nothing to do with slavery, Lead Belly begins with John Hardy standing on the "Freestone Bridge" because "there he thought he would be free." His "purty little wife" arrives after his arrest to assure him, "Johnny I been true to you." His mother and father try to pay his bail, but it is not allowed "for a murderin man." The song ends, sadly, with the prisoner standing in his cell, "tears are rolling down his eyes." Reconciled to his fate, he says, "Now I'm ready to die, poor boy, saying now I'm ready to die."

Over the years, a few other singers, notably Woody Guthrie, have tried to paint a sympathetic picture of John Hardy. But the task has proven difficult: his murderous act was too cruel, too cold-blooded, and there are few if any biographical details that might explain it, much less justify it. Only the remorse he expressed as he faced the hangman, and perhaps the tears his mother shed,

The Carter Family, 1927. *Left to right*:
A. P., Maybelle, and Sara Carter.

somehow seem to soften the image of a man whose actions had been both pitiless and cruel.

> John Hardy, he was standing in his cell
> With tears rolling down his eyes
> Been at the death of many poor men
> Now I'm ready to die oh boy
> Now I'm ready to die.

CHAPTER 14

RAILROAD BILL (1896)

Railroad Bill, Railroad Bill
He never worked and he never will
And it's ride, ride, ride

His name was Morris Slater, but they called him Railroad Bill. Born a slave in North Carolina, he later moved to Florida, and in the 1890s he became a notorious holdup man, robbing trains, chiefly in southern Alabama, and taunting those who tried to capture him. He became a folk hero to many blacks, often giving away his plunder, but at the same time he became the target of a furious manhunt by the authorities, and after eluding the law for more than three years he was finally gunned down. His corpse was then put on display, taken from town to town for all to see, finally desecrated. He was laid to rest in Pensacola, Florida, but his grave was not discovered until the summer of 2012, more than 115 years after his death.

Slater's name appeared only one time, it seems, in the Florida census rolls—in 1885, when he was thirty-five and working for the Northern Railroad. He reported that he was born in North Carolina in 1850. He was married: his wife, Catherine, nine years younger, was born in Tennessee and listed her occupation as housekeeper. She too had almost certainly once been a slave. The couple had a six-year-old daughter, but oddly the census taker only listed her initial—E—not her full name. The family resided in Suwannee, a small fishing village on the Gulf of Mexico midway between Tampa and Tallahassee, or, as the Chamber of Commerce later boasted, "where the salt waters of the Gulf of Mexico intertwine with the spring fed waters of the majestic Suwannee River." The river itself was made famous by Stephen Foster's song "The Swanee River (Old Folks at Home)," which he wrote in 1851, the year after Slater was born.

The Louisville & Nashville Railroad, the target of Slater's robberies, had been chartered by Kentucky in 1850, and within forty years the company had constructed or acquired existing lines so that its tracks stretched through Ohio, Missouri, Alabama, Louisiana, and Florida. Its cars helped build the city of Birmingham; large deposits of iron ore and coal were located nearby, and the railroad was there to transport them. In 1883, a brand-new 170-mile link was completed between Pensacola and Chattahoochee, Florida. Many years later, Jean Ritchie wrote a song, "The L&N Don't Stop Here Anymore," which talked about the coal cars "standin' in a rusty row all empty," but in the early 1890s the company was thriving, operating more than 2,614 miles of track with 436 locomotives, 339 passenger cars, and 12,534 freight cars.

It was in the town of Bluff Springs, in the Florida Panhandle, that Slater—who apparently had earlier run-ins with the law—became a wanted man. In October 1892 a twenty-three-year-old deputy sheriff named Allen W. Brewton accosted him outside the shack in which he lived and told him that he would have to buy a license—it cost five dollars—for his .38 Winchester rifle or else give it up. "I don't think so," Slater said and started walking away. Brewton demanded he stop, and when he didn't, the deputy fired at him but missed. Turning, Slater started to fire back, slightly wounding one of the men accompanying the deputy. Then he fled into the nearby swamp. The local newspaper reported that Slater had "bid defiance to the world in general."

> Railroad Bill, goin' down the hill
> Lightin' cigars with a five-dollar bill
> And its ride, ride, ride

For more than three years he remained at large, moving from place to place, riding L&N boxcars, robbing trains and freight stations, and occasionally shooting it out with the guards, the police, and the special detectives hired by the railroads. Sometimes he kept the loot, and sometimes he gave it away or sold it at cut-rate prices to poor people nearby. In March 1895, after a man found sleeping on a water tank along the railroad line was accosted but escaped, the company began posting armed guards on the most vulnerable lines. In April, it began putting up "most wanted" signs in depots, and that very month a posse cornered a man thought to be Railroad Bill at Bay Minette, Alabama, a station on the L&N, just a few miles from the Florida border.

There, late on a Saturday night, Slater had gotten into a gunfight with two white men, wounding one slightly. He was then tracked down by a posse that included Deputy Sheriff James H. Stewart, only twenty; a midnight shootout took place in which the deputy "received a rifle ball through his heart," while Slater slipped away. Sheriff Edward McMillan set bloodhounds on the scent, but a heavy rain had fallen the night before, and Slater escaped. As the papers told it: "Every effort has been made to capture the daring and reckless negro, but without success." Reports a few days later that he had been killed in another gunfight proved to be founded on nothing but rumor.

By July 4, McMillan, tipped off by an informant, managed to locate Slater in a house near Bluff Springs, Florida. Backed by Pinkerton Agency detectives, L&N officers, and volunteer vigilantes—not to mention bounty hunters—the lawman came face to face with his prey. From behind a tree someone shouted, "Who's there?" and then fired. Turning toward the tree, McMillan leaned forward when a second shot hit him near his heart. Asked if he was hurt, the sheriff replied, "Yes, I'm killed." McMillan was carried back to town, where he died even before his wife arrived on a specially chartered train. Meanwhile, Slater, who may have been wounded, again got away, disappearing into the woods.

The local newspapers reported that McMillan's hometown offered condolences by canceling its Independence Day festivities. "Our town instead of being in holiday attire would be appropriately decked in crepe, out of respect to Sheriff McMillan, who had been ruthlessly murdered at Bluff Springs the previous night." Praising the sheriff as "a fearless official," the papers talked of his "aged mother" and "devoted wife" and reported the entire town bathed in "deep

Sheriff E. S. McMillan.

gloom." The papers also announced that the ante was being raised: a reward of $1,250 was now being offered for information leading to Railroad Bill's capture, $350 of it pledged by the L&N railroad, which, as an added incentive, also offered a free lifetime railroad pass. "That $1250 reward will attract the slickest 'sleuth-hounds' in the country," the papers said.

> Railroad Bill made a mighty dash
> Shot McMillan by a lightning flash
> Talkin' bout that Negro, Railroad Bill

So a posse was formed and it set out on a search, recruiting volunteers from as far away as Texas and Indiana. On July 9, the newspapers claimed "about two dozen well-armed and indignant citizens left for the scene of the killing for the avowed purpose of avenging the killing of our highly esteemed and brave officer of the law." A day or two later, the number in pursuit of the "badly wanted scoundrel" had risen to fifty, and by August, it was said, he was being hunted by a "small army" of a hundred men. Yet despite the size of the search parties, and the lure of the large reward, Slater was nowhere to be found. In August the *Pine Belt News* reported—in the racist vernacular so typical of the times—"One thing is for certain, Bill is still a free nigger and wanders at his will."

Although the search failed to find Slater, posses created a virtual reign of terror, harassing, arresting, or beating blacks, blameless though they may have been, who were suspected of shielding Slater. According to one news account, "The posse that went out in pursuit of him found quite a number of Negroes who had been harboring the Negro desperado, and . . . they took them out in the woods and whipped them soundly, with the admonition that they might expect something more severe if they persisted in their conduct." On August 1, 1895, it was reported: "A number of Negroes have been arrested. None of them will be permitted to go about for fear that they might sneak some information to Railroad." The sheriff of Conecuh County, Alabama, explained: "We are guarding all trains and arresting all Negroes who come along." Another report from Alabama stated: "Several suspicious negroes have been arrested within the past few days. Two or three boys have been released, and one or two are in jail. Some seem to think they are pals of Railroad." To the authorities, any black individual who resembled the wanted man was fair game: "The number of negroes who were killed under the impression that they were Slater will never be known. Several were shot in Florida, Georgia, Mississippi and even out in Texas, but only one was brought here to be identified."

Blacks who admired Slater's audacity, and whites who feared it, sometimes attributed magical powers to him. Some believed he was a conjurer who made his getaways by assuming the form of a hound, a horse, or a hawk. Legend had it that he could catch bullets in his hands, and that only a silver bullet could kill him. He was said to be so skilled a marksman that he could shoot a hole through a dime and that he once "shot all the buttons off the brakeman's coat." There were those who believed that to touch him would bring good luck. A trickster beyond compare, he led a charmed life, had the knack of dodging the law and, some thought, could use hoodoo so the bloodhounds could not track him. Blacks and whites alike, at least many of them, "are firmly convinced that Railroad Bill has the superhuman power of easily transforming himself into any object, animate or inanimate, that he wants to."

The pursuit of Slater was made more difficult by conflicting accounts of his appearance. At first he was described as having light skin, as being a "yellow negro" of a "gingerbread color." A wanted poster described his face as "dark yellow as if sunburned or smoked," while his "breast and stomach to the waist [are] light yellow." But as time went by he came to be described as "coal-black" or as "black as ebony." Newspapers eventually resorted to emphasizing his blackness, terming him a "black Negro," a "black scoundrel" who "thirsted for blood," or "the dusky desperado," or "the dusky demon" who committed "deeds of darkness"—all terms that tended to ignite feelings of racial hatred.

Through it all, Slater remained at large. He was reportedly seen at various locations: Flomaton and Bay Minette in Alabama, Bluff Springs in Florida. Tracked by bloodhounds, he somehow seemed always to stay one step ahead of his pursuers. There were more train robberies, more shootouts with lawmen. One of his regular tactics was to break into a railroad car, throw valuables onto the track while the train kept moving, and return to collect the items afterward. But then, on March 9, 1896, the headline in the *Pine Belt News* read: "Dead With His Boots on. Railroad Bill, the Noted Desperado, Bandit and Assassin. Railroad Bill is Dead."

It happened at nine in the evening in Tidmore and Ward's general store in Atmore, Alabama, a town on the L&N railroad line a few miles from the Florida border. Slater entered, sat down on a barrel, and began eating some crackers with cheese. He was packing a Winchester rife in the leg of his pants, and two loaded pistols around his waist. Accounts of what happened next differ. Some claim that the storekeeper recognized Slater but was afraid to confront him, so he went outside and shot him through the window. Others said that a posse happened to be in the store at the time. That version appeared in the *Atlanta Constitution*, which reported that lawmen opened fire with double-barreled guns: "He was literally perforated with shot and was instantly killed." Whether Slater was able to reach for his gun as he toppled over did not much matter. As the papers reported: "About fifteen pistol, rifle and gunshot wounds were found."

Railroad Bill lyin' on de grocery floor
Got shot two times an' two times more
No more lookin' fer Railroad Bill

The body of Morris Slater, his face and right hand mangled, was then exhibited far and wide. Shipped by train to Brewton, Alabama, it was viewed by large crowds, and then was sent to Montgomery, where it was met by "a perfect mob of curious people"—so large a mob, in fact, that the coffin had to be closed and access temporarily denied. But soon the body was "placed on exhibition in an empty freight car," and an admission fee of twenty-five cents was charged. The corpse was also displayed elsewhere in Alabama and Florida. An observer recalled that blacks and whites came from miles around to view the remains, adding: "I would conservatively estimate the crowd at 5,000 people. It looked like a big crowd on circus day."

There is a photograph of Slater's body strapped to a board, his Winchester rifle next to him, with the barrel resting on his shoulder and his pistol placed conspicuously on top of him. Standing alongside gazing down at the victim is Sheriff J. L. McGowan, one of the men who killed him, and he too is holding his

Leonard McGowan standing next to the body of Morris Slater, known as "Railroad Bill," March 1897.

rifle. From underneath a shed, a man who appears to be black is hunched over looking out on the scene. People who wished to have their pictures taken alongside the body were able to do so, and photographs of the "Dead Bandit" sold well. Despite whatever precautions may have been taken, the papers reported, "many cut buttons off his clothes, scraps of cloth, cartridges etc. as souvenirs." The cadaver, embalmed, was shipped to Pensacola, where it was again displayed. Then, at last, Morris Slater was buried in St. John's Cemetery.

While he remained at large, white newspapers often referred to him in a half-mocking way—as "William," or "the Wanted William," or simply as "Railroad," and wrote dismissively of "THE WONDERFUL NEGRO POPULARLY SUPPOSED TO BE SUPERHUMAN." Yet the flippant language merely betrayed the anxiety whites felt when faced with a black outlaw who successfully defied white authority. That anxiety played itself out when the police sometimes arrested blacks merely on suspicion of having concealed Slater, or, worse yet, actually gunned down men they suspected—wrongly, as it turned out—of being the bandit. A deputy sheriff in Montgomery, for example, arbitrarily jailed seven men and women, "all Negroes, charged with harboring and protecting Bill."

Not long after his death, songs started to be written about Railroad Bill. Verses were collected as early 1909 and, two or three years after that, were published by E. C. Perrow and by Howard W. Odum. Newman I. White's *American Negro Folksongs*, which appeared in 1925, included verses in a chapter titled "The Seamier Side": "Railroad Bill did not know / Dat Jim McMillan had a forty-fo'." The first recordings also appeared in the 1920s: by Roba and Bob Stanley; by Will Bennett (the first by a black singer); and by Gid Tanner, Riley Puckett, and the Skillet Lickers. Puckett was born in 1894, just about the time Morris Slater began his career as a criminal, a career that three years later would lead to his death. The last line of each verse, as Puckett sang it, was "and it's ride, ride, ride."

CHAPTER 15

BETTY AND DUPREE (1921)

Betty told Dupree, "I want a diamond ring"
Betty told Dupree, "I want a diamond ring"
Dupree told Betty, "I'll give you most anything"

In 1922 there were 144 executions in American prisons; the first such death took place three days after New Year's, and the last three days before Christmas. All those who were executed were men—except for Pattie Perdue, a black woman who was hanged in Mississippi. Most of the condemned had been convicted of murder, but nine had committed rape, and two black men (in Virginia and Maryland) were even executed for attempted rape. On a single day, four bootleggers who were found guilty of murder went to the electric chair in Tennessee. Electrocution, in fact, had become the generally preferred method of execution, but hanging was a close second, and Utah still used firing squads. Of those who were killed, fifty were African Americans, three were Asians, ten were Hispanics, and the others were whites. The oldest to die was sixty-five, the youngest, only sixteen. In all, seven teenagers were put to death that year.

One was nineteen-year-old Frank B. Dupre. His father, Frank A. Dupre, described as "a small, retiring, mild-looking sort of a middle-aged man," was a blacksmith, in his early fifties, who had worked, when work was available, in the navy yard in Charleston but had then moved to Abbeville, South Carolina, about one hundred miles east of Atlanta. The younger Dupre's mother was recently deceased, a victim of pellagra; his older brother, Joe, had lately returned from military service. Frank was born in August 1903, and after attending school he made his way to Atlanta. That is where, in December 1921, he happened to see Betty Anderson (her last name was usually given, incorrectly, as Andrews) playing the piano at Child's Hotel, a downtown landmark that provided lodging for passengers using the railroad terminal, and apparently told her how much he liked the music she was making.

Barely eighteen years old, Betty had been married at fifteen to a barber, E. J. Anderson, but had filed for a divorce. Her father, Ed Guest, was a house painter in Gainesville, Georgia, but she had moved to Atlanta, working first for the telephone company and then dancing in the chorus line of *Chu Chin Chow*, a popular musical comedy based loosely on the story of Ali Baba and the Forty Thieves. The show featured scantily clad young women as well as a camel, a donkey, chickens, and snakes. According to her father, she was a poor student as the result of having come down with a high fever, and so had dropped out of school; her mind, he said, "is blank at times." Betty later confirmed she had met Frank Dupre at Child's Hotel, and although she had known him for only four days, "he fell in love with me but it was not my fault and I did nothing to encourage him to do so." The "details" of her doings on a certain day, the *Atlanta Constitution* smugly reported, "could not be printed in even the most risqué publications."

Shortly before one o'clock on the afternoon of December 15, 1921, Dupre sauntered into Nat Kaiser's Jewelry Store on Peachtree Street and asked to look at a diamond ring. This was not the first time he planned to take something that wasn't his. A few months earlier, he had stolen $140 from a cousin; he had also lifted two diamond rings from a store and sold them to a fence. Now, to fortify himself, he "drank half a pint of whisky," and, as he later said, "I was just about broke, and wanted to get that ring for Betty." Entering the store, he told the clerk, "I am going to get married and I want to see some diamond rings." The clerk called the owner, who showed Dupre a diamond ring. But Dupre said it was too small and asked to see a larger one on display in the window. The owner, his suspicions aroused, indicated to the store detective, Irby C. Walker, that he should station himself near the entrance. When the ring, valued at $2,500, was brought out, Dupre grabbed it and bolted for the door.

But Walker, a Pinkerton agent, grabbed him and pushed him back into the store. Momentarily panicked, Dupre drew his revolver, a .32 Colt automatic, "thrust the muzzle against Walker's abdomen and pulled the trigger." He fired two shots, and Walker fell to the ground dead. Continuing to blaze away, he dashed into the street, where he encountered Graham West, the city of Atlanta comptroller, who tried to seize him. So Dupre shot him, too, hitting him in the chin and stomach and leaving him "desperately wounded." Then he made his getaway, vanishing in a crowd of pedestrians and Christmas shoppers. As Dupre recalled the event: "Well, as soon as I got the ring in my hand, I made a break for the door, and about that time, Walker grabbed hold of me, . . . and I believe if I hadn't shot him he would have killed me right there on the spot; that's the last thing that I remember."

Then he got his pistol, went to the jewelry store
Then he got his pistol, went to the jewelry store
Killed a policeman and he wounded four or five more

While the police were checking the railroad stations, roads, and freight yards, newspapers provided a description of the killer—medium height, slender, clean-shaven, stylishly dressed in a gray overcoat and cap, "and possessed of a clean-cut, lean face"—whom they called the "overcoat" bandit and after a while the "Peachtree" bandit. But Dupre got away, went to see Betty, and gave her a few dollars. Then he hired a taxicab to take him to Chattanooga, Tennessee, where he pawned the ring for $445, and eventually made his way to Detroit. After eluding the law for a month, he sent a boastful letter to an Atlanta newspaper: "I would like to say that I think Atlanta has a bunch of boneheads for detectives; they don't seem to be able to catch any body. I gave them several chances to get me, and they have failed so far. . . . I am not in hiding and don't intend to be." He added that the taxi driver "did not know I was the bandit, and what would any taxicab driver do if he had the chance of taking a passenger to Chattanooga?" And of Graham West: "Sorry I had to shoot him, but he insisted on stopping me, and there was no other way out of it. I think he will mind his own business hereafter, which will be much better for him if he does."

He wrote that letter on January 12, 1922, and the very next day he was arrested in Detroit. After four exasperating weeks—following leads that led nowhere, detaining the cab driver for want of anyone better, recovering the ring from the pawnshop, and offering an unclaimed $2,000 reward—the police successfully traced another letter Dupre had written to the pawnbroker asking for the money he still had coming, and so at last they found him. Two detectives, with drawn revolvers, seized him on the street late in the afternoon. "I'll blow you back to Atlanta if you move," one of them said. Told he could remain silent, Dupre blurted out, "I think I'll tell you all about it." For the first time he disclosed Betty's name, admitted he had shot Walker, and waived extradition. "I never went around the jails much in Georgia," he said to the detective who questioned him. "Is it the chair or the rope there?"

Then he went to the post office to get the evening mail
Then he went to the post office to get the evening mail
Sheriff caught poor Dupree and put him in that old Atlanta jail

Once Betty's name was mentioned, she became a suspect as an accessory, and so she attempted to distance herself from the robbery. "God knows I am sorry for the boy," she said, adding, "I was in no way responsible for his crimes."

Even so, she accompanied Dupre's father—who had traveled to Atlanta to assist the defense—to the train station when his son arrived in handcuffs ("it appeared that half the city saw Dupre detrain," the papers reported), and she smiled, waved, and was permitted to see him at the police station: "Both began crying as soon as they beheld each other." But on January 19 she, too, was arrested and jailed as an accomplice. Taken from the women's ward in the Fulton County Tower to the district attorney's office, she was interrogated, then dissolved in tears and admitted that her clothing was indeed purchased with money Dupre had given her. Betty's husband, from whom she was separated, announced he would file his own suit for divorce.

Confined in the Fulton Tower, Dupre hired two lawyers, Lewis Foster and H. A. Allen, to represent him. "The boy has a good face, an intelligent face," Allen said. "He is naturally all unstrung now." He added that Dupre would confess to murder but ask for mercy on the grounds that he had acted "on a wild impulse, engendered by whisky and by fright" and, more generally, out of "just woeful ignorance, bad environment, unthinking boy impulsiveness." But the prosecution saw matters differently. Solicitor General John A. Boykin said: "We would stultify ourselves and bring the law into contempt if we agree to anything except the death penalty." The claim of insanity, he added, the very notion of remorse, was nothing but a pretense. Boykin's voice fairly

Betty Andrews, 1921.

dripped with contempt when he spoke of "the maudlin sob stuff that has been written about this innocent and baby-faced boy."

The trial began before Judge Henry A. Mathews and a jury of twelve men on January 26, a Thursday. "The crowd pushed, and shoved, and hammered, and howled to get in the courtroom all day," the papers reported. Boykin began by presenting evidence of the shootings and "the general reign of terror inspired by the bandit," while defense attorneys tried to find a flaw in the prosecution's case. The widow of the slain detective, Irby C. Walker, took the stand, as did the undertaker who had buried him. The Chattanooga pawnbroker was asked why he had bought the ring from Dupre without asking for identification; he answered, "The boy looked like a good boy." Graham West testified that Dupre had shot him from a distance of only a few feet. Dupre also took the stand "to declare that Betty Andrews, or as he properly called her, Betty Anderson, knew nothing of his career and in no way was responsible for his crimes." (Some in the audience considered his statement "a particularly noble act.") According to the newspapers, he smiled and "seemed like a schoolboy out for a holiday, instead of a felon fighting for his life." But his father, seated beside his son, appeared "palpably nervous and depressed."

> They took Dupree and carried him to that big rock jail
> They took Dupree and carried him to that big rock jail
> He didn't have no body, not a soul to go his bail

Dupre's attorneys, hoping for a verdict of manslaughter rather than murder, claimed that "he hasn't brains enough to think logically himself," and that "sending this boy to the gallows" would not ease the widow's pain. But in the end the defense's chief argument was that it was all Betty's fault. Dupre, they said, had robbed the jewelry store not to enrich himself but to please the vanity of the woman he loved. "He came to get a wedding ring for a girl with whom he was infatuated. He had no thought of money for himself." To be sure, Dupre had sinned, but he was no more blameworthy than such biblical figures as Adam, David, and Solomon, all of whom had succumbed to temptation, and so "what can you expect of a boy at his age when he is so peculiarly susceptible to the wiles of a woman?"

When it came to sounding the theme of misogyny, however, the prosecution easily outdid the defense. Claiming that Dupre's "soul is so steeped in sin that he would go out and wash his hands in the life blood of a fellow being to give a scarlet woman the fripperies and fineries that her rouged soul craved," the prosecutor denounced Betty as worse than a harlot: "Why that frizzy headed rag and bone and hank of hair had no more thought of marrying DuPre than she had of being faithful to the man she had married. All she wanted out of him was the money that his thefts brought in to her." To no one's surprise, Solicitor General Boykin concluded by demanding the death penalty: "It's up to you gentlemen to put a rope around this murderer's neck," he said. "We need some old-fashioned rope in Fulton County, before we ever halt this growth of crime."

Lasting only two days, the trial concluded late Friday, and the next morning, at 10:45, the jurors returned. At first they had been closely divided, some favoring the death penalty and others life imprisonment. But by Saturday morning, only one juror still held out for life, so a few of the others "formed a group and prayed constantly and fervently for three hours." The twelfth juror finally joined the majority. As the judge pronounced the death sentence, Dupre's father, his arm resting on his son's shoulder, "put his hand to his forehead, his head sank toward his breast and his eyes filled with tears. . . . He said he had nothing to say except that his heart was broken." Dupre himself, a "half-sneering smile" on his face, made a feeble attempt to comfort his father. When a newspaper reporter broke the news to Betty, she begged to be allowed to see Dupre, and said the jury "must be the hardest hearted and cruelest men in the world." "I don't believe God is that unjust," she declared, adding, "This old world is going to sink anyhow and I hope it does." Returning to his cell, Dupre was asked by a fellow prisoner: "What was it Frank?" and he answered: "They're going to stretch me."

Although the judge fixed an execution date for March 10, appeals slowed the procedure. Dupre's attorneys began by approaching the Georgia Supreme Court, but on July 13 that court upheld the verdict, ruling that the judge's charge to the jury was proper and that he had "submitted the issues of murder and voluntary manslaughter in language more favorable to the accused than the evidence required." Although the justices were evenly divided—three to three—the verdict was allowed to stand. They also rejected the defense's claim that four members of the jury were not impartial because "each of them had expressed opinions substantially to the effect that the accused ought to be hung, and that if they were selected on the jury they would stand for a verdict of guilty without recommendation." While the court believed the trial judge's charge to the jury "may be subject to some criticism," it was not so faulty as to require a new trial. The jury's verdict, the court declared, was "amply justified. Indeed, a case is rarely encountered where there is so nearly no defense."

There was one especially striking paragraph in the ruling that revealed the justices' view of their role in maintaining law and order, and in soothing the public's concern with a burgeoning crime wave: "We are reminded that human life is involved. It is true that the life of the accused is immediately and vitally affected. But this must not and cannot obscure the further fact that the lives of millions of peaceful and law-abiding citizens, engaged in the effort to earn an honest living for themselves and their dependents, are menaced by gunmen and bandits intent upon unlawfully obtaining their own ends, although its result be bloodshed and the making of widows and fatherless children. In the firm administration of the law by the courts lies the only protection to society."

Having failed to sway the state's highest court, Dupre's lawyers turned in August to the Georgia Prison Commission, asking merely that the sentence be commuted to life. They made several points: that the trial occurred too soon after the crime to have been impartial; that newspaper publicity had "inflamed the public mind" against Dupre; and that he was "completely under the influence of evil associates and the bad liquor which had been given him." They also submitted petitions urging clemency, signed by 12,308 women in Atlanta, one of whom asked that "the boy who has been without the counsels of mother-love be given another chance to learn of moral responsibility." Those on the other side—Walker's widow and his friends, Graham West, and an assistant solicitor general who deplored "maudlin sentiment"—made equally passionate arguments. Dupre's father was again in attendance. The very next day, August 11, the three-member commission rejected the plea for clemency, and Governor Thomas Hardwick gave no indication he would intervene.

Dupre received the bad news in his cell, the papers reported, "just after being baptized by Episcopalian ministers." "There is nothing I can say," was his response: "I can only trust in God." With the execution date set for September 1, Dupre's father gave a final interview to the press, saying he would visit his son the day before he died: "It will be the last time I'll see him on earth. I'll say goodbye then, and I won't go back—. . . I won't go back—unless he asks for me. Then I'll go to him but God knows how can I stand it." Nevertheless, he indeed visited his son again, as did Frank's brother, Joe, who had earlier telephoned the governor, vainly begging for a reprieve. As Frank Dupre walked from his cell to the gallows, he could see Betty Anderson, imprisoned on the third tier, and she could see him, and he called out, "Be a good girl Betty and meet me in heaven."

> Give mama my clothes, give Betty my diamond ring
> Give mama my clothes, give Betty my diamond ring
> Tomorrow is Friday, the day I'm going to swing

Several people witnessed the execution—the sheriff, a few deputies, ministers, newspapermen, and a friend—while thousands who had waited outside the prison since early morning strained to get the news. An eyewitness said of the crowd: "They were of every race, and every color, and of every social and financial degree." Dupre was accompanied to the scaffold by clergymen. A minister sang "Mother's Prayers Have Followed Me," a hymn Dupre had requested; there followed a reading from the Book of Common Prayer: "Despair not of God's mercy, though trouble is on every side." Then his legs and ankles were bound, his hands cuffed behind him, the noose fixed around his neck, and his face covered with a black hood. "I'm going to heaven," he said to one of the clergymen, who replied, "I am sure of it, Frank." "The trap was sprung and the body dropped, twitched horribly, and it was seen that the thin neck of the law's victim had not broken." Two doctors rushed over to him, "but it was fourteen never-ending minutes before they pronounced him dead." It was 2:18 in the afternoon.

Dupre's body was transported the next day to Abbeville, where last rites were performed. Betty, still in prison, quickly vanished from the news, and although she eventually was released, neither her whereabouts nor her doings were reported. Yet both Frank Dupre and Betty Anderson were, within a very few years, immortalized in song, first by a prolific composer and evangelist, Andrew W. Jenkins. Born in Georgia in 1885, nearly blind because in childhood he was given the wrong medicine for an eye ailment, he went on to become a Methodist preacher and wrote eight hundred songs, most but not all of them religious. Performing with his stepchildren, he made many recordings and in 1922 began appearing on an Atlanta radio station. He wrote "The Fate of Frank Dupre," recorded it in 1925, and several other versions of the song appeared shortly thereafter.

Frank Dupre, August 1922.
© Bettmann/CORBIS.

In 1926, a year later, Howard W. Odum and Guy B. Johnson published *Negro Workaday Songs*. It included several variants, with Frank's name now for some reason spelled "Dupree." Some of the lyrics strayed far from the facts of the case, but others were accurate: "Dupree, we got hangin' for you / Sorry, Dupree, we got to hang po' you." A few years later, in 1930, more people surely learned about the case when the first blues recordings appeared, usually with the title "Dupree Blues." In November, "Kingfish" Bill Tomlin cut a version for Paramount; and in December, "Blind" Willie Walker and Sam Brooks recorded it, fittingly, in a studio in Atlanta, Georgia.

Tomlin's version only vaguely described events on that December afternoon in 1921, but Walker's offered a reasonably credible account of what had happened. One of the finest guitar players in South Carolina, Walker recorded only a few songs before his premature death in 1933, but one of them was "Dupree Blues." He was accompanied by Sam Brooks, who also played the guitar and interjected comments:

> He had to kill a policeman and wounded a detective too (oh sugar)
> Killed a detective, wounded a policeman too (oh babe)
> "See here, mama, what you caused me to do"
>
> Hired him a taxi said, "Can't you drive me back to Main" (say taxi)
> Then he hired him a taxi, said, "Carry me back to Main" (oh baby)
> "I've done a hangin' crime yet I don't never feel ashamed"

There is no way to know whether Frank Dupre ever felt remorse for his crime. Given what he said in the weeks following his arrest and his behavior at the trial, it does not appear he did, although his comments and conduct in the days prior to the execution indicate that, at the very end, he may well have had a change of heart. Nor is there a clear indication of what may have been running through Betty Anderson's mind from the time she first set eyes on Dupre until, less than a year later, she caught a glimpse of him as he walked to his death. And there is surely no way of knowing what she may have thought, in later years, if by chance she happened to hear the song that was written about them:

> Wrote a letter to Betty and this is the way the letter read (oh baby)
> Wrote a letter to Betty and this is the way the letter read (oh baby)
> "Come home to your daddy, I'm almost dead."

Railroads

CHAPTER 16

JOHN HENRY (1870s)

When John Henry was a little baby
Just a sittin' on his mammy's knee
Said, "The Big Bend Tunnel on that C&O Road
Gonna be the death of me, Lord God
Going to be the death of me"

In February 1870, tracks for the Chesapeake and Ohio Railway were being laid through the Appalachians. Ten miles east of Hinton, West Virginia, the workers reached Big Bend Mountain, which was too high to go over and too large to go around. So a tunnel had to be cut through a mile of solid rock, some of it red shale that tended to disintegrate when exposed to air. When finally completed on September 12, 1872, the tunnel was 6,450 feet long, 17 feet high, and 13 feet wide. The entire project took more than two and a half years and required nearly a thousand workers, some of whom were prisoners leased by the state to private contractors. Many workers were injured, others lost their lives in accidents and landslides, and still others collapsed because of the backbreaking nature of the labor. One of those who died, most likely in the fall of 1870, was a black man named John Henry.

The work he was doing was by its very nature hazardous and occasionally lethal. "One was almost smothered so great was the heat," an observer who entered the tunnel said. "The smoke from the blasts became so thick that the light of the lamps was visible no farther than a few steps." Blasting produced "an infernal noise. . . . One would have said that ten thousand hammers were falling simultaneously on their anvils. A sharp whistling sound made itself heard above this clamor, piercing you to the very marrow." Clouds of "yellow smoke come pouring through the tunnel in such density and volume as to be positively painful," noted a report in December 1870. "The scene in the scantily lighted tunnel grew to resemble an inferno, men going about naked in the intense heat."

Various explosives were used for blasting—nitroglycerine, dualin (based on nitrogenized cellulose using sawdust or wood pulp), and gunpowder—all of which created grave hazards, leading *Scientific American* in 1871 to complain about the site's "black record." There were many other dangers as well: falling rocks, "tunnel-sickness," fetid air, and the fragility of the timber arches that supported the roof of the tunnel (wood was not replaced by brick until the 1880s). To quote Brett Williams's account: "The thick stone dust, the noxious blasting fumes from the 833 pounds of nitroglycerine used daily, and the smoke from the lard and blackstrap oil which fueled each day's 115 pounds of candles, were nearly intolerable." As the temperature in the tunnel became oppressive, workers sometimes took ill, visitors were usually barred, and workhorses died at the rate of ten a month.

Although songs about John Henry were probably being sung shortly after his death, the first printed version did not appear until 1909 when Louise Rand Bascom's "Ballads and Songs of Western North Carolina" was published in the *Journal of American Folklore*. She quoted only two lines: "Johnie Henry was a hard-workin' man, / He died with his hammer in his hand." Thereafter, versions turned up regularly in essays by folklorists. In 1911 Hubert Shearin and Josiah H. Combs said the song was being sung in Kentucky, and in 1913 E. C. Perrow—he claimed to have heard some of the lines ("This ole hammer killed John Henry, / Drivin' steel, baby, drivin' steel") as early as 1905—published adaptations from Indiana, Tennessee, Mississippi, and Kentucky. A year later, the lyrics turned up in South Carolina; in 1915 "John Henry, or the Steam Drill" was reported in Kentucky; and in 1916 a former governor of West Virginia quoted several stanzas. By then, about a dozen versions had been published.

The earliest recordings of the song were made in 1924, when several musicians—Fiddlin' John Carson, Sam Jones (a blind street musician), Ernest Thompson (who was also blind), and Gid Tanner and the Skillet Lickers recorded versions, although not all of them were released. Carson, in "John Henry Blues," sang, "Lord, he lay down his hammer and he cried, Oh, Lord," and "John Henry sunk a fo'teen foot / the steam drill only made nine." One verse went: "John Henry said to his captain / I ain't nothing but a man / Before I let that steam drill beat me down / I'll die with my hammer in my hand." At about the same time, Gid Tanner and the Skillet Lickers issued a recording of "John Henry (the Steel Drivin' Man)" with some lyrics that would later become familiar: "The hammer be the death of me, papa, / The hammer be the death of me"; "If I miss this piece of steel, / Tomorrow be your buryin' day"; and when the captain said he believed the mountain was falling in, John Henry "turned around and said / It's my hammer fallin' in the wind." In their version, John Henry had a son: "Last words that John Henry said, / 'Son, don't be a steel-drivin' man.'"

By the early 1920s, Louis Watson Chappell, a professor of English at West Virginia University, embarked on a "folk-lore study" of the man and the song. He interviewed a few workers, all of course quite elderly, who had known, or seen, or heard John Henry when he was working on the tunnel. Their recollections were strikingly similar. "He was the best steel-driver I ever saw," one man recalled. "John Henry was always singing or mumbling something when he was whipping steel. . . . He'd sing 'My old hammer ringing in the mountains, / Nothing but my hammer falling down.'" Another man said, "He was a great singer, and always singing some old song when he was driving steel. He was a black, rawboned man, 30 years old, 6 feet high, and weighed near 200 pounds." A teenage boy who had worked in the tunnel with his father recalled: "I saw John Henry drive steel. He was black and 6 feet high, 35 years old, and weighed 200 or a little more. He could sing as well as he could drive steel, and was always singing when he was in the tunnel—'Can't you drive her,—huh?'" Another worker: "Always singing when he worked. He was a sort of song-leader. He was 30 or 35 years old." Yet another: he was "the singingest man I ever saw."

Memories are often imperfect, but Chappell found widespread agreement with respect to "John Henry himself, his name, race, and prowess as a

Professor Louis Chappel, West Virginia University, 1920s. Courtesy of the West Virginia and Regional History Center, WVU Libraries.

gang-leader, a great worker and singer." Equally important, the interviewees agreed "he was well fitted for his popular role, a young man, powerful and generous." With one exception, all those who provided information to Chappell were white, and in the late 1920s, when Guy B. Johnson, a sociologist at the University of North Carolina, conducted his own set of interviews, every one of his informants was, too. Although he had once believed the story of John Henry was a myth, he quickly changed his mind. Johnson not only sent notices to newspapers in five states seeking information but also staged "John Henry contests" to obtain texts and information.

In his book, *John Henry: Tracking Down a Negro Legend*, Johnson pointed out that the story "is now known in one form or another to about nine-tenths of the Negro population." He came to several conclusions: "There was a Negro steel driver named John Henry at the Big Bend Tunnel," "he competed with a steam drill in a test of the practicability of the device," and "he probably died soon after the contest, perhaps from fever." Johnson heard from people who claimed they had known John Henry, or knew people who had known him. He cited a letter from an elderly black man who had worked with John Henry forty-five years earlier: "He driv against a steam drill and beate it down . . . Just as true as you see the sun. there was a real man John Henry. He was the champon of the wowld with a Hammer. . . . the steem Drill Beat men of every other Race down to the sand." Johnson also interviewed men who had once worked at the Big Bend Tunnel, who recalled that "steel-driving contests were pretty common," and who believed there was "a pretty good chance that a man such as John Henry is said to have been, could have excelled a steam drill in the early days of power drills." Whether or not such drills were used at the time, Johnson wrote, "there remains the fact that the legend itself is a reality, a living, functioning thing in the folk life of the Negro."

As Richard M. Dorson has shown, Johnson was among those who recognized the significance of John Henry for art, music, literature, and the theater. "I marvel that some of the 'new' Negroes with an artistic bent do not exploit the wealth of John Henry lore," Johnson said. "Here is material for an epic poem, for a play, for an opera, for a Negro symphony. What more tragic theme than the theme of John Henry's martyrdom?" In fact, within a relatively short time, John Henry would appear in all of those fields, and by the 1940s would become a favorite character in such children's books as *John Henry, the Rambling Black Ulysses*, or *John Henry and the Double-Jointed Steam Drill*, or *John Henry and His Hammer*.

Carl Sandburg, although best known as a poet, historian, and novelist, also had an abiding interest in folklore. In 1927, he published a version of "John Henry" in *The American Songbag*, providing a characteristically vivid description: "In southern work camp gangs, John Henry is the strong man, or the ridiculous man, or anyhow the man worth talking about, having a myth character somewhat like that of Paul Bunyan in work gangs of the Big Woods of the North." The song, Sandburg wrote, "evokes the atmosphere in which the powerful titan, John Henry, 'does his stuff,'" and he included the line in which John Henry asked for "A twelve-poun' hammer wid a fo'-foot handle / An' I beat yo' steam drill down." Sandburg provided many verses of the song, which on occasion he would also perform for audiences:

> John Henry tol' his cap'n,
> Dat a man was a natural man
> An' befo' he'd let dat steam drill run him down,
> He'd fall dead wid a hammer in his han'
> He'd fall dead wid a hammer in his han'

During the 1930s, radical artists, some of them members of the Communist Party, drew on the legend of John Henry to indict both racial and economic inequality. Two of those artists were brothers, Lawrence and Hugo Gellert, both of whom had emigrated from Hungary to the United States. "Negro culture is perhaps the most genuine workers' culture in America," Lawrence Gellert wrote, and he managed, somehow, to gain entrance to southern prisons, where he recorded inmates' songs, many of which were bitingly sarcastic. He later released them on an album called *Negro Songs of Protest*. Hugo Gellert, who drew cartoons for such radical periodicals as *New Masses* and the *Daily Worker*, also employed John Henry–like figures, all of them muscular, all representing a threat, at least implicitly, to wealth and privilege. Other African American artists, too, such as Fred Becker and Frank W. Long, drew, painted, or engraved John Henry, invariably a figure with bulging muscles, to demonstrate the radical potential inherent in the working class.

In 1940, a musical about John Henry, based on a novel by Roark Bradford, with Paul Robeson playing the lead role, reached Broadway. Bradford, who had been a journalist in New Orleans, had published his book in 1931 and had recently won a Pulitzer Prize for an adaptation of another of his plays, *Green Pastures*. He wrote the libretto, and Jacques Wolf composed the music. The play opened in January (but received dreadful reviews and closed within a few days). Robeson played John Henry, with a cast that included Josh White and Bayard Rustin. Robeson later recorded his version of John Henry in a 1945 album, *Songs for Free Men*:

> John Henry went to the mountain
> To beat that steam drill
> But the rock was high
> John Henry was so small
> That he laid down his hammer and he died
> Yes, he laid down his hammer and he died

Popular interest in the legend of John Henry persisted after the war, eventually attracting the interest of MacEdward Leach, an anthropologist at the University of Pennsylvania. In 1967 he published an essay claiming that Henry had not died in the United States, but rather in Jamaica. Leach recognized John Henry had become "a symbol of the Negro people, supreme in valor, strength, love, the conqueror of the white man's machine," but found "a tissue of contradictions" in what had been written about him. On a trip to Jamaica in 1957, he was shown a map, drawn in 1894, on the back of which was a song with the lines, "Ten pound hammer it crush me pardner . . . ; Somebody dyin' every day." He concluded that between the years 1894 and 1896, "a man named John Henry was killed during construction work on the Garden Town–Newcastle road and specifically at Number 9 tunnel" while at work "on the "construction of the Kingston–Port Antonio railroad." Leach wrote: "The oldest objective data concerning John Henry are the Jamaican songs. They are older than any in the United States by at least ten years. . . . the Jamaican material must be considered in any theory of the genesis of the John Henry legend and songs."

In recent years, several historians have revisited the legend, without, however, reaching a consensus. Scott Reynolds Nelson's *Steel Drivin' Man: John Henry*, published in 2006, generally accepted Chappell's earlier version of how, where, and when John Henry died, while adding important details to the story. But Nelson's account elicited a sharp response from John Garst, a retired chemistry professor. Garst claimed that "there is no indication that anyone raced a steam drill," that the song's setting was not Virginia but Alabama, and that the man who died was John Henry Dabney, an ex-slave from Mississippi, who was boring tunnels through the Oak and Coosa Mountains while working for the Columbia and Western Railway. He also maintained that the incident did not even happen in 1870—but, rather, in 1887 or 1888. Regarding John Henry, he concluded: "We may have to drive a stake through his heart to stop his perambulating and get finally rid of his ghost at Big Bend Tunnel and those other places."

Yet it does not appear that John Henry will ever be far from the minds of Americans. What was true in 1941—when John and Alan Lomax said he was "probably America's greatest single piece of folklore"—remains true today. As Dorson explained: "He comes from Tennessee most often, but also from East Virginia, Louisiana, and Mobile, Alabama. His hammer weighs nine, ten, twelve, sixteen, twenty and thirty pounds; sometimes he carries a hammer in each hand." Ultimately, John Henry remains a protean figure, meaning different things to different people at different times, but many who sing the song may still believe that "this old hammer killed John Henry / But it won't kill me, it won't kill me."

There are some songs that seem to defy time. In April 1926, Uncle Dave Macon recorded "Death of John Henry." The first verse explained, "People out West heard of John Henry's death / Couldn't hardly stay in bed." So they carried him to the graveyard and "looked at him good and long." But somehow John Henry then began talking to his coworker, and then he told his captain, "I am a Tennessee man," and then he said that before he'd let the steam drill beat him down, he'd "die with the hammer in my hand." As the song ends, the steel-driving man may inevitably succumb, but still he sings:

> John Henry hammered in the mountain
> Till the hammer caught on fire
> Very last words I heard him say,
> "A cool drink of water 'fore I die
> A cool drink of water 'fore I die."

CHAPTER 17

ENGINE 143 (1890)

Along came the FFV, the swiftest on the line
Running o'er the C&O Road, just twenty minutes behind
Running into Souville, headquarters on the line
Receiving her strict orders from a station just behind

On May 11, 1889, the Chesapeake and Ohio Railway Company's passenger train, known as the Fast Flying Virginian—or FFV—made its inaugural run. Starting out in Washington, D.C., it continued on through Virginia's Shenandoah Valley, then passed through the beautiful Blue Ridge Mountains and into West Virginia, eventually crossing the Ohio River into Cincinnati. One of the first trains to have steam heat, electric lights, water coolers, and ceiling fans, it also boasted a dining car and enclosed "vestibules," flexible covered passageways that allowed passengers to move safely from one car to another. Luxuriously appointed, the interiors were made of mahogany, rosewood, and cherry, and the seats were covered in leather. The line's president was Melville E. Ingalls, a Harvard-trained lawyer, who remained in charge for many years. He carried out many modernization projects, enlarging tunnels, building steel bridges, and providing larger cars and locomotives.

The coaches on the FFV, unlike other trains on the line, were painted in eye-catching colors, orange with maroon bands, and red wheels. Driven by huge, powerful steam locomotives, the cars were capable of hauling heavy loads over steep grades. Hundreds of stations and signal towers dotted the train's route. Starting in the early 1880s, Pullman sleeping cars were affixed to C&O trains, and soon the first dining cars were added. For breakfast, which cost a dollar, passengers were offered a gourmand's choice of baked apples and cream, broiled sea fish, sirloin steak, spring lamb chops, shirred eggs, and Saratoga—that is, potato—chips. The line boasted: "Our table water is from the celebrated Healing Springs of Virginia."

FFV menu.

However elegant the train's furnishings, the Interstate Commerce Commission reports left little doubt that working on the railroads, or even riding as a passenger, meant taking your life in your hands. The lack of uniformity in the use of safety mechanisms, especially car couplers, constituted, according to the ICC, "a death trap." The commission's report for the year ending June 30, 1890, showed there was one death for every 306 employees, and one injury for every 33 employees. But those figures included all railway employees, including office workers. Among trainmen alone—engineers, firemen, and conductors—there was one death for every 105 employees and one injury for every 12. The death rate for 1890 actually increased by 14.29 percent over the previous year. As the commission concluded: "This fearful increase is worthy of serious consideration. Among no other class of organized labor is it so great or the risk incurred so hazardous."

Moreover, the passenger cars were still heated by stoves during the winter months, sometimes with horrific consequences. Although several states had begun requiring trains to use steam heat instead of stoves, the changeover was by no means complete. In January 1891, the ICC reported that "a fearful instance of the sacrifice of human life" occurred when trains collided in a tunnel in New York City. The accident was "rendered still more horrifying by the fact that the wreck caught fire and, beyond a doubt, of the 6 persons killed several lost their lives in the flames. It is not positively known whether the holocaust was due to the stove or heater, or to the breakage of the kerosene lamps which were used on the ill fated train." The commission looked toward the day when, it hoped, kerosene would be abandoned and a safer means of heating would be used.

In 1890, the railroads employed 750,000 people, slightly over 3 percent of the nation's labor force. One of those employees was George Washington Alley, born in Richmond, Virginia, in July 1860, whose father, Leonidas Salathiel Alley, had begun his career with the Virginia Central Railroad, the predecessor of the C&O, in 1852. After moving his family to Staunton and then Clifton Forge, Virginia, Leonidas eventually settled in the small town of Wolfcreek, in the southeastern corner of West Virginia. After his wife died when George was a boy, he remarried. In all, there were seven children in the family. Like his father and two of his brothers, George went to work for the railroad; he began as a fireman, working with his father, but by the time he was nineteen he informed the census taker he was an "engeneare." Six feet tall, lean and lanky, he had a dark complexion, black eyes, and straight black hair. He was married at twenty-one, and within a few years he and his wife were raising four children of their own.

On October 23, 1890, George Alley was driving the cab of Engine 134, a heavy ten-wheeler, out of Hinton, West Virginia, a town not far from his home. The fireman on board was Lewis Withrow, and Robert Foster was also there to help. When Alley's shift began, the train was already running an hour behind schedule, so he was trying to make up lost time. It was 5:40 in the morning, still dark and gloomy. Suddenly, only three miles east of Hinton, the headlight revealed a huge boulder left by a landslide on the tracks just ahead of the train. Hitting the brakes, Alley told Withrow and Foster to jump. Foster leaped from a window and was only injured, but Withrow did not get out before the engine crashed into the rock, and he was severely burned.

Alley was injured worst of all, pinned to his seat, unable to move, his left arm and right leg fractured. Scalded by escaping steam and hot water from the cracked boiler, he probably lost consciousness. By the time rescue workers arrived, it was too late to help him, and he died after five hours of acute suffering. His wife, who hurried to the scene, arrived after he was already dead. The local newspaper, which regarded him as a hero for refusing to jump and attempting to stop the train, said: "A brave and noble Christian spirit passed from earth leaving behind a noble example of unselfish devotion to duty and principle." The paper also commented on his devotion to his family. "He spoke of them

continually every few minutes asking, 'Are they coming? Are they coming?'"
The passengers, none of whom were hurt, "expressed their appreciation for his
valor in staying at his post and risking his life to save others, and collected $103
in donations for his family."

> Oh Georgie said to his fireman, "There's a rock ahead I see
> Oh there's death awaiting to receive both you and me
> All from this engine you must go your darling life to save
> For I want you to be an engineer when I'm sleeping in my grave"

The local newspapers published relatively brief accounts of the crash, the
fourth serious accident on the FFV in less than eighteen months. The *Huntington Daily Advertiser* reassured its readers: "No one else, either of the crew or
passengers, was injured, though all of them had a shaking up and a bad scare.
No particular damage was done to the passenger cars and at 9:30 the track was
cleared and the train started east." Another local paper reported: "This morning, as the east bound vestibule train was going round a curve near the mouth
of Greenbrier river, it ran into a rock that had fallen from the cliff, and the
engine, tender, baggage car and postal car were derailed, the baggage car and
tender going over embankment. Three of the train men were injured, one of
them fatally, but none of the passengers were hurt." There was an acknowledg-
ment, in passing, that Alley's last-ditch effort to apply the brakes had done some
good: "The passengers had a narrow escape as but for the slackening of the
train's speed at the curve, all the coaches would have gone over the embankment into the river. The railroad company should have extra watchmen at the
points of the road where land slips are likely to occur, in such weather as we had
last night, and perhaps some of these costly accidents might be avoided."

The first attempt to recount George Alley's tragic fate came not in the form of
a song but rather a poem. It was composed within a week of his death by his aunt,
Mittie Frances Clark Point, who wrote under the pen name of Alex McVeigh
Miller. Born in 1850, she became one of the best-known authors of the day, writing about eighty dime novels over a period of thirty-five years, with such alluring
titles as *The Bride of the Tomb* and *Queenie's Terrible Secret* and *Dainty's Cruel
Rivals; or the Fatal Birthday*. Her memorial poem, appearing a week after Alley's
death in the *Clifton Forge and Iron Gate Review*, included the lines

> He is dying! Are they coming?
> Ah, there is some strange delay!
> And the iron horse lags hourly
> While his weak life ebbs away

But the brave young martyr murmurs
Messages for home and wife
Planning for their future welfare
When he shall be done with life

Surely a tragic poem, but one that at least held out a ray of hope: "And the heavenly hosts gave welcome / To that life that never ends."

Most of the songs about George Alley were written much later, probably about 1910, although the collector Robert Winslow Gordon received a copy from a man who claimed he had heard the song in Baltimore in 1896 or 1897. In any event, George Reneau of Knoxville, Tennessee, made the first recording in September 1924. Born in 1901, Reneau was known as "the blind musician of the Smoky Mountains." He cut a total of seventy songs, including "The Lonesome Road" ("I'm going down the road feeling bad") and novelty songs such as "I'm Glad My Wife's in Europe" ("and she can't get back to me"). Reneau met a sorrowful end in December 1933 when, after playing his guitar in frigid weather, he caught pneumonia and died, while still in his early thirties. In his version of the song, Alley's mother urged him to be careful, and he promised to heed her advice, only to decide, "O'er this road I'm going to go at the speed of a cannonball"; then the fatal crash ensued. Reneau's version did not spare the gruesome details: "His face was all covered up in blood and his eyes you could not see / And the last words poor Georgie said were 'nearer my God to thee.'"

Two years after Reneau's recording, a musician named Roy Harvey recorded his version of the song. He was born in 1892 in Greenville, West Virginia, less than fifteen miles from where Alley had once lived. And like Alley, he spent his early years as a railroad worker, starting as a fireman and eventually becoming the line's youngest engineer. But in 1923, he walked out during a rail strike and lost his job. So he began working in a music shop, where by chance he met Charlie Poole and became the guitar player with Poole's North Carolina Ramblers. Then he began making records of his own. In 1926 he recorded "The Brave Engineer" for Columbia, in which he told how George's mother warned him to be careful, "for many a man has lost his life trying to make lost time / if you run your engine right you'll get there just on the time." Harvey made his last record in 1931 and eventually went to work for the Florida East Coast Railway.

Ernest V. Stoneman also recorded the song in 1926. He had begun making records nearly two years earlier with members of his family. Stoneman was generally known as "Pop," perhaps because he and his wife, Hattie, had twenty-three children (thirteen of whom survived to adulthood). In Stoneman's version, George Alley had "curly golden hair" and a mother who advised him: "Pray to God, George my son, be careful how you run." Although promising to take her

Roy Harvey, ca. 1930.

advice, once he was driving the engine he exclaimed: "Yes, o'er this road I mean to fly, with speed unknown to all." When he saw the rock on the tracks he told his fireman to jump, but he remained in the cab: "His head was on the firebox door, while burning flames rolled o'er / 'Glad I was born an engineer to die on the C. and O!'"

In 1932 Alfred V. Frankenstein, a critic who wrote for the *San Francisco Chronicle* (and who also played clarinet in the Chicago Symphony Orchestra), compared the versions sung by Stoneman and Harvey. He believed that Stoneman's was a "human interest story" while Harvey's, closer to the folk tradition, was a "plain, unvarnished narrative," and, moreover, that Stoneman's song contained the "who, where, what, when, why and how" of the accident while Harvey's was almost exclusively concerned with the "what." "The Stoneman version is the story of a hero," he wrote; "The Harvey version is the story of a wreck." By the time his article appeared, however, the Carter Family had recorded what came to be the classic version of the song, and the one that would reach the widest audience.

Alvin Pleasant ("A.P.") Carter, his wife Sara, and sister-in-law Maybelle began making records in the summer of 1927. Success came quickly. They recorded "Engine 143" (although Alley's engine number was 134) at the RCA Victor Studio in Camden, New Jersey, on February 15, 1929. According to legend, the first time A. P. Carter saw Sara she was singing "Engine 143," accompanying herself on the autoharp; whether the story was true or not, their version of the song, with Maybelle, only nineteen, playing lead guitar, became well-known and widely imitated. The Carter Family used the themes made familiar by earlier singers, sparing none of the gruesome details: "Upside-down the engine turned, poor Georgie's breast it smashed / His head was against the firebox door, the flames were rolling high." One line in the song, however, was new, and bone-chilling. After the doctor told George his life could not be saved, the song said that he was "murdered upon the railroad and laid in a lonesome grave." None of the earlier versions had used the word "murdered" to describe George Alley's death.

Eventually, by the early years of the twenty-first century, railroad fatalities fell dramatically. Fewer than half a dozen employees died each year while on the job. In 2012, only eighty-two people perished in railroad accidents. Most fatalities occurred not among railroad workers, but among pedestrians who crossed the tracks unsafely; there were 442 such deaths in 2012. The head of the Federal Railroad Administration, Joseph Szabo—the first former trade union official to hold that position, and someone who had once worked as a yard switcher, road trainman, and conductor—boasted that 2012 was "a monumental year for American rail—one of the greatest in generations. It was the safest year in railroad history."

Even so, long after the fatal crash in West Virginia, "Engine 143" continued to be performed by folk and country musicians, including Joan Baez, Lester Flatt and Earl Scruggs, Ralph Stanley, Doc Watson, and the David Grisman Bluegrass Experience. Johnny Cash, who had listened to the song on the radio as a young boy in Dyess, Arkansas, recorded it on a 1964 album and again on August 21, 2003, just three weeks before his death. It would, in fact, be the last song he ever recorded. In a quivering voice he sang

> His face was covered up with blood
> His eyes, they could not see
> And the very last words poor Georgie said were
> "Nearer, my God, to thee."

CHAPTER 18

CASEY JONES (1900)

Come all you rounders, if you want to hear
The story told of a brave engineer
Casey Jones was the rounder's name
A high right-wheeler of mighty fame

At the turn of the twentieth century, railroads were the largest industry in the United States, employing more than one million workers. Railroads were also the industry that killed the most people. From 1895 to 1905, 78,152 people died in crashes and accidents, and many more were severely injured. In 1900 alone, 7,865 people died in train wrecks: 249 of them were passengers, 5,066 were trespassers and pedestrians on the tracks, and 2,550 were railroad employees. One of those ill-starred employees—Jonathan Luther Jones, nicknamed "Casey"—was destined to become famous. A song written about his death by his friend, an African American engine wiper named Wallace Saunders, would be sung over the years by countless numbers of people, undergo countless changes, and be recorded countless times.

At the time, on-the-job accidents, the single largest cause of violent death among blue-collar railroad workers, claimed more lives than measles, diabetes, dysentery, typhoid fever, or venereal disease and nearly as many as diphtheria. From 1882 to 1912, 48 percent of all fatalities among railroad laborers resulted from accidents. Even passengers took their lives in their hands. As trains became longer, heavier, and faster—speeds increased from about thirty miles per hour in 1870 to sixty miles or more an hour in the 1890s—they became harder to control. Although more efficient high-speed brakes were introduced in 1894, the changeover took years to complete, and even the new mechanisms did not keep pace with the increased speed and weight of trains. As Mark Aldrich explains in *Death Rode the Rails*, "Outside of wartime never before had such large groups of individuals been subject to such fearsome risks from manmade causes."

Although many of those risks were avoidable, some locomotive drivers were willing to take them anyway. One who did was thirty-six-year-old Jonathan Luther Jones. He was born in March 1863 in southeastern Missouri. His parents moved the family to the town of Cayce, Kentucky, just across the border from Tennessee, and so the youngster got the nickname, "Casey." By the age of fifteen, standing six feet, four inches tall, with dark hair and gray eyes, he began working as a telegrapher for the Mobile and Ohio (M&O) Railroad. At twenty, he moved to Jackson, Tennessee, about ninety miles east of Memphis, where the line promoted him to a position as flagman. He resided in a boardinghouse and fell in love with the proprietor's daughter, Mary Joanna "Janie" Brady; she was Catholic, and he decided to convert so they could have a church wedding. They were married in November 1886, in St. Mary's Catholic Church in Jackson, Tennessee, bought a house, and raised two sons, Charles and John, and a daughter, Helen.

Quickly moving up the ranks at the M&O, Jones was promoted to brakeman and then to fireman. In the summer of 1887, a yellow fever epidemic struck many crews on the neighboring Illinois Central Railroad, creating opportunities for promotion, and early in 1888 Jones moved to that line. On February 23, 1891, at twenty-seven, he got the job that he had always dreamed of: engineer. He ran a freight service between cities in Mississippi, and in 1893, when the World's Columbian Exposition opened in Chicago, Jones spent the summer there, shuttling thousands of visitors. He also learned to operate No. 638, a powerful new freight engine with eight drive-wheels and two pilot wheels. When the Columbian Exposition closed, Jones got permission to drive the engine back to Mississippi. Eventually he was transferred to a passenger run between Memphis and Canton, Mississippi, a distance of 188 miles, one leg of the run that linked Chicago and New Orleans.

> Another driver had called in sick
> Asking Casey to do a double trick
> Casey smiled, said, "I'm feelin' fine
> Gonna ride that train to the end of the line"

In the early morning hours of April 29, 1900, Casey Jones pulled into Memphis's Poplar Street Station, a "magnificent red stone structure" originally designed as a terminal on the transcontinental railroad that magnate Collis P. Huntington dreamed of building. By chance, the engineer for the run to Canton was ill, so Jones agreed to substitute for him. The trip usually took five hours. The train, the Cannonball Express, left the station at 12:50 a.m., ninety-five minutes behind schedule, but Jones and his fireman, Simon "Sim"

Webb, were determined to make up the lost time. As they neared Vaughan, Mississippi, eleven miles from their destination, the speeding train was only two minutes late. "Oh, Sim!" Casey said, "the old girl's got her high-heeled slippers on tonight. We ought to pass way on time." But the night was damp, the fog was thick, and unknown to Jones a freight train with a burst air hose was stalled on the tracks, unable to move onto a siding.

As he continued at breakneck speed, perhaps seventy-five miles per hour, Jones suddenly caught sight of the lights of the caboose looming just ahead, told Webb to jump, and tried frantically to apply the brakes. The *Memphis Commercial Appeal* described what happened next: Jones's engine "was running under a full head of steam when it crashed into the rear end of a caboose and three freight cars which were standing on the main track. . . . The caboose and two of the cars were smashed to pieces, the engine left the rails and plowed into an embankment, where it overturned and was completely wrecked, the baggage and mail coaches also being thrown from the track and badly damaged." So at 3:52 a.m., the clash of the engine colliding with the caboose echoed across the Mississippi countryside.

Casey Jones.

"I was unconscious when they picked me up," Webb recalled. "They found Casey with one hand clutching the throttle and the other the air-brake control. Casey was the only one killed." As one passenger said, "The mystery was that the passengers, in coaches and sleepers, were disturbed so little and hurt not at all." But while no one else was seriously injured, Jones was fatally wounded because either a metal bolt, or a piece of splintered wood, pierced his throat. The newspaper, though, said he was found "lying under the cab with his skull crushed and the right arm torn from its socket." Crewmen from nearby trains carried him on a stretcher half a mile to the depot, which is where he died. His body was first taken to Canton, and the next day a service was held in the same church in Jackson where he and Janie Brady had been married. Fifteen enginemen traveled more than one hundred miles to pay their last respects at his funeral.

While many people mourned Casey Jones's passing, officials of the Illinois Central Railroad were not among them. The company's investigation into the crash concluded matter-of-factly: "Engineer Jones was solely responsible for the accident as consequence of not having properly responded to flag signals." The company noted that since Jones had been promoted to the rank of engineer in 1890 his safety record was wanting. He had been suspended on nine occasions for periods ranging from five to thirty days. He was held responsible for a collision, for running through switches, for "striking flat car in siding," for "gross carelessness in handling orders . . . in violation of rules," and for "not recognizing flagman who was protecting work train extra . . . as required by train rules." His last infraction, less than a year before the fatal crash, was for "having left switch open at cross over in north yard, resulting in train No. 21 running in on siding."

Nevertheless, Casey Jones was destined to become a legendary figure—the blast of his calliope whistle, people would say, sounded like a whip-poor-will in the night—a folk hero about whom songs, stories, and poems would be written. Evidently, Jones's friend Wallace Saunders composed the earliest such ballad—he did not copyright the lyrics—using a popular tune, "Jimmie Jones," and emphasizing Jones's resolve to reach his destination on time:

> Fireman say, "You running (too) fast,
> You ran the last three lights we passed"
> Casey say, "We'll make it through,
> She's steamin' better than I ever knew"

The version of the song that would become most widely known first appeared in *Railroad Man's Magazine* in 1908, with a note stating that "the song is supposed to have been sung by his negro fireman." Some of the verses are similar to Saunders's, though others are not:

'Twas around this curve he spied a passenger train
Reversing his engine, he caused the bell to ring
Fireman jumped off, but Jones stayed on—
He's a good engineer, but he's dead and gone

A year later, two vaudeville performers, T. Lawrence Seibert and Eddie Newton, published their version of "Casey Jones, the Brave Engineer," in which they acknowledged Saunders's importance as writer. Looking back, they claimed they had relied on "an old negro song. . . . Nobody knows how many verses it had, and as near as we can trace it back it started about an old engineer named John Luther Jones. . . . We have searched back, and so far as we can learn, an old darkey by the name of Wallace Sanders, working in a roundhouse, started the first of the Casey Jones song." Their verses, while shorter than Saunders's, still captured the essence of the story:

Dead on the rails was a passenger train
Blood was filling up Casey's brain
Casey said, "Hey, now, look ahead!
Jump, Sam, jump or we'll all be dead!"

Their version also included the well-known refrain, "Takin' the trip to the promised land."

Recordings of the song soon started to appear, one of the earliest a version by Billy Murray in 1911. Born to Irish immigrants in Philadelphia—he later quipped, "I squalled for the first time in 1877, and so did the phonograph. I didn't do very much for ten years after that; but neither did the phonograph"— Murray spent most of his childhood in Denver, and as a young man began recording such popular songs as "In My Merry Oldsmobile," and "Alexander's Ragtime Band." His recording of "Casey Jones" included a verse, similar to one cited by Siebert and Newton, but now available to a significantly larger audience. Murray suggested that Mrs. Jones had found someone to replace Casey.

Miss Casey Jones setting upon the bedside
When she received the message that her Casey had died
Says, go to bed chillun' and ahush your crying
For you've got another poppy on the Salt Lake Line

The song was so popular that several other record companies, including Columbia, brought out their own versions.

Within twenty years of Jones's death, many versions of the song had appeared, millions of recordings had been sold, and the sheet music, too, was widely available. By 1921, when Carl Sandburg began thinking about putting together a book of American folk songs, he decided to include "Casey Jones, the Brave Engineer" which, he said, was the "greatest ballad ever written." As he wrote to a friend: "I am reading poems and singing Casey Jones, Steamboat Bill, and medleys. This whole thing is only in its beginnings, America knowing its songs. . . . It's been amazing to me to see how audiences rise to 'em." His collection, *The American Songbag*, appeared in 1927, and it naturally included a version of "Casey Jones." Sandburg declared, "The laughter of the railroad man at death and mutilation runs through many of his songs. The promise of a wooden kimono, a six foot bungalow, is with him on every trip whether he's on a regular run or the extra list, and no matter what his seniority."

By the time Sandburg's book was published, several commercial recordings of "Casey Jones" had already been made. Two of the earliest—by Fiddlin' John Carson and George Riley Puckett, both natives of Georgia—appeared in 1924. Puckett, who was blind as the result of a childhood accident, played guitar and banjo and later joined Gid Tanner and the Skillet Lickers. It was Carson's version, though, that contained nearly all the elements that came to typify the song. He has

Engineer Casey Jones in the cab of Engine No. 638, ca. 1898. © Bettmann/CORBIS.

Casey saying to his fireman: "Pick your place to jump / For there's two locomotives that are bound to bump!" He has Casey going to heaven, where St. Peter tells him: "Well, you're looking mighty bold / I guess we'll have to put you back to shoveling coal." And he has Casey's wife finding another man: "Go to bed, children, before you cry yourself hoarse / I got you another daddy on the police force."

Black musicians also began recording the song in the 1920s, but what they included, and what they left out, differed considerably from the version sung by whites. Unfortunately, Mississippi John Hurt's recording of the song in February 1928 was not released (although later, in the 1960s, he would often sing it). But Walter "Furry" Lewis's recording made in August 1928 was widely available. The title was deliberately misspelled as "Kassie Jones," to avoid a copyright violation. The lyrics, however, are only loosely connected to Casey Jones's actual fate. In Lewis's telling, the song contains no description of his efforts to avoid the crash or his decision to remain in the engine. Even the fatal accident is mentioned in passing quite late in the song: "Under the boiler lay Mister Casey Jones / Good old engineer, but he's dead and gone." Moreover, Casey's wife remains faithful: "She loved Mister Casey, 'cause she told me so," and she reassures her children, "Children, children want you to hold your breath / Draw another pension from your father's death."

Meanwhile, an entirely different version of Casey Jones, one having nothing to do with the actual event but making the most of the song's popularity, had begun circulating among members of the radical union the Industrial Workers of the World. "Casey Jones—the Union Scab" was a parody—although the tune was identical—by Joe Hill, an IWW organizer, in 1911. He wrote it in San Pedro, California, at the start of a nationwide walkout of forty thousand railway employees. It told a story about a railroad worker who refused to support a strike, died, went to heaven, was told by St. Peter that he could get a job as a scab since the musicians in paradise had gone on strike, but instead was sent by the angels' union to hell, where he found his just reward:

> Casey Jones went to Hell a-flying
> "Casey Jones," the Devil said, "Oh fine;
> Casey Jones, get busy shoveling sulfur
> That's what you get for scabbing on the S.P. line"

The song, after its initial use during the California strike, was largely forgotten until Pete Seeger recorded it with the Almanac Singers in 1941 on an album called *Talking Union*.

Joe Hill's satire aside, in nearly all the versions of what is one of the best-known American songs, Casey Jones's wife does not remain faithful. Rather, when informed that her husband is dying—not even dead, merely dying—she tells her children to go to bed "and hush your crying / Cause you got another papa on the Salt Lake line." The implications of those words offended Janie Jones, who raised her children, supported the family by running a boarding-house, and lived a long, blameless life. Occasionally, over the years, she would be remembered, even honored. She was invited to the World's Fair in New York in 1939, appeared on Ripley's *Believe It or Not* radio show, and took part in a ceremony at Vaughan, Mississippi, when a historical marker was dedicated beside the scene of the crash. She was present on Casey Jones Day in Tennessee in 1950 when a three-cent stamp honoring her husband went on sale. She died in 1958 at ninety-two, in a rest home, and was buried alongside her husband in the Catholic cemetery in Jackson, Tennessee.

She had made her last public appearance in 1956 when the Casey Jones Rail-road Museum opened in Jackson and she cut a red ribbon that opened the door of her former home, now restored, to the public. Yet even now, sightseers in Jackson can visit Casey Jones Village, which includes the Historic Casey Jones Home & Railroad Museum, Casey Jones Village Amphitheatre, the Shoppes at Casey Jones Village—and, of course, Casey Jones Mini-Golf. In 2013 the Broth-erhood of Locomotive Engineers and Trainmen decided to mark the 150th anniversary of the birth of "an American hero and one of the BLET's most leg-endary figures." Not to be outdone, the state of Tennessee proclaimed March 14, 2013, as "Casey Jones Day" to commemorate the birthday, not of the man who recklessly exceeded the speed limit, but of "the American railroad hero."

CHAPTER 19

WRECK OF THE OLD 97 (1903)

Well they gave him his orders in Monroe, Virginia
Sayin' Steve you're way behind time
This is not 38, this is ole' 97
You must put her into Spencer on time

In 1879 Charles Francis Adams, the writer and former minister to England, declared that American railroads were extraordinarily safe: "There is no more creditable monument to human care, human skill, and human foresight than the statistics of railroad accidents." But over the next quarter century, as more trains began carrying more passengers over ever-longer distances at increasingly faster speeds, neither the care, the skill, nor the foresight was much in evidence. In only one year—1903—a total of 9,840 men, women, and children died in train crashes or because of other rail mishaps. Eleven of those deaths occurred on a Sunday morning in late September 1903, when a speeding mail train plunged off a trestle at Danville, Virginia. Five photographs of the crash were printed in newspapers throughout the country. The Danville train wreck, unlike other railroad disasters, also led to a long, drawn-out legal battle, lasting nearly forty years, which began in federal district court, then moved to the federal appeals court, and finally reached the United States Supreme Court.

Among the casualties was the engineer, Joseph Andrew "Steve" Broady. (His nickname was derived from Steve Brodie, who in July 1886 claimed that he had jumped off the Brooklyn Bridge from a height of 135 feet, and survived.) The son of a Confederate war veteran, Broady was born in Virginia in 1870, and by twenty-one had begun working on the railroads, first as a fireman, then as a brakeman, and finally as an engineer. Highly regarded for his ability, he was described as "tall and slim, prematurely balding with a twinkling eye and a mouth constantly ready for a smile." He started out with the Norfolk and Western Railway, but then moved to the Southern Railroad. Like all engineers,

Broady was supposed to be well-informed about the engine, the air brakes, the roadway, the speed limits, the rights of way, the weather conditions, and the placement of signals. The rules stated that engineers "must maintain, as far as practicable, regular and uniform speed," avoid excessive speed on downgrades, and make every effort consistent with safety "to make up their running time and to recover time lost."

On the morning of September 27, 1903, Broady was driving Fast Mail Train No. 97 out of Monroe, Virginia, heading toward Spencer, North Carolina, and was already an hour behind schedule by the time he departed. He was in Engine 1102, a ten-wheeler that had four pilot wheels in the front and six sixty-eight-inch driving wheels under the boiler. The train was equipped with a Westinghouse air brake system. "A steam pump stored air in the lines that connected all the cars, and when air in the line was released, air stored in reservoirs on each car automatically pushed against the wheel brakes to slow the train." This was supposedly a safe system because any break in the lines while the train was moving would bring it to a stop. But as Larry Aaron has noted in his study of the crash, there was a problem: "Applying the brakes too often without allowing air to build back up in the reservoirs caused the brakes to fail when they were needed."

Broady had made the trip from Monroe to Danville, Virginia, twenty-two times, day and night, so the road was familiar to him. Even so, the run remained treacherous because of the changes in elevation as the train reached Stillhouse Trestle—a wooden bridge 45 feet high and 325 feet long—and because of the curves in the track. As a Southern official noted, engineers had to manage "a bad entrance, and a bad grade, and a bad trestle." Although eyewitnesses gave varying estimates of the train's speed that morning—ranging from thirty-five to sixty miles per hour—most agreed that Broady did not slow down sufficiently. In fact, the engine abruptly jumped the track and flew off the trestle into midair, dragging the other cars behind it in a cloud of steam, dust, and flames. One observer reported: "The engine went first splintering a telegraph pole and sailing about 100 feet before thudding into the mud. Each of the cars behind came crashing on top of the engine—one, two, three, four—pounding it into the earth."

> It's a mighty rough road from Lynchburg to Danville
> It's a line on a three mile grade
> It was on that grade that he lost his airbrakes
> You can see what a jump he made

The crash occurred at about 2:45 on Sunday afternoon, and residents who happened to be in their backyards, in churches, on their porches, or on the streets heard the frightful sound. Almost immediately, as bells in the churches, the cotton mill, and the courthouse began pealing loudly, people rushed to the scene. And a dreadful scene it was, "weird beyond description." As the *Danville Bee* reported: "The bodies of the dead men were broken almost entirely in pieces and horribly mangled, particularly about the head and face. The impact of the steam against the bodies of the engineer and fireman caused the skin and hair to fall away from their bodies. . . . All the cars except one are battered into kindling wood." The train had also been transporting hundreds of canaries, which were used in coal mines to detect toxic gases, especially carbon monoxide, and now, their crates having been "cracked open by the impact," the birds were "circling around the engine, flying back and forth and chirping loudly."

Nine men—the engineer, the conductor, the firemen, the flagman, the apprentice, and the postal clerks—all of them in their twenties or thirties, lost their lives. Most perished instantly, but some lingered for days. One victim was discovered only later at the bottom of the wreckage. Rescue workers found seven members of the crew who had been injured, some of them severely, but

Wreck of the Old 97.

had survived. Broady himself met a horrific fate. "The skin [and hair] came off his arm just like a chicken that's scalded," one person reported, and another said: "His skin was black from the fire and steam. He couldn't talk." His brother, arriving at the scene to maintain a vigil, instead witnessed Broady's death.

> He was goin' down that grade makin' 90 miles an hour
> When his whistle broke into a scream
> He was found in the wreck with his hand on the throttle
> Scalded to death by the steam

Within a few years after the crash, a legal contest got under way that pitted the families of the deceased and those who survived against the officials of the Southern Railroad. In some cases the line agreed to settle; in other cases juries made awards—as much as $8,000—to victims' families. Then in July 1905, the estate of Joseph Broady brought suit against the railroad. A trial was held in Danville before Judge Archibald Murphey Aiken, who was best known for having spearheaded the drive to restore white rule to the state during Reconstruction (or, as one account put it, "How Judge Aiken Struck First Blow for Restoration of White Man's Rights"). Broady's relatives claimed the railroad trestle was known to be unsafe, while the attorneys for the Southern countered that "the blame for this fearful disaster must rest with him," with Broady himself. Broady's heirs had asked for damages of $10,000, but the jury instead awarded $4,500.

As the years went by, recordings of the song, sometimes titled "The Wreck on the Southern Old 97," began to appear, modeled, to some degree, on "The Ship That Never Return'd," written in 1865. Henry Whitter, a cotton mill worker from Virginia, who played several instruments, was the first to record the railroad song, in December 1923, and it was released a month later. It included the verse

> He turned around and said to his black greasy fireman
> Just shovel in a little more coal
> And when we cross that White Oak Mountain
> You can watch ole' 97 roll

Within a matter of months, two other recordings followed: one by Ernest Thompson, a musician from Winston-Salem, North Carolina, who had lost his sight while working in a sawmill and who did the song for Columbia, and the other by George Reneau of Knoxville, Tennessee, also a blind singer, who traveled to Vocalion's New York studio to cut the record (although it is possible that he only provided the guitar accompaniment, since on many of his records the singing was done by one Gene Austin).

On May 14, 1924, Marion Try Slaughter made the most popular early recording, and it was distributed later that summer. During his long career, Slaughter used nearly one hundred pseudonyms—one of them, certainly the most common, being Vernon Dalhart. Born in Jefferson, Texas, in 1883, he studied opera at the Dallas Conservatory of Music, then moved to New York City and proceeded to make hundreds of classical and popular recordings— among the latter was "Hard Hearted Hanna (the Vamp of Savannah)"—before turning to country music. Proficient on the guitar and the harmonica, he was also a talented whistler. He mainly copied Whitter's lyrics, including his final admonition:

> Come ladies you must take warning
> From this time, now and on
> Never speak harsh words to your true loving husband
> He may leave you and never return

The Hawaiian guitarist Frank Ferera accompanied Dalhart, whose recording sold more than a million copies in just a few years.

On October 1, 1924, shortly after these recordings appeared, the song was copyrighted, in Whitter's name, and before long a series of legal battles erupted—dragging on for fifteen years—over such matters as who had written the song, and, equally crucial, who was entitled to royalties from its sale. It all began in 1927, when David Graves George, a Danville resident and telegraph operator who had witnessed the crash scene, wrote a letter to a newspaper claiming that he and others had composed "the poetry of 97." He brought suit against the Victor Talking Machine Company, which had released Dalhart's recording, claiming that he was entitled to royalties. Not surprisingly, the company refused to settle. Instead, at the pretrial hearing in April 1929, it turned to the Library of Congress musicologist Robert Winslow Gordon, who had done much research on the song and thought that the company had purchased the rights from two men, Danville residents, who had composed it, paying each of them $100.

The men, Charles Weston Noell and Frederick Jackson Lewey, testified for the defense at the hearing, held in Greensboro, North Carolina, and later at the trial. Lewey claimed that he had written the song, that he had performed it for Noell and others, and that in October 1925 he had given the text to Gordon. For his part, Gordon said he had transcribed the words, including some of the most famous lines, such as "mighty bad road from Lynchburg to Danville," and

Vernon Dalhart.

"He was found when she wrecked with his hand on the throttle / Where he'd scalded to death from the steam." Lewey also reiterated his claim of having used the tune of the older song, "The Ship That Never Return'd."

In the spring of 1931, after numerous delays, *George v. Victor Talking Machine Co.* finally reached federal district court in New Jersey. The judge was John Boyd Avis, who had served in both houses of the state legislature before his appointment to the bench. At the trial, George endeavored to prove he had composed the song in 1903, while Victor tried to prove he could not have done so. The company's lawyers showed that the carbon paper George said he had used to write the song was not yet in existence; that his handwritten lyrics, allegedly from 1903, had in fact been written in 1927; and that he had promised a witness who was about to give evidence that "If I win, you'll get a piece (of the pie)."

Gordon also testified for Victor, after being informed by the company's lawyer, Louis B. Le Duc, that all that was required was to describe "the several versions of the song, their dates and places of publication and circulation." His role, the lawyer advised, "will be solely that of the expert dealing with hypotheses and not at all that of the fact investigator." So when he took the stand, Gordon asserted that purely on the basis of internal evidence he could "determine the relative date of any given text"; in fact, he said, a folklorist could use such evidence in the same way "as the philologist goes about the study of language." Although, as he told the attorney, he had attempted to find out everything he could about the crash, he testified only that he was certain that George's version was written at a much later date.

Notwithstanding these arguments, on March 11, 1933, Judge Avis ruled in favor of George. His opinion rejected the record company's claim that George had taken the text of the song from Vernon Dalhart's recording; instead, the judge held that George had written the ballad in the aftermath of the wreck, and that it was essentially the song that Victor had recorded. While he respected Gordon's testimony, and that of the handwriting expert, Avis said, he found they "erred in their conclusions." The folk music scholar Norm Cohen has criticized the ruling, with good cause, noting that Avis lacked a sufficient understanding of how songs are orally transmitted: "Thus, ironically, Avis based his decision solely on his (incorrect) analysis of internal evidence and ignored the external data."

By the time the judge had ruled, the Radio Corporation of America had purchased the Victor Talking Machine Company and decided to appeal. So the case moved to the Third Circuit Court of Appeals in Philadelphia, which, on January 3, 1934, reversed the lower court's judgment. Judge J. Warren Davis, who had been appointed to the court in 1920 by President Woodrow Wilson, delivered the opinion. Davis went into extraordinary detail, noting that the song could be heard everywhere, "at country gatherings, in plank taverns, and under electric lights on street corners on summer nights." He compared George's lyrics to virtually every version of the "The Wreck of the Old 97," including those that had been recorded by Whitter and Dalhart. The "real question in this case" was whether George had written the song, Davis said, and decided that it was "established beyond doubt" that Noell and Lewey had composed it.

The judge had scathing things to say about the alleged author. He thought that George had been "disingenuous" in describing his writing of the song—that it was "impossible for a person of his experience and training" to have written it. The judge believed that the record company's lawyers had shown that George had copied the song "largely from Dalhart's rendition of Whitter's record. This conclusion depends not so much upon the veracity of witnesses as upon documentary evidence." Davis then proceeded to examine particular phrases in the song, which convinced him that George "shows signs of copying, even mistakes which appear only in Dalhart." He also noted that George could only offer "a long, rambling, but incredible explanation" of why he substituted "average" for "airbrakes" in his text. To Davis, it was "too plain for argument" that George had copied Dalhart's record; the documentary evidence alone, he said, "discredits his testimony."

The ruling by the Court of Appeals, however, did not end Old 97's legal odyssey. In December 1934 the United States Supreme Court weighed in, ruling that the Third Circuit Court of Appeals had failed to hear the case within the required time and was "without jurisdiction," and therefore reversed Davis's ruling. And so the matter returned, in July 1938, to the district court. A "master" was appointed to take additional testimony. He determined that Victor had realized a net profit of $130,591.11 from the sale of the recording of "The Wreck of the Old 97" (the flip side contained both "The Prisoner's Song" and "Sourwood Mountain"), and that one half of that amount—$65,295.56—was to be given to George. In September, the district court awarded him that sum, with the judge declaring, "We see no reason for departing from our conclusion on the merits of the controversy as to the authorship of the song set forth in our previous opinion."

There the story might have ended, but a final act, or acts, had yet to unfold. In July 1939 the case once again was appealed to the Third Circuit. Judge Davis was no longer there—in fact, he was no longer on the bench; he had resigned in March, in disgrace, after being indicted by a federal grand jury for allegedly accepting a bribe. Judge Albert B. Maris now wrote for the court. He ruled that it did have jurisdiction to review the defendant's liability, and concluded: "We see no reason for departing from our conclusion on the merits of the controversy as to the authorship of the song set forth in our previous opinion." He said "the evidence established beyond question" that George had not written the song, "and that the District Court erred in finding that he was its author and holding the defendant liable to account to him for its use."

So the district court's award was reversed, and efforts to take the matter again to the Supreme Court failed. Late in 1939, the justices twice refused to consider the case, and in January 1940 they denied a rehearing for the last time. Years later, George's son claimed that the Victor Talking Machine Company would have settled out of court for $50,000, and that his father should have taken the offer. But George would not hear of it, declaring, "I'll live on wild onions before I accept that amount from them," and so he never realized a penny.

It took nearly four decades after the mishap in which Joseph Andrew Broady and eight other young men lost their lives for all the legal wrangling to come to an end. Yet even more than a century after the Danville crash, there are those who recognize there is still money to be made from the tragedy. A railroad station through which the train once passed was converted into a restaurant named the "Old 97 Steak House." Someone has marketed a "Wreck of the Old 97" coloring book for children. A country rock band that calls itself the "Old 97s"—its label is "Bloodshot Records"—has released "Wreck Your Life," "Blame It on Gravity," and an album called *Hit by a Train*.

Fortunately, railway fatalities have declined and now number in the hundreds each year and not the thousands. But the carnage once caused lives on in the nation's memory, and in its songs.

> The people waited at the depot
> Till the setting of the sun
> It was hours and hours the dispatch was waiting
> For the fastest train ever run.

Workers

CHAPTER 20

COTTON MILL BLUES (1930s)

And it's hard times, cotton mill girls
Hard times, cotton mill girls
Hard times, cotton mill girls
Hard times everywhere

The blues musician B. B. King—he would use the initials instead of his first name, Riley—was born on a Mississippi plantation in 1925. As a young boy, he picked cotton, up to 480 pounds a day, earning, for that hard day's work, $1.75. "Cotton didn't make me or my people rich," he later said. "But cotton got us through." In fact, cotton got lots of people through—those who planted and picked the bolls, and also those who worked in the mills spinning the cotton into yarn and then weaving it into cloth. When the United States entered the First World War, the mills employed about 310,000 workers—145,000 men, 125,000 women, and 40,000 children. More than 80 percent of them worked in only ten states, all in New England or the Deep South.

Most of those workers put in a sixty-five-hour week, twelve hours every weekday and five hours on Saturday. The pay was usually twenty or twenty-five cents an hour, though men always made more than women, whereas children earned the least. Working conditions were particularly hazardous because cotton dust and fibers as well as flax and hemp fibers were present everywhere. The mills had inadequate ventilation, and inhaling the fibers often caused byssinosis, commonly known as brown lung disease. The illness caused wheezing, coughing, even difficulty breathing. Other injuries on the job occurred, too, typically when clothing got tangled up in the machinery.

I'm a-gonna starve, and everybody will
'Cause you can't make a living at a cotton mill

Mill workers especially detested the "stretch-out," a system that required them to operate several different machines, often at increasingly rapid speeds. "Men and women are being killed inch by inch with this terrible system," a worker wrote to President Franklin D. Roosevelt in 1934: "I ask you to read of the cruelty of Pharaoh to the Israelites to get a comparison. . . . The time is near at hand where there will be no old people in the mill villages because of the stretch-out system." The system remained in place, however, despite protests. As another worker said: "They'd put more work on you for the same pay. More work; they don't know when to quit. And they got to where people couldn't stand it no longer."

Hard as it may have been for the men and women in the mills, it was infinitely harder on the children, some as young as seven, whose parents sent them to work. Boys usually began either as sweepers, going from room to room with brooms to clean up the lint that covered the floors, or as doffers, replacing the filled spools on the spinning machines with empty ones. Some of the spools were too high to reach, so the smaller boys had to climb onto the machines, usually barefooted for better traction, but always at risk of losing their balance and being caught in the equipment. Girls, thought to be more patient, worked as spinners, piecing together the broken ends of the thread; they "would walk up and down the aisles, brushing lint from machines and watching the spools or bobbins for breaks." Accidents were more common among children than among adult workers.

In 1908, and again in 1913, Lewis Hine published a series of photographs of the children who worked in the mills. Employed at the time by the National Child Labor Committee, Hine visited plants chiefly in the Carolinas, capturing the looks on the youngsters' faces and also their bearing—startling images, the subjects at once proud and pitiful, defiant and despondent, nearly all of them, however, cheerless. The children are seemingly dwarfed by the size of the machines. Hine commented on "the indifference of most of the mill officials to the investigation and their apparent unconsciousness of anything either wrong or criminal in the employment of children." He also noted that the state law regulating child labor, inadequate at best, was usually ignored; as a mill proprietor said, "Not over ten per cent of the mills observe it." The pitiful tales he had been told, Hine said, "corroborated by the photographic fidelity of the camera [are] unassailable."

Those photographs—documenting the "abuse of childhood"—were disturbing enough, but Hine added equally unsettling captions: "I met one boy during the day at his home who said he is working nights and is ten years old." Of another photograph, he said it "shows a little spinner at work on the day shift. She was 51 inches high, runs 4 sides, earns 48 cents a day and has been in

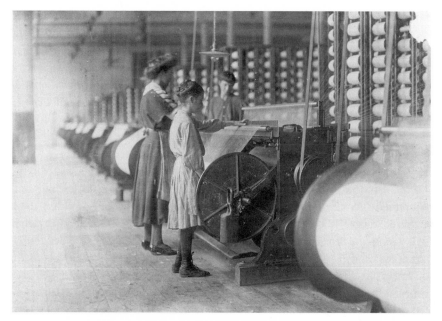

Lewis Hine photo of girls working in a cotton mill, Gastonia, North Carolina, 1908. Courtesy of the Library of Congress.

the mill for two years." He photographed another boy, thirteen years old, who "has worked since he was six. He has lost part of a finger in machinery." The conditions under which the children worked, bad enough in North Carolina, were even worse in South Carolina, where school attendance was irregular and illiteracy was rampant. At one mill, "one of the children confessed to the age of ten and another to the age of eight, while five children out of six examined were unable to read or write." Hine concluded: "The children are helpless, and their only appeal for protection must he made to those who make and execute the laws."

> Those babies all grew up unlearned
> They never went to school
> They never learned to read or write
> They learned to spin and spool

Conditions, therefore, were ripe for protest. From 1919 to 1921, as the historian John A. Salmond has written, "industrial strife rocked the Piedmont as workers flocked to join the AFL's United Textile Workers (UTW)." Since the bosses were unwilling to meet the union's demands, workers went out on strike, violence frequently erupted, calls went out to the state militia to maintain order, and workers made few gains. By 1928 a new, rival union was formed, the National Textile Workers Union (NTWU). Although considerably more radical in its outlook—the leadership included some members of the Communist Party—the NTWU supported such traditional goals as shorter hours, better pay, union recognition, elimination of the stretch-out, and the abolition of child labor. By early 1929 the union launched an organizing drive in North Carolina.

On the first of April, eighteen hundred mill workers went on strike, many of them in Gastonia, a town twenty miles west of Charlotte. The focus was the Loray Mill, the largest in the South, a building that was six stories high and contained fifty thousand spindles and sixteen hundred looms. Within days, Governor Oliver Max Gardner sent for units of the National Guard. The troops, 250 strong, quickly arrived and arrested some of the strikers, men and women alike. But many workers decided to remain on the job, and the strike seemed to be collapsing when, on April 18, a large group of masked men—some witnesses claimed there were as many as two hundred—attacked the building that was being used as strike headquarters, smashing it to pieces. When the city council prohibited parades without a permit, five hundred strikers defied the ban and were viciously attacked by sheriff's deputies; some workers were stabbed with bayonets or beaten with rifle butts, and many more, men and women alike, were taken to jail. By the end of May the strike was fizzling out and the mills were again operating.

Yet some union members stood firm—marching and picketing—until, in September, a tragic incident occurred near the American mill in Bessemer, a town not far from Gastonia. One of the workers who had gone on strike was Ella May Wiggins, twenty-nine years old and the mother of nine children (four of whom had died at an early age, one a victim of pellagra). Separated from her husband, she cared for her children during the day and worked a twelve-hour night shift, earning nine dollars a week. In May, in the company of a small group of workers, she had traveled to Washington, D.C., hoping to persuade a Senate committee to investigate conditions in the southern textile industry. When the delegation chanced upon North Carolina senator Lee Overman, Wiggins spoke up: "How can I send my children to school when I can't make enough to clothe them decently? When I go to the mill at night I have to lock them up by their lone selves. I can't have anyone to look after them."

Back home in North Carolina, she became known for writing songs—the words were harsh, often bitter, the melodies, based on folk tunes, were usually quite lovely—that described working-class life. One of them was "The Mill Mother's Lament":

Ella May Wiggins during trip to
Washington, D.C., May 1929.
Courtesy of Millican Pictorial
History Museum.

We leave our home in the morning
We kiss our children goodbye
While we slave for the bosses
Our children scream and cry

How it grieves the heart of a mother
You every one must know
But we can't buy for our children
Our wages are too low

On September 14, 1929, as she was riding to a rally in an open truck along with
other striking workers, a mob opened fire with shotguns and rifles. Struck by a
bullet, Wiggins died almost instantly. Although seven men were arrested and
charged with conspiracy to commit murder, none of them were convicted. At her
funeral, a friend sang "The Mill Mother's Lament" as a dirge, while her children
tried to hold back their tears.

Shortly thereafter, equally tragic events took place in the town of Marion, only eighty miles from Gastonia. In July, two thousand workers had gone on strike, and soon several mills were encircled by "thousands of singing workers in line." The owners obtained an injunction to prevent picketing, the National Guard was called out, and martial law was declared. On September 11, a settlement was reached, calling for a reduction from sixty-five to fifty-five hours a week, with a corresponding cut in pay. But demonstrations resumed when union members were not rehired, and on October 2 deputies hurled tear-gas bombs and opened fire on the workers, killing six and injuring twenty-five. A mass funeral for the fallen was held. Charges were brought against the sheriff and deputies, but they were either exonerated in a preliminary hearing or later acquitted by a jury.

The novelist Sinclair Lewis, who was on the scene, wrote *Cheap and Contented Labor*, a pamphlet describing the death of a sixty-eight-year-old striker who "wounded badly, was taken to the hospital with handcuffs on, was placed on the operating table, with handcuffs still on, and straightway he died on that table . . . with his handcuffs on." Lewis, expressing the sentiments of many mill workers, wrote: "To such an open declaration by the Marion businessmen that they will assist Capital to choke Labor, can there, on the part of workers, be any conceivable answer save the most militant and universal and immediate organization of trade unions?" Other strike supporters expressed their anger, and their dismay, in song:

'Twas in Marion, North Carolina
In a little mountain town
Six workers of the textile mills
In cold blood were shot down

'Tis ever the same old story
With the laborers of our land
They're ruled by mighty powers
And riches they command

By the early 1930s, as the nation sank more deeply into the Great Depression, workers who still had jobs, including those in the cotton mills, were understandably reluctant to go on strike. But with the advent of the New Deal their mood changed dramatically. Many expected that the Roosevelt administration would support their efforts to improve wages and working conditions. The administration had indeed gotten Congress to pass the National Industrial Recovery Act, which created codes of fair competition for many industries; the cotton code required a forty-hour work week, a minimum wage of twelve dollars a week, and an end to child labor. In practice, though, employers found ways around the codes, cutting costs and maximizing profits by speeding up the assembly lines, resorting to piecework, and requiring, in effect, that workers produce more in less time.

There were, unfortunately, more ways to circumvent the code than anyone could have imagined. The stretch-out system still forced workers to put in unreasonably long hours. That system, one worker protested, was "killing people": "In 1929 I run 10 Looms Now I Run 50 looms." Far from benefiting from new opportunities, fifty thousand cotton workers actually lost their jobs within a year's time. Employers still found ways to avoid paying the minimum wage by reclassifying jobs as "yard help," for example, and even workers who had been in the mills for many years might find themselves listed as "apprentices" and paid accordingly. One worker told government officials that his company "is not paying code wages at all, and nearly all the Hands even those that was raised in this mill are put on apprentice Pay Roll." There were so many ways for employers to evade the codes, he said, that it would "take a week to tell it all."

The predictable result was a wave of strikes throughout the country in 1934, many producing violent clashes between workers and police. In April, a stoppage by automobile workers in Toledo led to a pitched battle with the Ohio National Guard in which several workers were killed and more than two hundred were injured. In May, a nine-day strike by Minneapolis teamsters brought trucking to a standstill and also led to clashes, leaving two workers dead and more than sixty others injured. In July, San Francisco municipal workers called a general strike that shut the city down for four days; ultimately, 150,000 workers in the Bay Area became involved. On what would be known as "Bloody Thursday" in San Francisco, two strikers were slain and the California National Guard blocked major thoroughfares with machine-gun-mounted trucks.

The largest strike that year—in fact, the largest strike the nation had ever witnessed—was that of the United Textile Workers. It began on Labor Day in 1934, involved more than four hundred thousand workers, and lasted for three weeks. Originating in the southern cotton mills, the strike quickly spread northward to New England. The workers' demands included the restoration of cut wages, union recognition, elimination of the stretch-out, and the reinstatement of workers fired for their union activities. The strike started in North Carolina, and within a few days the *New York Times* reported: "Moving with the speed and force of a mechanized army, thousands of pickets in trucks and automobiles scurried about the countryside in the Carolinas, visiting mill towns and villages and compelling the closing of the plants. . . . Strikers in groups ranging from 200 to 1,000 assembled about mills and demanded that they be closed."

In many states, governors responded swiftly by calling out the National Guard, and, risking nothing, the cotton manufacturers hired their own private deputies and guards. In a tense atmosphere, violence was inevitable. In Rhode Island, the governor declared a state of martial law when striking workers "armed with rocks, flowerpots and broken headstones from a nearby cemetery battled troops armed with machine guns." In Georgia, the governor, also declaring martial law, ordered the National Guard to arrest pickets and hold them in a former World War I prisoner-of-war camp to await trial. The National Guard was mustered in North Carolina, while in South Carolina sheriff's deputies and strikebreakers opened fire on picketing workers, killing seven of them. As the newspapers reported: "Without warning came the first shots, followed by many others, and for a few minutes there was bedlam. Striker after striker fell to the ground, with the cries of wounded men sounding over the field and men and women running shrieking from the scene."

After three weeks of bloodshed, the textile workers' union called off the strike, declaring it had won a victory when in truth it had virtually nothing to show for its efforts. The union had neither gained recognition nor won better conditions for the workers. Most mill employees sullenly returned to their jobs, although many firms (ignoring President Roosevelt's request) both refused to reinstate many workers who had supported the strike, and blacklisted union organizers. The administration created a Textile Labor Relations Board, but it lacked authority to improve conditions, as did a new mediation panel. The strike, one scholar wrote, was "unquestionably the greatest single industrial conflict in the history of American organized labor," but in the end there were few tangible gains to show for it.

By late September the strike had ended, but not the difficulties encountered by many workers who wanted to return to work. Beth English's study of the cotton industry, A Common Thread, describes how employers retaliated against workers in the aftermath of the strike. In some instances, the companies simply dismissed them, declaring, "You're blackballed. Get on out!" Willing hands were readily available from the ranks of the unemployed. To keep their jobs, workers sometimes had to agree not to join a union, or if they had already joined, to renounce their association. Working conditions also continued to erode, to such an extent that, by January 1935, the Textile Labor Relations Board had received sixteen hundred complaints against 579 mills. Nationwide, union membership in the cotton mills also dropped sharply; by the spring of 1937 only thirty-eight thousand members remained.

For the most part, cotton mill workers remained poorly paid and nonunionized until the United States entered the Second World War. Only then did federal agencies provide the needed backing for unions, while management, flush with military and civilian orders, was chiefly concerned with maintaining productivity. Some of the older workers, however, undoubtedly remembered the lethal conflicts of 1934 and 1929, and even the earlier struggles in the mills. They may also have remembered the songs that were once so much a part of those struggles:

> When I die, don't bury me at all
> Just hang me up on the spoolroom wall
> Place a knotter in my hand
> So I can spool in the Promised Land.

CHAPTER 21

CHAIN GANG BLUES (1930s)

Take these stripes, stripes from around my shoulder
Take these chains, these chains from around my legs
Lord, these stripes, it sure don't worry me
But these chains, these chains gonna kill me dead

He was arrested in Texas in 1915 at the age of twenty-seven, convicted of carrying a pistol, and sentenced to thirty days on the county road gang. He escaped after three days, found someone to cut his leg irons with an ax, and took an alias, "Walter Boyd," to cloak his identity. Then, in December 1917, he got into a fight with a man, shot and killed him, was arrested, broke out of jail, was recaptured, and was sentenced to Shaw State Prison Farm in Texas. In August 1919, he escaped, only to be tracked down by bloodhounds within a day. He was transferred to "Sugar Land," a state prison farm just southwest of Houston. But he was also a musician who played the twelve-string guitar, so he serenaded Governor Pat Neff, begging for release by singing "What a Friend We Have in Jesus," and in January 1925 the governor granted him a pardon.

Five years later, now residing in Louisiana, he stabbed a white man, was nearly lynched, and was given six to ten years of hard labor. This time he was sent to Angola Penitentiary, fifty miles northwest of Baton Rouge, a prison described as "a swampy hell" and "uninhabitable." He arrived in February 1930, worked picking cotton while shackled like a slave, and once received ten lashes for "laziness" and another time fifteen lashes for "impudence." In August 1934, his time finally up, he was granted release by Governor O. K. Allen. His name was Huddie Ledbetter, his nickname, "Lead Belly," and he began traveling with folk song collector John A. Lomax, who soon realized that the former prisoner knew a wealth of songs.

The chain gang, including the one to which Lead Belly was sent, was designed as a replacement for—and an improvement on—the existing convict lease system. That system had originated in Mississippi in 1868 when a wealthy businessman obtained custody of convicts by paying their fines, hiring guards, providing housing, and then forcing them to work his land. The state assumed no responsibility other than paying for their maintenance and transportation. Convict leases soon spread to every southern state except Virginia. Prisoners, the vast majority of them blacks, were leased to the highest bidders and forced to do all kinds of arduous work from sunup to sundown. They picked cotton, built levees, cleared swamps, mined coal, and labored in sawmills.

They were typically housed in run-down, dilapidated camps, where whipping was commonly employed, not only to punish insubordination or attempts to escape, but also to enforce labor discipline. Convicts could be strapped for failing to work quickly enough, for "slow hoeing" or for "sorry planting." Often suffering from malaria, sunstroke, or dysentery, as well as exhaustion, they received little if any medical care but were sent out to work no matter how weak or ill they were. As the historian David Oshinsky has written: "A doctor sent by the state on a rare visit to a Delta plantation wrote that the word 'unsanitary' did not begin 'to express the filthy conditions of the convict cage': bloodstained dirt floors, overflowing waste buckets, and vermin-covered walls." The system was as merciless as it was cruel.

After many years, convict leasing gradually ended as government inspectors, social reformers, and journalists exposed its evils. In 1900 the United States Industrial Commission reported that the system "should not be tolerated in any civilized community." In 1907, Mary Church Terrell, herself the daughter of former slaves, wrote that convict lease camps housed "thousands of colored people, men, women, and children, who are enduring a bondage, in some respects more cruel and crushing than that from which their parents were emancipated forty years ago." In 1908, a Justice Department investigator declared convict leasing was in effect a system of involuntary servitude. Mississippi abolished leasing in 1894, and so did most other southern states in the early twentieth century, although Alabama, incredibly, retained the system until 1928.

To replace leasing, southern states usually set up prison farms where convicts, in chains, worked in the open under the watchful eyes of guards, usually on mounted horseback. In 1892, North Carolina established the first such facility—Caledonia Correctional Institution—and the next two decades saw the creation of many others: Angola Prison Farm in Louisiana, Cummins and Tucker in Arkansas (one for blacks, the other for whites), State Prison Farm in Georgia, Harlem Prison Farm and Imperial State Prison Farm (known as Sugar Land) in Texas, Moffett Prison Farm (later renamed Atmore) in Alabama, Raiford Penitentiary (State Prison Farm) in Florida, and Parchman Farm in Mississippi. The South Carolina Penitentiary left it up to the county supervisor and judge to decide whether prisoners would go to a road camp.

Men permanently shackled in leg irons were invariably treated as less than fully human, and catastrophes predictably resulted. One ghastly example was provided by the Texas Department of Corrections: "In September 1913 guards at Harlem State Farm punished twelve black convicts by confining them in the 'dark cell,' an enclosure nine feet three inches long, seven feet 3½ inches wide, and six feet 11½ inches high. The inside temperature of the sun-drenched box rose to well over 100 degrees. The confined inmates screamed for help, but the guards later testified that they 'had no reason to think there was anything wrong or that any of the convicts were in distress or suffering.' Eight of the twelve convicts suffocated. The guards were charged with negligent homicide, but a preliminary investigation found that they had violated no law. A commissioners' investigation suggested that the prison officials had exercised 'bad judgment.'"

> Judge gave me life this morning
> Down on Parchman Farm
> Down on Parchman Farm
> I wouldn't hate it so bad
> But I left my wife and my home

The institution most closely associated with the chain gang was the Mississippi State Penitentiary, commonly known as Parchman Farm, located in Sunflower County about ninety miles south of Memphis. Governor James K. Vardaman established the prison in 1904, a year after his election. "No politician exploited the Negrophobia of the state's down-trodden white electorate more successfully," one historian said of the man usually known as the "White Chief": "No man defended the racial status quo more zealously." Mississippi acquired large tracts of land for the prison, more than fifteen thousand acres by 1917 and eventually nearly double that amount. The number of inmates grew as well, from thirteen hundred in 1907 to nearly two thousand in 1937. The prison farm was lucrative, a money-making venture for the state. In 1912 a Mississippi legislator who visited Parchman declared it "a very monument to labor that our state can boast of, and one of which we might well be proud."

Parchman Farm was divided into fifteen field camps, segregated by race and sex. Adults and juveniles were mixed together, as were first-timers and habitual criminals. Nine of ten prisoners were African American. Each of the camps contained wooden barracks—cheaper, by far, than cells—where the inmates ate and slept. The prison eventually put the inmates to work in a sawmill, a brickyard, a slaughterhouse, a vegetable-canning plant, a cotton gin, and, of course, on the roads and in the fields. In some respects, the prison resembled an antebellum plantation: "Both systems used captive labor to grow the same crops in identical ways. Both relied on a small staff of rural, lower-class whites to supervise the black labor gangs. And both staffs mixed physical punishment with paternalistic rewards in order to motivate their workers."

Labor discipline was maintained by overseers, who were themselves prison employees, and also by inmates who had been chosen as trustees—usually long-term prisoners who were "picked for their ability to intimidate other convicts, and their willingness to use force." Granted certain privileges—better food, for example, and more freedom to move about—and wearing uniforms with vertical rather than horizontal stripes, the trustees carried high-powered

A southern chain gang, ca. 1900–1906. Courtesy of the Library of Congress.

Winchesters to ensure that no one escaped. In 1925, a Mississippi official told a meeting of the American Prison Association that in the event prisoners attempted to flee, "we have two ways of stopping them: order them to halt and if they don't, our trusties have a shotgun for short range to shoot in their lower limbs, and if they get out of reach, they use a high powered rifle."

> We go to work in the mornin'
> Just at dawn of day
> Just at dawn of day
> Just at the settin' of the sun
> That's when the work is done

Prisoners who were captured while attempting to escape, who broke the rules, or who disobeyed guards were punished brutally, as were those who failed to meet their work quotas, or were accused of stealing, or were disrespectful to the authorities. Punishment took the form of a whipping on the bare back or buttocks with a leather strap, known as "Black Annie," three feet long, four inches wide, and a quarter of an inch thick. Five to fifteen lashes were usually given while other prisoners looked on. Black convicts administered the whippings. In 1909, the Parchman superintendent justified the beatings, saying it was "absolutely necessary to whip a convict" when he failed to do his work. A year later, a physician told the American Prison Association that whipping was "the only effective method of punishing the class of criminals in the Mississippi penitentiary." The swish of the lash cutting through the air and striking flesh was a sound that prisoners frequently heard and rarely forgot.

Although most of the prisoners were African Americans, some white men were also incarcerated at Parchman Farm, as were a number of black women. Since segregation was the rule, separate—although not equal—facilities were provided. Whites accounted for about 10 percent of the prison population, somewhat more during the 1920s and early 1930s when Prohibition was the law of the land. By the mid-1920s, there were 280 white inmates, of whom 87 had been arrested for violating the federal ban on the manufacture or sale of booze. At the time, only about sixty women were incarcerated at the facility, most serving time either for murder or grand larceny. They were put to work canning vegetables, doing laundry, sewing clothes, making linens, mattresses, and uniforms, and helping in the fields.

The work done by prisoners, both inside and outside the prison grounds, undermined the status and livelihood of free workers. Convict labor not only tended to depress wages generally, but also thwarted union organizing efforts. As one investigator told Congress, convict workers gave employers "a club over organized labor." Workers were naturally reluctant to make demands or go on strike when they feared companies would replace them with prisoners. Moreover, it was evident to state officials and private employers that "the use of forced convict labor in road work was more economically efficient than using . . . free labor, because convicts could be worked harder, for longer hours, and over a more sustained period of time."

Parchman prisoners who worked outdoors would usually sing as they wielded their axes, picks, and shovels. One man acted as the leader, or "caller," and the others would respond to the phrases he chanted. This not only made the time pass more quickly, but also synchronized their physical movements and provided an outlet for pent-up tensions. The leader could slow the tempo, if necessary, and thereby protect a man from being punished for working too slowly. It was less important for callers to have good voices—although some indeed did—than for them to maintain a steady rhythm and come up with enough verses to keep the song going. In 1933, John A. Lomax recorded the prisoners on a chain gang in Texas asking the sun—"old Hannah"—to set:

> Go down, old Hannah,
> Won't you rise no more?
> Go down, old Hannah,
> Won't you rise no more?
>
> Oh, did you hear, what the captain said?
> Oh, did you hear, what the captain said?
> That if you work He'll treat you well
> And if you don't He'll give you hell

While the convicts' songs sometimes carried messages of protest, they were sufficiently indirect not to provoke the guards' animosity. Lead Belly's version of "Old Hannah," for example, contained the line: "And if you do rise in the morning / Set this world on fire."

In August 1933 Lomax and his eighteen-year-old son, Alan, spent three days at Parchman Farm, talking to the prisoners and recording many of their work songs. "It would require many months to secure all the song material available among those two thousand black men," Lomax said, so he and Alan returned a number of times. One of the songs they recorded that summer was "Rosie." It was, Lomax said, "the most stirring of all prison work songs," as it was "filled full of a fierce and bitter despair." He reported that a group of convicts "sang it for us late one evening after they had come in from a day's work in the fields, and what they sang is essentially unreproducible; for along with the singing one

On the chain gang, Thomasville, Georgia, ca. 1890. Courtesy of the Library of Congress.

must hear the beat of the hoes on the hard ground, the shouted exclamations at intervals in the song."

> Stick to the promise girl that
> You made me
> You made me
> You made me
> Won't got married til' (uh)
> I go free
> I go free, Lordy, I go free
> Won't got married til' (uh)
> I go free

In the years that followed, other collectors with recording equipment also ventured onto prison grounds or taped southern road gangs. One such individual, Lawrence Gellert—who was as radical as his more famous brother, the artist Hugo—had emigrated from Hungary as a youngster and settled in North Carolina. From 1933 to 1937, he made his way through the Carolinas and Georgia, collecting songs from black Americans, including many from prisoners. Traveling in a touring car that housed his audio equipment—a mechanical phonograph, a sawed-off megaphone, and a bundle of blank aluminum records—he recorded men in a prison in Greenville, South Carolina, thankful that the guards seemed indifferent to what he was doing. "I gathered more than 300 songs of the black folk," Gellert said. Among the songs he taped—they would not be released for forty years—were "Cold Iron Shackles," "There Ain't No Heaven," "Cap'n Got a Pistol," and "Negro Got No Justice." "Mail Day I Gets a Letter" contained particularly heartbreaking verses:

> I asked my captain, "captain won't you have a little mercy"
> I asked my captain, "captain won't you have a little mercy"
> "Upon a man, oh my Lord, upon a man?"
> My captain cried out, "we don't have no mercy"
> My captain cried out, "we don't have no mercy"
> "On no one man, oh my Lord, on no one man"

Huddie Ledbetter, because of his association with Alan Lomax, had ample opportunity to record his music. Lomax began taping the former inmate in the early months of 1935, at a farmhouse in Connecticut, arranged further sessions with him in the years that followed, and brought him to the Library of Congress in June 1937 and again in August 1940. Lead Belly sang and played his twelve-string guitar. He recorded scores of songs, not only his rich repertoire of blues, spirituals, dance tunes, folk songs, and children's play party songs, but also topical songs, some of which he had composed: about the Scottsboro Boys, for example, or President Franklin D. Roosevelt. Perhaps more surprising, at least to Lomax, was an early eighteenth-century English religious song, "Must I Be Carried to the Sky on Flowered Beds of Ease?"

In 1947, Lomax returned to Parchman Farm, his mind set on recording additional songs. "Only a few strands of wire separated the prison from adjoining plantations," he wrote on his arrival: "Only the sight of an occasional armed guard or a barred window in one of the frame dormitories made one realise that this was a prison." The lyrics he heard—"It ain't but the one thing I done wrong, / I stayed in Mississippi just a day too long," or "I'm choppin' in this bottom with a hundred years, / Tree fall on me, I don't bit mo' care"—were, he said, "a vivid reminder of a system of social control and forced labor that has endured in the South for centuries: one listens to verse after verse of sardonic irony and of veiled protest." As always, Lomax reported, workers who could not maintain the pace were punished: "I heard everywhere of men working till they dropped dead or burnt out with sunstroke. In the pen itself, we saw that the songs, quite literally, kept the man alive and normal." Yet he also feared that the tradition of singing in prison was dying out. "The old-timers had lost their voices," he wrote, "and most of the young prisoners regarded the practice as 'old fogeyism.'"

Perhaps so, but more than a decade later, in 1959, another folklorist, Harry Oster, then teaching English at Louisiana State University, traveled to Angola Penitentiary, where he recorded several talented blues musicians: Robert Pete Williams, Roosevelt Charles, Matthew "Hogman" Maxey, Otis Webster, and Robert "Guitar" Welch (dubbed the "King of the Blues"). Oster improvised, setting up a studio in a tool room and taping songs he later issued on *Angola Prison Blues*, an album that appeared on his own record label. He recorded Robert Pete Williams singing: "Some got six months, some got a solid year / But me and my buddy we got lifetime here," and Guitar Welch doing his version of "Electric Chair Blues": "Wonder why they'll execute a man at the one o'clock hour at night / Because he's much stronger, people turn out all the light."

Several musicians, after being released from Parchman Farm, would go on to make names for themselves during the blues revival of the 1960s. One of them, Eddie James "Son" House, had been sent to the prison in 1928, at twenty-six, for killing a man in a juke joint after having himself been wounded in the leg. Although he received a fifteen-year sentence, he somehow gained his release after serving only two years, was eventually "rediscovered" in 1964, and thereafter toured extensively and cut several records. Booker Washington White, known as "Bukka," had first recorded for Victor Records in 1930. In 1937, after he shot and killed a man in a fight, White was convicted and sentenced to serve "the balance of his natural life in the State Penitentiary." He was sent to Parchman, yet, like House, he was released after two years and succeeded later in restarting his recording career.

Significant changes eventually came to Parchman Farm but only because the federal courts intervened. In 1971 four inmates brought suit, alleging that their civil rights were being violated by the infliction of cruel and unusual punishment. In *Gates v. Collier* (1972)—Nazareth Gates was an inmate, John Collier the prison superintendent—Federal District Judge William C. Keady found that conditions in the prison violated the Eighth Amendment and were "an affront 'to modern standards of decency.'" Reports showed that "inmates subject to disciplinary action for alleged violations of prison rules are deprived of any semblance of procedural or substantive due process."

The judge ordered an end to the practice of placing inmates in a dark hole without toilet facilities, or "beating, shooting, administering milk of magnesia, or stripping inmates of their clothes, turning fans on inmates while they are naked and wet, depriving inmates of mattresses, hygienic materials and/or adequate food, handcuffing or otherwise binding inmates to fences, bars, or other fixtures, using a cattle prod to keep inmates standing or moving, or forcing inmates to stand, sit or lie on crates, stumps or otherwise maintain awkward positions for prolonged periods." Mississippi was also required to integrate the prison, abolish the trustee system, hire African American staff, and construct new prison facilities. On December 5, 1973, the Fifth Circuit Court of Appeals, in an opinion by Judge Elbert Tuttle, upheld the lower court ruling.

Tuttle condemned the punishments used at Parchman, which, he said, "offend contemporary concepts of decency, human dignity, and precepts of civilization which we profess to possess." That comment was equally true of the system of convict leasing, the use of the chain gang, and the other punitive practices that had lasted the better part of a century. In the wake of *Gates v. Collier*, several other states—Arkansas, Alabama, Louisiana, and Texas—were forced to abolish the trustee system. But the pain and indignity, the humiliation and degradation—all of it gratuitous—that so many men and women had experienced for so long should be remembered. Surely, Bukka White spoke for everyone who was ever imprisoned at Parchman Farm when he sang, "I hope some day / I will overcome."

CHAPTER 22

ONLY A MINER (1930s)

He's only a miner been killed in the ground
Only a miner and one more is found
Killed by an accident, no one can tell
His mining's all over, poor miner farewell

During every year of the first three decades of the twentieth century, more than half a million men worked as coal miners. In the boom years of the 1920s the number rose to more than three quarters of a million, peaking in 1923 at 862,500. The majority worked the Pittsburgh seam of coal, "perhaps the most valuable body of minerals ever discovered by man, certainly in the United States and perhaps in the world," which ran from Pennsylvania through West Virginia, Kentucky, Tennessee, and parts of Alabama. Many miners worked at hazardous jobs in cramped, dust-laden surroundings. From 1900 to 1930, more than two thousand men lost their lives every year while working underground—well over seventy thousand altogether.

The fatalities could be counted, but not the number of miners who suffered life-threatening injuries, respiratory damage, and lung cancer, as well as such job-related illnesses as coal workers' pneumoconiosis (CWP, also known as black lung disease), progressive massive fibrosis (PMF), and damaged hearing. The prevalence of coal dust, silica, fibers, and beryllium caused other diseases, too, such as asbestosis and silicosis. The Centers for Disease Control, which were established in 1946, would eventually find "an epidemic of occupational lung disease in underground coal miners. In nine studies undertaken in various regions of the U.S. in the 1960s, the prevalence of CWP among those with 30 or more years in mining ranged between 10 percent and 60 percent depending on the coal field."

In addition to poor health, there were also lethal disasters: cave-ins, blasts, and explosions. The deadliest year was 1907, when eighteen accidents—ten in

Pennsylvania and West Virginia—took the lives of 3,242 miners. That December alone, mine explosions killed 239 men, women, and children in Rostraver Township, Pennsylvania; 84 workers in Stuart, West Virginia; and 362 men in Monongah, West Virginia. (The most recent study of Monongah, in fact, places the number of deceased closer to 500.) The years that followed saw further carnage. Mishaps caused the death of 154 miners in Marianna, Pennsylvania (1908); 259 in Cherry, Illinois (1909); 128 in Littleton, Alabama (1911); 263 in Dawson, New Mexico (1913); 181 in Eccles, West Virginia (1914); 115 in Layland, West Virginia (1915); and 172 in Castle Gate, Utah (1919). The number of fatalities was appalling, was, indeed, horrific.

Coal miners at work, 1906. Courtesy of the Library of Congress.

The Monongah explosion occurred at two mines located on a fork of the Monongahela River, six miles south of Fairmont, West Virginia. On the morning of December 6, 1907, a blast "ripped through the mines . . . causing the earth to shake as far as eight miles away, shattering buildings and pavement, hurling people and horses violently to the ground, and knocking streetcars off their rails." At one entrance, "explosive forces rocketed out of the mine mouth like blasts from a cannon, the forces shredding everything in their path." Fire and smoke billowed more than sixty feet into the air. Rescue teams, suffering from headaches and nausea, were hampered by "choking coal dust, rubble, and wrecked equipment," by intense heat, and by fumes from the explosion. "The stench of death was barely tolerable, and became overpowering as the search dragged on. Embalmers worked around the clock in shifts. Caskets lined both sides of the main street. The bank served as a morgue. Churches conducted funeral services several times a day as dozens of men dug long rows of graves on nearby hillsides."

At the time, an eyewitness said, "it seemed to me the smoke was afire," while another described the explosion as "the worst catastrophe in the history of coal mining in West Virginia or in any other section of the world." Company officials tried to play down the number of casualties, but the truth could not be concealed. More than 250 women were left widowed by the explosion, and more than 1,000 children lost their fathers. The day after the tragedy, five railroad cars filled with coffins arrived. As J. Davitt McAteer has explained, since each body had to be buried "within the correct ethnic graveyard, a double barbed-wire fence was stretched down the hill to separate the graveyards: Polish graves on the left and Italian graves on the right. . . . Further south of the Polish graveyard, the bodies of other ethnic groups, Greeks and Turks, were interred. . . . Black victims and other nationalities were buried further away from town." In one instance, "an Italian laborer offered his services for carrying the dead to the church yard. He spoke to a Slovak and said that everyone is the brother of the other, no matter what nationality he belongs to. He said it in broken English."

In the aftermath of the disaster, President Theodore Roosevelt and former West Virginia governor Aretas Brooks Fleming proposed creating a government research bureau to study mines and make recommendations regarding safety. In 1910, Congress passed the Federal Mine Safety Act, which created the Bureau of Mines within the Department of the Interior. Dr. Joseph A. Holmes, a former professor and North Carolina state geologist, became its first director. The bureau had a dual purpose: to boost productivity and to provide information on blasting materials and safety techniques. Cutting down on accidents, however, was not its chief concern, and the bureau did not have "any right or authority in connection with the inspection or supervision of mines." Although it could offer suggestions, the industry was free to ignore them, which it usually did. Not until 1941 did Congress finally authorize federal inspectors to enter mines.

In 1927, "Blind" Alfred Reed recorded a song about the Monongah tragedy called "Explosion in the Fairmount Mines." Born in 1880, Reed, who recorded between 1927 and 1929, drew on an earlier version by Vernon Dalhart, which in turn was based on an older English song, "Don't Go Down in the Mine, Dad," about a mining disaster in South Wales. In that song, a child begged his father not to go to work in the mine, and the father, heeding the plea, "return'd home again to his wife and his child." In Reed's version, too, the father remained at home:

> One bright morning, the miner just about to leave
> Heard his dear child screaming in all fright
> He went to her bed, then she looked up and said:
> "I have had such a dream, turn on the light"
>
> "Daddy, please don't go down in that hole today
> For my dreams do come true some time, you know
> Oh, don't leave me, daddy, please don't go away
> Something bad sure will happen, do not go."

The song concluded with an account of the disaster: "There came an explosion and two-hundred men / Were shut in the mines and left to die."

Coal miners, who took life-and-death risks whenever they went down in the shafts, took risks of a different sort, nearly as dangerous, when they organized unions and went on strike. From World War I to the Great Depression, miners who sought to improve their conditions were often met with violence from local and state authorities as well as from guards hired by the coal companies. Although there were dozens of strikes by coal miners during those years—some successful and others not—the names, the dates, and the locations of a few were especially noteworthy: Ludlow, Colorado, 1914; Matewan, West Virginia, 1920–1921; Herrin, Illinois, 1922; Indiana County, Pennsylvania, 1927; and Harlan County, Kentucky, 1931. Many of those conflicts would be memorialized in song.

On April 20, 1914, the Colorado National Guard, along with men hired by the Colorado Fuel and Iron Company—many of them from the Baldwin-Felts Detective Agency—attacked striking coal miners and their families in the town of Ludlow, located 175 miles south of Denver in the foothills of the Sangre de Cristo Mountains. The strike, which had begun the previous September, sought

Young coal miner photographed in 1908 by Lewis W. Hine. Courtesy of the New York Public Library.

traditional ends: union recognition, a wage hike, an eight-hour day, and improved safety rules. But violence eventually broke out when some of the detectives, who rode around in an armored car mounted with a machine gun, fired into the miners' tents. A daylong gunfight then erupted between the guardsmen and workers.

Seeking safety, several women and children hid in a pit beneath a tent. But the tent was set on fire, as were most of the workers' tents, and two of the women and all eleven children—one of them a three-month-old infant—suffocated and burned to death. In all, perhaps twenty-five people died that day, three of them members of the militia, the rest strikers and family members. In response, some labor leaders urged union members to take up arms, and a renewed battle, lasting ten days, ensued, with still more casualties. Hearing of Ludlow, strikers elsewhere prepared to do battle. After ten days, the governor of Colorado finally called for federal troops to quell the violence.

Many years later, Ella Reeve "Mother" Bloor, a radical labor organizer and member of the Communist Party, wrote about the strike in her autobiography, *We Are Many*. Published in 1940, her account profoundly affected many readers, including Woody Guthrie. Relying on her description of events, he composed a song, "Ludlow Massacre," which he wrote in the first person, as if he were one of the miners. He described how the miners were moved into tents, and then, with bullets flying everywhere, "so afraid they would kill our children / We dug us a cave that was seven foot deep." He claimed that the soldiers had doused the workers' tents with kerosene, and then opened fire with their "Gatling guns," killing many children. The miners armed themselves, Guthrie concluded, and "mowed down them troopers." The song concluded: "I said, 'God bless the Mine Workers' Union' / And then I hung my head and cried."

In the years after World War I, the violence that had marked the Ludlow strike in 1914 erupted in other coal regions. In fact, the term "war" and similar martial metaphors—"massacre" and "battle"—were applied, and aptly so, to the labor struggles that took place in West Virginia in 1920 and 1921. Those conflicts came to be known as the Matewan Massacre and the Battle of Blair Mountain. In May 1920, Matewan, a town in Mingo County about seventy-five miles southwest of Charleston, was the scene of a deadly shootout between local miners and agents of a private detective agency. Then, late in the summer of 1921, the Battle of Blair Mountain saw ten thousand coal miners confront thousands of strikebreakers and policemen in what was the largest armed rebellion since the Civil War.

The Baldwin-Felts Detective Agency, which had been involved in the Ludlow strike, played a similarly lethal role in Matewan. The agency had been created years earlier by William Gibboney Baldwin, a detective, and by Thomas Lafayette Felts, a lawyer. Their headquarters were in Bluefield, Virginia. The two men started out by investigating railroad crimes, but quickly placed their services at the disposal of the mining companies, supplying strong-arm men to infiltrate unions, block the work of organizers, and suppress strikes. Seven detectives who worked for the agency would be killed in Matewan during the shootout with union workers.

That encounter occurred on May 19, 1920, when Baldwin-Felts detectives and a dozen other men went to Matewan to evict several miners who had occupied houses belonging to the Stone Mountain Coal Corporation and refused to leave. One of the union's leaders, Sid Hatfield, tried to have the detectives arrested, and when he found that was not possible, remarked: "We'll kill the God damned sons of bitches before they get out of Matewan." When the detectives evicted the men and their families, Hatfield, who was also the city's police chief, intervened on their behalf, and even claimed authority to arrest the detectives. As the situation grew more volatile, armed miners surrounded the detectives, and both sides opened fire. The casualties included two miners, several townspeople, two of the Felts brothers, Albert and Lee, and the mayor, Cabell Testerman. As the turmoil continued into the fall, Governor John J. Cornwell called out the state police and imposed martial law, declaring Mingo County to be "in a state of insurrection." In January 1921, Hatfield was tried on a trumped-up charge of murder but was acquitted in March.

He was a marked man, however, and in August, Baldwin-Felts detectives shot him down in cold blood as he was approaching a courthouse, thereby igniting the Battle of Blair Mountain. Mass meetings and marches were held, and as many as ten thousand coal miners, many armed, gathered in Logan County, where they confronted about three thousand policemen and privately hired guards. Martial law was declared, and hundreds of miners were arrested and deprived of basic legal rights. Then word came that union sympathizers were being gunned down in Sharples, also in Logan County, just north of Blair Mountain, and, worse yet, that women and children had been caught in the crossfire. So the miners headed there, and gunfights broke out, continuing on and off for a week. As one historian said, "The sound of gunfire became a continual roar." Men on both sides were killed, and hundreds more were injured.

By September 2, 1921, more than two thousand federal troops—and even reconnaissance aircraft—had arrived. The miners soon began surrendering, and order was restored. In all, about a thousand miners were indicted for complicity in the insurrection, for murder, for conspiracy to commit murder, and for treason against the state of West Virginia. Although sympathetic juries acquitted most of the defendants, hundreds of others were imprisoned, some for several years, and a few were not paroled until 1925. In the end, the mine owners won an overwhelming victory, and membership in the United Mine Workers declined sharply, a trend that would continue for the rest of the decade.

Within a year of Blair Mountain, another deadly confrontation took place, this time in Herrin, a small town in southern Illinois. Called by one writer "the most brutal and horrifying crime that has ever stained the garments of organized labor," the clash took the lives of twenty-three men—twenty guards and strikebreakers, and three union members. The mine owner was William J. Lester, who owned the Southern Illinois Coal Company (and was a graduate of Cornell University). In June 1922, he broke an agreement he had made with the union not to load coal (he stood to make a hefty profit of $250,000 if he sold it), fired miners who had joined the union, hired replacements, and began making shipments. He also retained guards, armed with machine guns.

But it was the union miners who did most of the shooting. Seeing the mines operating again, they marched to the scene, apparently determined to deal with the workers who had replaced them. A union official said, "Listen, don't you go killing these fellows on a public highway. There are too many women and children around to do that. Take them over into the woods and give it to them. Kill all you can." And that is what happened: "The union members took turns beating the men and then shot each one as the others looked on." There were even reports that some of the strikebreakers had their throats slashed. Several miners were arrested and stood trial for murder in county court, but by April 1923 sympathetic juries had acquitted all of them.

Four years later, bituminous coal miners in western Pennsylvania, faced with a wage cut, again went on strike. But after a struggle lasting nearly a year and a half, the workers were defeated by the combined power of the coal companies and the state courts. The company recruited strikebreakers, and then served eviction notices on thousands of miners and their families who resided in company housing. The county sheriff banned gatherings of three or more people, and a judge issued a sweeping injunction that undermined the strike by forbidding picketing, marching, gathering for meetings, and disbursing union funds to assist those who were on strike. The judge prohibited hymn singing or holding services on two lots owned by the Magyar Presbyterian Church, which happened to be situated opposite the mouth of the mine.

In February 1928, members of the Senate Interstate Commerce Committee arrived at the scene to investigate conditions and to hear from some of those on strike. Senators Robert Wagner of New York and Burton K. Wheeler of Montana were especially sympathetic to the workers' point of view. Wagner believed the injunction violated the right of free speech, and said that had he not seen the situation for himself, "I would not have believed that in the United States there were large areas where civil government was supplanted by a system that can only be compared with ancient feudalism." Other senators also criticized the injunction, but to no avail. The coal company refused to negotiate, and by the end of August 1928, virtually every mine in the region was operating on a non-union basis. The strike was called off in October, the union having suffered a major defeat. Membership in the United Mine Workers declined precipitously, sinking to eighty-four thousand in 1929.

Coal miners in Harlan County, Kentucky—an area just north of the Cumberland Gap—had no union representation at all, and as the Depression worsened, so too did their conditions. From 1929 to 1931, coal production in the region plunged from 14.1 to 9.3 million tons, employment in the mines fell from 10,831 to 9,932, and average earnings dropped from $1,235 to $749 a year. So in February 1931, the workers, many of whom had signed up in the union, decided to strike. At issue was the very right to unionize, as well as wages and working conditions. In mid-February, the Coal Operators Association cut wages by 10 percent, fired workers who were suspected of being union members, and evicted them from company-owned homes. Violence was predictable: miners and deputies clashed, and state and federal troops were summoned to restore order.

Workers who supported the strike—nearly six thousand of them—found that one of their chief adversaries was the sheriff, John Henry Blair, who had nearly 170 deputies, most of them paid by the coal companies. Blair was later quoted as saying: "I did all in my power to aid the coal operators. . . . There was no compromise when labor troubles swept the county and the 'Reds' came into Harlan County." One day, he and his deputies arrived at the home of a union organizer, Sam Reece, and, not finding him, ransacked the house. His wife, Florence, reported: "Afterward I tore a sheet from a calendar on the wall and wrote the words to 'Which Side Are You On?' to an old Baptist hymn, 'Lay the Lily Low.' My songs always goes to the underdog—to the worker. I'm one of them and I feel like I've got to be with them. There's no such thing as neutral. You have to be on one side or the other." Her song become a union anthem:

> You go to Harlan County there is no neutral there
> You'll either be a union man or a thug for J. H. Blair
> Which side are you on? Which side are you on?
>
> They say they have to guard us to educate their child
> Their children live in luxury our children almost wild
> Which side are you on? Which side are you on?

To Reece, and probably many miners, the choice was clear: "Will you be a gun-thug, or will you be a man?"

The spring and early summer of 1931 saw clashes between the miners and the authorities that left several people dead. In addition, union members were arrested without cause, and others were brutally attacked. As tensions increased, the police used tear gas to disperse an orderly meeting outside the Harlan County Courthouse; a minister was jailed for having said that the sheriff and his men were "with the operators. The operators bought and paid for them on Election Day"; a union member was charged with criminal syndicalism for possessing radical literature; a car being used to distribute food to the miners was dynamited, and so was the home of a union sympathizer. Violence sometimes erupted out of the blue. As late as February 1932, a sheriff's deputy who also worked for the coal company shot Harry Hersh (who used the surname Simms), a twenty-one-year-old radical labor organizer from Massachusetts. A ballad, "The Death of Harry Simms," was written about him:

> Come and listen to my story, come and listen to my song
> I will tell you of a hero, who's now dead and gone
> I will tell you of a young boy, whose age was nineteen
> He was the bravest union man, that I have ever seen

For some time, the region remained in the news, partly because a committee made up of well-known writers, including Theodore Dreiser and John Dos

Passos, traveled to Harlan to investigate conditions; in 1932 they issued a lengthy report titled *Harlan Miners Speak: A Report on Terrorism in the Kentucky Coal Fields*. In addition, singers from the area, notably Aunt Molly Jackson and her younger half-brother Jim Garland, went on tour to raise funds for the strikers. Jackson, who lost her first husband, her brother, and her son in mine cave-ins, wrote many songs, including "I am a Union Woman":

> The bosses ride fine horses
> While we walk in the mud
> Their banner is the dollar sign
> While ours is striped with blood

Even after it was evident that the strike had failed, some miners continued to support the action, but by June 1931 most had no other choice than to return to work. The union had not obtained its objectives, and, predictably, both its membership and influence temporarily declined. By the spring of 1939, however, the union had gathered its strength and began a strike lasting six weeks. In the end, most of the Appalachian coal companies agreed to a union-shop contract, and others soon followed suit. John W. Hevener's study of Harlan County concluded, "The Roosevelt administration's support of the Harlan strike accounted in large part for the difference between union defeat in 1931 and union victory in 1939."

The union's status improved further as the nation prepared for, and then entered, World War II. The need for workers led the federal government to offer strong support to the labor movement. By 1945, the United Mine Workers had grown to half a million members, and, led by John L. Lewis, forcefully pressed for better wages and working conditions. In succeeding years, though, with the introduction of mechanization, computerization, and technological advances, the number of miners steadily declined. By 1975, union membership had fallen to 150,000; by 2005, to 75,000; and more recently, to only 60,000. Now there is only one miner for every ten who were working a century ago—but that one miner can produce twice as much coal as ten miners once did.

Miners now work under much safer conditions: although more than two thousand miners used to die in accidents every year, now about twenty do. Federal health and safety acts in 1969 and 1977 offered new protection in the workplace. Moreover, in 2006—following three mining tragedies that claimed nineteen lives—Congress passed the Mine Improvement and New Emergency Response Act (MINER). It required operators to develop emergency response plans in underground mines, and provided for well-trained rescue teams and the sealing of dangerous areas. In 2014 the Labor Department adopted rules that cut by 25 percent the amount of coal dust to which a miner could be exposed and required miners in areas where there were high levels of dust to wear tracking monitors.

In June 1938, long before most of these modern safety measures were in place, the Carter Family recorded a version of "Coal Miner's Blues":

> These blues are so blue, they are the coal black blues
> These blues are so blue, they are the coal black blues
> For my place will cave in, and my life I will lose

Considering all the miners' lives—more than one hundred thousand—that were lost, and all the illnesses and accidents, and all the widows and fatherless children, and all the sorrow and anguish, the song evokes the dreadful price that many coal miners and their families paid in the not-so-distant past.

CHAPTER 23

HOUSE OF THE RISING SUN (1930s)

There is a house in New Orleans
They call the Rising Sun
It's been the ruin of many a poor girl
And me, O God, for one

Who wrote the "House of the Rising Sun"? And when was it written? Unfortunately, no one knows. The earliest mention occurred in 1925 when an itinerant railroad worker sent the lyrics to a song he knew as "The Rising Sun Dance Hall" to Robert Winslow Gordon, at the Archive of American Folk Song at the Library of Congress. Seemingly elated, Gordon replied, " 'The Rising Sun' is bully, and I'm glad to have it"—but he then promptly filed the lyrics away in a cabinet. The first recording, called "Rising Sun Blues," was made eight years later, in September 1933. The singer, thirty-eight-year old Clarence Ashley, said that he had learned the song as a child from his grandfather; Ashley played the guitar, and Gwen Foster accompanied him on the harmonica. Since then, Woody Guthrie, Nina Simone, Bob Dylan, Dolly Parton, Pete Seeger, and the Animals have all recorded the song. By now, several hundred versions of it exist.

Once there actually was a Rising Sun Hotel in the French Quarter of New Orleans, but it burned to the ground in 1822. A few other structures in the city later went by that name, or by a very similar one. The "House of the Rising Sun," however, is explicitly a song about a bordello. Although there is no surviving evidence of a building by that name, a red-light district known as Storyville, in which prostitution was allowed, did exist in New Orleans. (Because the women used red lightbulbs to indicate their trade, it became known as "the red light" district.) The area was created by the city council in 1897 and began to operate legally on January 1, 1898.

Named for Sidney Story, the city alderman who drafted the law creating the district, it comprised a thirty-eight-block area in one of the poorer sections of town. Eventually, there were about two thousand prostitutes in Storyville, residing in more than 230 houses, cabarets, and "cribs," although as the years went by the number somewhat declined. Segregation was the rule, with black and white prostitutes inhabiting separate houses. As Emily Epstein Landau has written in *Spectacular Wickedness*: "Men flocked to Storyville to hear music, to drink, to gamble, and to have sex with prostitutes." In theory, at least, prostitution was prohibited elsewhere in the city.

Naturally, there were many residents who objected to setting aside an area in which sex was for sale. One of them, a well-to-do lumber manufacturer named George L'Hote, brought suit against the city in September 1897. He claimed that such a district would damage the neighborhood and injure his family, which resided there. In January 1898, a lower state court judge, Fred D. King, ruled in L'Hote's favor. So the city appealed to the Supreme Court of Louisiana. In November 1898, in *L'Hote v. City of New Orleans et al.*, the court, in a decision by Judge Henry C. Miller, found that the city indeed had the power "to assign the limits beyond which houses of prostitution shall not be permitted." Such an ordinance, the judge said, "merely asserts the municipal functions to secure public order, decency and morals" and did not violate the rights of property owners. Although L'Hote had argued that the many brothels would "render his property unfit for his family dwelling" and lessen its value, the court found that confining the brothels within a geographical area did not violate any state constitutional guarantees. Declaring the ordinance to be an "exercise of lawful power," the court, by a vote of two to one, dismissed L'Hote's suit.

Having lost at the state level, L'Hote appealed to the United States Supreme Court. But in May 1900, in a decision by Justice David Brewer, the Supreme Court ruled unanimously in favor of the city. Brewer began, however, by presenting L'Hote's allegations concerning the detrimental effects of the city's tolerant policy. Among other things, "the introduction of public prostitutes, women notoriously abandoned to lewdness, in said locality, authorizing them to occupy, inhabit, live, and sleep in houses and rooms situated therein" would not only lessen the value of his property but would also "destroy the morals, peace, and good order of the neighborhood, drive out and turn away the law-abiding, virtuous citizens and their families from said locality, and dedicate the same to public and private nuisances *per se*, contrary to law and good morals." According to Brewer, L'Hote claimed that enforcing the ordinance "would work irreparable damage and injury to him in the depreciation in value of his property because it would cease to be a fit and proper place for the dwelling house of himself, his wife, and children, and necessitate their abandonment of the same and removal from the locality."

Having acknowledged the plaintiff's contention, Brewer then explained why L'Hote should, nevertheless, not prevail. The question was whether a property owner "can prevent the enforcement of such an ordinance on the ground that by it his rights under the federal Constitution are invaded." As the Court saw it, "one of the difficult social problems of the day is what shall be done in respect to those vocations which minister to and feed upon human weaknesses, appetites, and passions. The management of these vocations comes directly within the scope of what is known as the police power. They affect directly the public health and morals." Still, police power was reserved to the states, whose duty it was to protect public health and morals. In Brewer's view, "It is no part of the judicial function to determine the wisdom or folly of a regulation by the legislative body in respect to matters of a police nature." Granted, the exercise of the police power might cause some to suffer a financial loss, but "the mere fact of pecuniary injury does not warrant the overthrow of legislation of a police character." The Court therefore unanimously upheld New Orleans's residential ordinance.

> Just fill the glass up to the brim
> Let the drinks go merrily around
> We'll drink to the life of a rounder, poor boy
> Who goes from town to town

So the regulations that Sidney Story had proposed in 1897, now, in 1900, would finally be enforced, and Storyville became an area in which brothels operated openly. Many large American cities had red-light districts, but only in New Orleans did prostitution take place publicly in a clearly—indeed, in a legally—demarcated area. And the very size of the district in New Orleans meant that along with the brothels, sometimes on the same street, were homes, businesses, schools, and even churches. "Low-lying and swampy," Storyville was "largely populated by people without the resources to buy houses or pay rent in more desirable areas." It was, in general, "a residential working-class neighborhood of whites and persons of color with self-sustaining small businesses and vendors, and a significant business sector catering to drink, gambling, drugs, and prostitution."

Many city residents, including some advocates of social reform, believed brothels and saloons should be tolerated "as long as the venues associated with vice stayed inside designated geographic confines," which, in New Orleans, they did. So it was an easy matter for residents and visitors who wanted a guide to Storyville's houses of prostitution to turn to the New Orleans Blue Books, published between 1895 and 1915, which listed addresses and phone numbers, and even printed reviews, noting, for example, that one madam "has a lot of jolly good girls, who are indeed superfine." The editor claimed that it "puts the stranger on a proper grade or path as to where to go to be secure from holdups, brace games and other illegal practices usually worked on the unwise in Red Light Districts."

Many of the finest jazz, blues, and ragtime musicians performed in the city's brothels, many of which served as venues for cornet players "Buddy" Bolden and Joe "King" Oliver, trumpeters "Bunk" Johnson and Freddy Keppard, and pianists Tony Jackson and Ferdinand "Jelly Roll" Morton. Morton played at such establishments as Hilma Burt's "Mirror Ballroom," Emma Johnson's "Circus House," Flora Meeker's "Palace of Mirth," and Lulu White's "Mahogany Hall." He later recalled: "Lights of all colors were glittering and glaring. Music was pouring into the streets from every house. . . . I thought I had a very bad night when I made under a hundred dollars." By 1914, an estimated twelve thousand people earned their livings from the bars, bordellos, and bedrooms of Storyville. The income amounted to nearly a million dollars a month.

In February 1917, New Orleans attempted to make the brothels conform to the policy of strict racial segregation that was widespread throughout the South and in many parts of the country. The city decided to establish two districts: Storyville, to be reserved for white prostitutes, and a newly formed uptown district for black prostitutes. An African American Storyville bordello owner, Willie V. Piazza—who was "fully at ease in the English, French, Spanish, Dutch, and even the Basque languages"—brought suit to overturn the ordinance. The case reached the Supreme Court of Louisiana, which ruled against Piazza, holding that the rights of a property owner were not absolute: an owner may not "at all times, and under all circumstances, and in every way, use it as he pleases, regardless of the public morals, safety or welfare." Opposition to the city's plan, the justices said, was based on "the fear of the loss of trade of those debased white men on whose indulgence of their appetites in sexual intercourse with colored prostitutes the keepers of negro bawdy-houses hope to thrive and prosper." The court decided that "the legislature may lawfully forbid the prosecution of any business which, though not inherently vicious, or immoral, is regarded as contrary to public policy, or amounts to a depredation upon the rights of others."

The ruling took effect in March 1917, and in April the United States entered World War I. Within a matter of weeks four soldiers were murdered in the city's red-light district, and President Woodrow Wilson's administration decided the area was unsafe, a source of venereal disease and therefore a threat to the health of servicemen. Secretary of War Newton D. Baker declared: "These boys are going to France. I want them adequately armed and clothed by their government; but I want them to have an invisible armor to take with them." A recently

Lulu White, ca. 1900.

formed Commission on Training Camp Activities sent investigators to New
Orleans, who quickly proposed that houses of prostitution be shut down.

Early in September, the mayor, Martin Behrman, met with Baker in Washington to urge that the district remain open, since, he said, it was the only effective way to control vice in the city. But he was not successful. Later that month,
Secretary of the Navy Josephus Daniels decided that men in the armed forces
"should be shielded from those temptations to immoral conduct which, in some
instances, have done more to undermine the fighting strength of an army than

the bullets of the enemy." He instructed the mayor: "You close the red-light district or the armed forces will." So, in October, Behrman introduced an ordinance to shut Storyville; the city council reluctantly agreed to close the brothels as of November 12. That was one day after the Supreme Court of Louisiana rejected a last-minute legal move to keep them open.

In the years after the war, prostitution persisted in New Orleans, in other parts of the city, but not in Storyville. Yet the district had earned a seedy reputation that was soon memorialized in song. In 1924, a talented New Orleans composer and musician, Spencer Williams, who had been born on Basin Street in 1899, wrote a song about Storyville called "Good Time Flat Blues." He would eventually leave the United States to reside in England, but in the 1940s Billie Holiday and Louis Armstrong recorded his song under the title "Farewell to Storyville," which is how it would be known:

> All, you old time Queens, from New Orleans, who lived in Storyville
> You sang the blues, try to amuse, here's how they pay the bill
> The law stepped in and call it sin to have a little fun
> The police car has made a stop and Storyville is done

The song concluded with the line: "They made you close-up they'll never let you back / Won't let you back."

Most of the songs about New Orleans bordellos closely followed the lyrics that Clarence Ashley had used in 1933 in the "House of the Rising Sun." In April 1935, though, a variation appeared, called "Rounder's Luck." The performers were Walter and Homer Callahan, brothers from western North Carolina. Walter played the guitar and Homer a variety of instruments including the banjo, fiddle, and mandolin. They sang about a rounder, who roamed from town to town, whose mother was a seamstress and whose father was a gambling man. Using verses closely patterned after Ashley's, they sang:

> There's a place down in New Orleans
> That's called The Rising Sun
> Where many poor boys to destruction have gone
> And me, oh Lord, for one

By the early 1940s, the song had made its way to New York City, where the Almanac Singers recorded it. Woody Guthrie, who was a member of the group, added a line commenting on the hard times, and the wandering, that marked the Depression: "The only pleasure that he gets out of life / Is a-hoboin' from town to town." The song also enjoyed a rebirth during the folk music revival of the 1960s,

New Orleans band, ca. 1905. *Top*: Jimmy Johnson, Buddy Bolden, Willy Cornish, Willy Warner; *bottom*: Brock Mumford, Frank Lewis. Courtesy of the Lebrecht Music and Arts Photo Library.

although it was significantly altered when the Animals recorded it in 1964. Their version, which sold more than a million copies in little more than a month, told the familiar story, but told it from the perspective of the male protagonist—"it's been the ruin of many a poor boy"—rather than from that of the woman; moreover, the "gambling man" of the song now had become a father, rather than a lover:

> Well, I got one foot on the platform
> The other foot on the train
> I'm goin' back to New Orleans
> To wear that ball and chain
>
> Oh mother tell your children
> Not to do what I have done
> Spend your lives in sin and misery
> In the House of the Rising Sun

The song could be made—and over the years has been made—to say different things. After it was changed to reflect a man's perspective, it was changed back again in the 1980s to reflect a woman's. In 1981, Dolly Parton sang it from the standpoint of the daughter:

> My father he was a gambler
> Mother died when I was young
> And I've worked since then
> To please the men
> At the house of the rising sun

Whatever the perspective, the song taught a lesson about the wages of sin, a lesson that some people took to heart and others probably did not. But the advice given in the song was unheeded in New Orleans in the early twentieth century, even though there surely must have been mothers who warned their daughters "not to do what I've done / to live a life of sin, shame and strife / In the house of the rising sun."

Disasters

CHAPTER 24

THE *TITANIC* (1912)

It was sad when that great ship went down
It was sad when that great ship went down
There were husbands and wives,
Little children lost their lives
It was sad when that great ship went down

On April 10, 1912, the *Titanic*, the grandest oceangoing liner that had ever been built—it was, in fact, "the largest manmade moving object on earth"— set forth on her maiden voyage from Southampton, England, to New York. There were 2,224 people on board—passengers, engineers, and crew. At 11:40 in the evening of April 14, when the ship was about four hundred miles southeast of Iceland, it struck an iceberg and in less than three hours sank to the bottom of the ocean. The lifeboats could not accommodate all those on board, and were never even filled to capacity. In all, 1,514 people perished—most of the deaths caused by hypothermia in the ice-cold water—while only 710 survivors managed to find refuge in lifeboats. The wealthy stood the best chance of survival. Of the 329 passengers traveling first class, 60 percent were saved; of the 285 in second class, 44 percent were saved; and of the 706 in third class, only 25 percent were saved. More than three-fourths of the crew perished, as did the captain, Edward John Smith.

Construction of the *Titanic* had gotten under way in Belfast, Northern Ireland, three years earlier, on March 31, 1909. It required eleven thousand workers, more than three million rivets, and three years to complete. A marvel of modern engineering and design, the ship was 883 feet long, 92.5 feet wide, and weighed 46,329 tons. Its two reciprocating engines—which burned nearly 160 tons of coal every day—were nearly four stories tall, allowing the ship to travel at 24 knots, or about 28 miles per hour (on the night of the tragedy, its speed was 22.5 knots). Steam was generated from three engines, 29 boilers, and 159 furnaces.

Constructed with an elaborate system of watertight doors to close off any compartments that might flood, the ship was designed to stay afloat even if water inundated three, or even four, of the sixteen compartments. A British shipping trade journal declared the *Titanic* was "unsinkable," a sentiment echoed by Captain Smith. "I cannot imagine any condition which would cause a modern ship to founder," he said. "Shipbuilding has gone beyond that."

The *Titanic* resembled a luxury hotel, complete with a gymnasium and squash courts, Turkish baths and lounges, an orchestra and dining salon, a library and post office, and the Verandah Café / Palm Court, an indoor area designed to look like an outdoor patio, reserved for passengers traveling first class. There were separate accommodations and dining rooms for first-, second-, and third-class passengers. There was also a first-class smoking room reserved only for males. The ship's décor was opulent, having an "airy lightness"—wicker furniture in the dining areas, pastel fabrics, palm trees and potted plants, wallpaper with floral patterns, and elegant lighting fixtures. The cargo, other equipment, and even the lifeboats were discreetly concealed so as not to detract from the ambience. Lifeboats were regarded as eyesores, and so

Titanic preparing to be launched, May 1911. Courtesy of the Library of Congress.

only sixteen (rather than the sixty-four originally proposed), along with four collapsible boats, were provided, which of course proved to be a colossal blunder.

Departing on its maiden voyage at noon on April 10, 1912, the *Titanic* picked up additional passengers at Cherbourg, Queenstown, and Cork Harbor and set out the next afternoon for New York, where it was due to arrive on April 17. But at 9:40 on the evening of April 14, as the ship was nearing Newfoundland, a warning came from the nearby steamer *Mesaba*—"saw much heavy pack ice and a great number of bergs, also ice"—a warning that was not forwarded to the bridge. Then at 10:55 another message was sent by the *Californian*, only twenty-one miles away: "Say, old man, we are stopped and surrounded by ice." But the *Titanic* continued at a speed of 22 to 22.5 knots—about 25 miles per hour—until, at 11:40, it smashed into a massive iceberg. Survivors later said they felt only a "slight shock" or "just a grating sensation," but in fact a hole had been gashed in the hull. Compartments began to flood, and at midnight an urgent message went out to a neighboring ship, the *Carpathia*, giving the *Titanic*'s location: "Come at once; we have struck a berg." Fifteen minutes later another, more ominous message: "Come as quickly as possible, old man, the engine room is filling up to the boilers."

> Oh, they built the ship Titanic, to sail the ocean blue
> They thought it was a ship that water would never go through
> It was on its maiden trip, that an iceberg hit the ship
> It was sad when that great ship went down

The hole in the *Titanic*'s hull was about twelve and a half square feet, large enough for five of the supposedly watertight compartments to become flooded. The ship began to sink, bow-first. In less than three hours, the forward deck was under water, and the ship started to break in half. Most of those on board who had not gotten into lifeboats were thrown into the icy water—four degrees below freezing—and perished within half an hour. The collision with the iceberg, lasting only a few seconds, had produced "a series of nonuniform, poking, prodding blows that served to disperse the force of the impact along the riveted seams of the ship—in effect, the weakest links." Modern forensic investigation has, in fact, placed much of the blame for the loss of life on the quality of the rivets. Had they been of better quality, the ship would have taken longer to go down, more passengers would have had time to board the lifeboats, and a rescue vessel could have arrived in time to save most, if not all, of those who perished.

It was 12:05 a.m. when Captain Smith ordered the lifeboats to be deployed. Fourteen of them were each able to hold sixty-five people, and two emergency sea boats could each carry thirty-five people; the four collapsible boats could each contain forty-nine people. It took forty minutes for the first lifeboat to be lowered, but only twenty-eight people were on board (all but two of them first-class passengers). Although some crew had practiced lowering the lifeboats, they had only let down two of them and did not know how long it would take to evacuate the passengers. Moreover, there were far too few lifeboats—their total capacity of 1,176 was little more than half the ship's total of passengers and crew—and they were not even filled. In all, 466 seats on the lifeboats were left empty. Worse yet, although lifeboats were supposed to be lowered from the deck with women and children aboard, and were then to take on additional women and children from gangways on the lower decks, many of the boats descended directly into the water without stopping, with disastrous consequences.

> They were off from England, And not very far from shore
> When the rich refused to associate with the poor
> So they threw them down below, where they were the first to go
> It was sad when the great ship went down

Even as things on the *Titanic* were going horribly wrong, many passengers seemed in a state of disbelief, even denial. One of them, forty-eight-year-old Mahala Douglas (whose husband refused to enter a lifeboat, saying it would make him "less than a man"), was traveling with her French maid. As she recalled, "once off, everything seemed to go perfectly. The boat was so luxurious, so steady, so immense, and such a marvel of mechanism that one could not believe he was on a boat—and there the danger lay. We had smooth seas, clear, starlit nights, fresh favoring winds; nothing to mar our pleasure." But appearances could not have been more deceptive, for once the collision occurred, events unfolded swiftly and irreversibly. "In an incredibly short space of time, it seemed to me, the boat sank," Douglas related. "I heard an explosion. I watched the boat go down, and the last picture to my mind is the immense mass of black against the starlit sky, and then nothingness."

Even though the fatalities were highest among third-class passengers, who had purchased the least costly tickets, the press and the public predictably paid most attention to the rich and famous. Among the well-publicized victims were Thomas Andrews, an Irish businessman and shipbuilder who was involved in developing the plans for the *Titanic*, and Major Archibald Willingham Butt, military aide to Presidents Roosevelt and Taft. One of the world's wealthiest men, forty-eight-year-old John Jacob Astor IV, perished, although his second wife, Madeleine (who was nineteen and pregnant), made it into a lifeboat.

Another American millionaire, Benjamin Guggenheim, and his valet, allegedly spent their final moments seated in deck chairs sipping brandy and smoking cigars. The press made much of his final remark: "We've dressed up in our best and are prepared to go down like gentlemen." He was traveling not with his wife but with a French singer, who managed to escape in a lifeboat with her maid. The owner of Macy's Department Store, Isidor Straus, and his wife, Ida, remained together on the deck. A passenger said he "had heard them discussing that if they were going to die they would die together. We tried to persuade Mrs. Straus to go alone, without her husband, and she said no." Both perished.

A passenger who was rescued, Daisy Minahan of Wisconsin, later described the pandemonium that reigned in the lifeboats: "The crowd surging around the boats was getting unruly. Officers were yelling and cursing at men to stand back and let the women get into the boats. . . . When the lifeboat was filled there were no seamen to man it. . . . At times when we were being lowered we were at an angle of 45° and expected to be thrown into the sea. As we reached the level of each deck men jumped into the boat until the officer threatened to shoot the next man who jumped. We landed in the sea and rowed to a safe distance. . . . The *Titanic* was fast sinking. After she went down the cries were horrible. . . . The cries continued to come over the water." When some of the women implored the officer in charge of the lifeboat to go back to rescue others, he snapped: "You ought to be damn glad you are here and have got your own life." Minahan concluded: "He had been so blasphemous during the two hours we were in his boat that the women at my end of the boat all thought he was under the influence of liquor."

The nearest ship was the *Californian*, but its wireless operator was unable to decode the signal from the *Titanic*, so another vessel, the *Carpathia*, nearly fifty-eight nautical miles away, was the first to arrive on the scene. By 4:10 a.m. it began picking up survivors, most of them shivering on the lifeboats, and over the next few days the grisly work of recovering the dead got under way—only 326 corpses, bloated and waterlogged, would be located. Testifying before a Senate committee investigating the tragedy, the captain of the *Carpathia*, Arthur Henry Rostron, described the scene on his arrival: "By the time we had the first boat's people it was breaking day, . . . I also saw icebergs all around me. There were about 20 icebergs that would be anywhere from about 150 to 200 feet high and numerous smaller bergs. . . . They were anywhere from 10 to 12 feet high and 10 to 15 feet long above the water. . . . From the boats we took three dead men, who had died of exposure. . . . We got all the boats alongside and all the people up aboard by 8:30."

In the days and weeks following the tragedy, both the United States Senate and the British Parliament launched inquiries into what had gone wrong. Both bodies reached similar conclusions: that the *Titanic* "had inadequate life-saving apparatuses onboard, and its designers and inspectors had been negligent and cursory in their evaluations." The Senate committee, after taking more than one thousand pages of testimony from eighty-six witnesses over eighteen days, focused not surprisingly on the issue of the lifeboats: "There was no system adopted for loading the boats; there was great indecision as to the deck from which boats were to be loaded; there was wide diversity of opinion as to the number of the crew necessary to man each boat; there was no direction whatever as to the number of passengers to be carried by each boat, and no uniformity in loading them. . . . The failure to utilize all lifeboats to their recognized capacity for safety unquestionably resulted in the needless sacrifice of several hundred lives which might otherwise have been saved."

The British government appointed John Charles Bigham, 1st Viscount Mersey, as the aptly named "wreck commissioner" to conduct its own inquiry. On July 30, in a report to Parliament, he insisted that all passengers, rich and poor alike, had been treated equally. Taking note of allegations "that the third class passengers had been unfairly treated; that their access to the Boat deck had been impeded, and that when at last they reached that deck the first and second class passengers were given precedence in getting places in the boats," his report resolutely if implausibly maintained that "there appears to have been no truth in these suggestions." Rather, the appreciably higher casualty rate among third-class passengers "is accounted for by the greater reluctance of the third class passengers to leave the ship, by their unwillingness to part with their baggage, by the difficulty in getting them up from their quarters, which were at the extreme ends of the ship, and by other similar causes. . . . They were not unfairly treated."

The magnitude of the disaster, the appalling loss of life, the publicity the event received—all ensured that the *Titanic* would enter the public's consciousness, and popular culture, in a way few other events had. Within a month, a ten-minute silent film, *Saved from the Titanic*, was shot and released. Cowritten by and starring twenty-two-year-old Dorothy Gibson, who was on board the ship and found safety in a lifeboat, the film incorporated actual newsreel footage. Gibson played a fictionalized version of herself, and even wore some of the same clothing she had worn on board the ship. (It would be her last film, as "she had practically lost her reason, by virtue of the terrible strain she had been under to graphically portray her part.") The story of the disaster would eventually be depicted not only in motion pictures but also in poems, novels, dramas, dance performances, and, of course, in song.

Perhaps the earliest musical recording about the disaster, however, was not a song but rather a liturgical chant: the Hebrew prayer for the dead, *El male rachamim (für titanik)*. The renowned cantor Josef "Yossele" Rosenblatt recorded it in July 1913. Rosenblatt had recently immigrated to the United States after serving as a cantor in synagogues in Hungary and Germany. Often called "the Jewish Caruso"—his voice was not only beautiful but also capable of expressing profound emotion—he was serving as cantor for a congregation in New York City when he made the recording for Victor, the proceeds of which he donated to the families of the victims. The prayer (translated) began: "God full of mercy who dwells on high / Grant perfect rest on the wings of Your Divine Presence / In the lofty heights of the holy and pure / who shine as the brightness of the heavens to the soul of . . . who has gone to his eternal rest."

There are indications that people started singing about the *Titanic* soon after it went down, but the first commercial recording, by Ernest "Pop" Stoneman, was not made until September 1924. It was not released, however, and so he recorded it again for Okeh Records in January 1925. Stoneman, who was born in Virginia in 1893, played a number of instruments and usually recorded along with several of his children. "It was sad when that great ship went down," he sang. "Husbands and wives, little children lost their lives / It was sad when that great ship went down." Stoneman's version also included lines that would appear, in one version or another, in later recordings: "The rich they decided they would not ride with the poor / So they sent the poor below / They were the first that had to go / It was sad when that great ship went down."

Several early recordings were made by African American musicians: Virginia Liston, who recorded "Titanic Blues" in May 1926; William and Versey Smith, a married couple, whose song "When That Great Ship Went Down" appeared in August 1927; and Richard "Rabbit" Brown, a New Orleans street singer, who cut "Sinking of the Titanic" in March 1927. Brown referred to a "gruesome iceberg" having caused the wreck, and included a story—never verified—about the last song by the ship's band: "The music played as they went down on that dark blue sea / And you could hear the sound of that familiar hymn, singing 'Nearer my God to Thee.'" Brown also provided other specific details, including the name of the ship that rescued the survivors and the very words—"come at once"—sent by telegraph from the *Titanic*:

> The Carpathia received the wireless SOS re distress
> Come at once, we are sinking, make no delay and do your best
> Get the lifeboats all in readiness 'cos we're going down very fast
> We have saved the women and the children and tried to hold out to the last

As Steven Biel has pointed out in *Down with the Old Canoe*, a fine study of the sinking of the *Titanic*, "Americans derived religious messages about sin and redemption from the disaster," and nowhere was this more evident than in Blind Willie Johnson's gospel version of "God Moves on the Water," recorded in December 1929. In all, Johnson recorded thirty songs, chiefly on religious themes, between 1927 and 1930, among them, "Dark Was the Night, Cold Was the Ground," about the Crucifixion (and one of the few songs chosen to be launched into space on *Voyager I* in 1977). "Ah, Lord, ah, Lord," his song about the *Titanic* began, with the refrain after each verse: "God moves, God moves, God moves, ah / and the people had to run and pray":

> Year of nineteen hundred and twelve
> April the fourteenth day
> Great Titanic struck an iceberg
> People had to run and pray

Then, after telling how "Captain Smith gave orders, women and children first / Many of the lifeboats piled right up, many were liable to crush," Johnson pleads on behalf of the victims, but to no avail:

> Ahh-ah So many had to leave their happy home,
> all that they possess
> Lord Jesus, will you hear us now,
> help us in our distress

> Women had to leave their loving ones,
> see 'bout their safety
> When they heard the liner was doomed,
> hearts did almost break

Although many songs about the tragedy were written and performed by black musicians, there was in fact only one black family on the ship. Twenty-six-year-old Joseph Philippe Lemercier Laroche, a French-educated engineer, had been born in Haiti into the royal family. Unable to find work as an engineer in France, he was moving his family back to Haiti. He was traveling with his wife, Juliette, who was white, and who was pregnant, and their two young daughters, two and three. "The sea is very smooth," Juliette wrote to her father as the voyage began, "the weather is wonderful." But when the *Titanic* began to take on water, he ensured that his wife and daughters were put aboard a lifeboat, promised to join them later, but sadly went down with the ship.

There was one black singer who pointed out that African American passengers were not welcome on the *Titanic*. Huddie Ledbetter wrote a song that claimed the black heavyweight-boxing champion, Jack Johnson, had been

Joseph Philippe Lemercier Laroche and family.

denied a ticket because of his race, although there is no evidence to support that idea. At the time, Johnson was preparing to defend his title and was also opening a Chicago nightclub. Lead Belly, who had been singing about the disaster for years, composed his own version sometime in the 1930s. In the spring of 1947, he explained: "When they was getting on board, was not no colored folks on there. . . . Jack Jackson [sic] went to get on board But boss shoved him back. . . . We are not hauling no coal so Jack Jackson didn't like what the big Boss did[.] He went out and tried to do something about it." When the newspapers told of the ship going down, Lead Belly continued, "you might have seen Jack Jackson doing the Eagle Rock, so glad that he was not on that ship. Ship hit the iceberg." In 1948, recording for the Library of Congress, he emphasized the issue of racism and how the prejudice of whites had fittingly boomeranged:

Jack Johnson want to get on board
Captain said, "I ain't haulin' no coal"
Cryin' fare thee, *Titanic*, fare thee well

Black man oughta shout for joy
Never lost a girl or either a boy
Cryin', fare thee, *Titanic*, fare thee well

Songs about the *Titanic* are still being sung after all these years, but public interest in the subject greatly intensified in September 1985 when Robert Ballard, an oceanographer and former navy captain, along with a French expedition, finally located the wreckage beneath the sea. Since then, seven more underwater expeditions have been launched, more than fifty-five hundred artifacts have been collected—many would later be auctioned—and a seventeen-ton section of the hull has been recovered and made part of a traveling exhibit. When all this activity began to cause the ship to break down at a faster rate than expected, UNESCO, on April 14, 2012—the hundredth anniversary of the sinking—made it a protected site to "prohibit the pillaging, sale and dispersion of the wreck and its artifacts." The forty-one signatory states, however, did not include the United States and Canada. And so an American company continues to offer trips in submersibles to the wreck, at a cost of $59,680, promising: "Experience for yourself the mystique and majesty of this poignant chapter in humanity's collective history." It was sad when that great ship went down, but sadder still that its resting place seems destined to be disturbed.

CHAPTER 25

THE BOLL WEEVIL (1920s)

Oh, the boll weevil is a little black bug
Come from Mexico, they say
Come all the way to Texas
Jus' a-lookin' for a place to stay
Jus' a-lookin' for a home
Jus' a-lookin' for a home

In 1880, an entomologist on a collecting trip for the U.S. Department of Agriculture in Mexico encountered a "small, dark-colored weevil" about 120 miles southwest of Laredo, Texas. The tiny insect had been devastating the cotton crop, and by 1892 it had crossed the Rio Grande into Texas. In 1894, the acting secretary of agriculture warned "there is imminent danger that it may spread into other portions of the Cotton Belt." Spread it did, over the next thirty years, into every southern state from Texas to the Atlantic Ocean. By the end of the twentieth century, the beetle had destroyed tens of billions of pounds of cotton, valued at nearly one trillion dollars. Books appeared with such titles as *The Insect Menace*, and writers declared that the boll weevil had "marched through Georgia like Sherman to the sea, and creating far more havoc."

Boll weevils are about a quarter of an inch in length, with reddish-brown and gray bodies, a long proboscis, spurs on their front legs, and "large, bulging black eyes." As James C. Giesen explains in *Boll Weevil Blues*, the weevil's life cycle "is centered around the cotton plant." The insects feed on the plant's fibers, lay eggs in its "squares," and grow in the enclosed buds. Weevils convert the plant's substances into pheromones that attract sexual partners, and "this reliance on a component of the plant to court mates for reproduction drives the boll weevil to spend its entire life cycle in and around the plant."

In June and July, after the cotton plant flowers, the female weevil punctures the boll with its proboscis, drops a single egg inside, and then seals the hole with

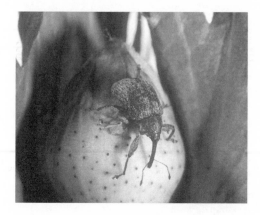

Cotton boll weevil.

a yellow wax that protects the egg. In three days the eggs hatch into larvae, which greedily devour the inside of the boll; in a week, the larvae enter the pupal stage, then become adult weevils, thereby destroying the boll, or "square." When the adults are ready, "they cut themselves free from the dead squares and begin their own search for food and a mate." When winter comes, they look for a hibernation site. They also reproduce at an astonishing rate. "A single pair of boll weevils can theoretically account for well over *twelve million* offspring during one growing season. (The most conservative of entomologists' estimates still place the number at two million.)"

In the fall of 1894 an observer in Corpus Christi, Texas, having detected the presence of boll weevils, told the Department of Agriculture that farmers "are at a loss to know what to do to overcome this pest." In desperation, farmers were urged to rotate their fields, to flood their land, to burn the bolls, even to stop the planting of cotton in certain areas, but nothing came of these measures. By 1895, the weevil was destroying large portions of the crop in southern Texas and seemed poised "to spread throughout the cotton-growing regions of Texas, if not to other states." The infestation did indeed spread northward, from San Antonio to Austin and then to Waco. By 1903, the weevil had moved east into Louisiana, and a year or so later north into Oklahoma, costing farmers in the affected areas anywhere from one-quarter to three-quarters of their cotton crop. In despair, an entomologist sent to study the insect remarked that he had "seen it frequently, . . . and have had it fly into my room through a third-story window."

A few feeble steps were taken to combat the weevil—Texas appointed a state entomologist in 1899, for example, and the United States Senate appropriated $250,000 to fight the pests in 1904—but they were inadequate. When a prominent entomologist was asked to devise ways to halt the infestation, his reasonable recommendations—to avoid planting cotton after a certain date in the spring, to widen the spaces between rows, even to destroy certain stalks—were not adopted, but instead were ridiculed. Texas then offered a $50,000 reward to anyone who could come up with a practical way to eradicate the insect; the prize was never awarded. "Meanwhile, the boll weevil ignored the hoopla and continued its methodical march to the north and east, oblivious to the social and economic havoc it left in its wake," Giesen wrote. "Boll weevils did not play politics, and they did not read newspapers. They lived and died for cotton, and they wouldn't stop until they had infested every last boll."

Songs about the boll weevil began to be sung not long after the insect appeared. Gates Thomas, an English professor at Southwest Texas State Teachers College, was one of the first to begin collecting African American work songs, and eventually he published lyrics about the boll weevil that he had heard from a black tenant farmer in 1897. Two of the verses read

> The boll-weevil says to the sharp-shooter,
> "Pardner let us go
> And when we strike that cotton patch,
> We'll take it row by row
> For it's our home, Babe, for it's our home"

> The first time I seen him
> he wuz settin' on a square
> Well, the next time I seen him
> he wuz a-crawlin' everywhere
> Just a-huntin' him a home, Babe, just a-huntin' him a home

(Thomas explained that the term "sharp-shooter" referred to "a small insect like a midge, contemporary with the weevil and once thought as harmful.") He believed that "the ballad is still imaginatively true to the time and region in which it arose communally."

Even as these songs were being sung, by the early twentieth century the boll weevil was relentlessly advancing northward. By the end of 1907, the beetle had swarmed into five states: Texas, Louisiana, Arkansas, Mississippi, and Oklahoma. By 1910, when it showed up in Alabama, it "had traveled more than eight hundred miles and destroyed an estimated 1.6 million bales of cotton, worth $107 million." Then, in 1913, the insect appeared in Missouri and Kentucky, and a year later it showed up in Tennessee, where it soon infested more than nine thousand square miles, demonstrating "a wonderful ability to adapt itself to colder climatic conditions." Boll weevils were sighted in Georgia in 1915, and two years later in South Carolina, where in some localities they "proved so destructive that cotton growing was practically discontinued." The beetles swarmed into North Carolina in 1919, New Mexico in 1921, and Virginia in 1922, where the infestation cut cotton acreage by half within ten years.

The experience of Georgia exemplified the scale of the problem. Although agricultural experts urged farmers to diversify, in 1911 the state nevertheless harvested its largest cotton crop: 2.88 million bales. By 1914, land devoted to cotton production peaked at 5.2 million acres, but by then the weevils were moving toward the Georgia border. By the summer of 1915 they crossed into the state; within two years they were present in every cotton-producing county, and production had fallen by 32 percent, to 1.9 million bales. By 1919, losses were estimated at $40 million. By 1920, despite the use of an insecticide, some areas in the southern part of the state lost 50 to 75 percent of the crop. A 1921 report said that the weevil "has disturbed our economic situation more than any other single factor since the conclusion of the Civil War; it is a pest of as great a magnitude as any which afflicted the Egyptians in the olden days."

Wherever the weevils went they left a trail of destruction. In many places, "panic set in, farms were abandoned, and whole counties were depopulated." Some growers moved west, seeking colder, drier regions where the weevils would be less of a problem, while others decided to stay put, managed as well as they could, reconciling themselves to losing a substantial portion of their crop. Some, seeking an effective pesticide, applied calcium arsenate without realizing its carcinogenic qualities. Still others made Herculean efforts to rid themselves of the pests: "The cotton plants of the infested area were pulled up, dipped in petroleum and burned. The ground was thoroughly cleaned after the removal of the plants, and saturated with crude petroleum, then plowed, harrowed, rolled and sprayed with oil again." In desperation, cotton plants were sometimes purposely flooded and left underwater for days at a time.

By the 1920s, the devastating impact of the boll weevil was readily apparent, and record companies sought to capitalize on the insect's notoriety. In 1921, two recordings of "Boll Weevil Blues" were made by white vaudevillians—Al Bernard and Ernest Hare—who usually performed in blackface. In 1924 the Arkansas Trio, consisting of Vernon Dalhart, Ed Small, and John Cali, recorded the song ("I got the weary I got the dreary / I got the mean boll weevil blues / Got no credit and I got no shoes") and so did Fiddlin' John Carson, who used the refrain: "we come to get your home, we're gonna get your home." In that year, as well, both Bessie Smith and Gertrude "Ma" Rainey came out with their own versions; Ma Rainey sang

Lewis Hines photo of children, some five or six years old, picking cotton in Bells, Texas, 1913. Courtesy of the Library of Congress.

> Hey boll weevil, don't sing the blues no more
> Hey hey boll weevil, don't sing the blues no more
> Boll weevils here, boll weevils everywhere you go

In 1927, Burl C. "Jaybird" Coleman, a harmonica player, recorded "Boll Weevil Blues" in which the anthropomorphized insect gives the farmer a very hard time:

> Boll weevil boll weevil,
> You think you treat me wrong
> Eat up all of my cotton,
> You done started on my corn
> Boll weevil's got mustache,
> Boll weevil's got hands
> Sometimes he's walkin' in the tall canes,
> Just like a natch'l man

Charley Patton recorded "Mississippi Boweavil Blues" for Paramount in June 1929, although the song had been in his repertoire for more than twenty years. "You can plant your cotton and you won't get half a cent," Patton sang, and he proceeded to describe the boll weevil's qualities: its mobility, its adaptability, and its destructiveness. Some of the verses were sung in the narrator's voice, some in the farmer's, and some in the boll weevil's itself:

> Well I saw the boll weevil, Lord, a-circle, Lordy, in the air
> The next time I seen him, Lord he had his family there, Lordy
>
> Boll weevil left Texas; Lord, he bid me "fare you well"
> I'm going down in Mississippi, gonna give you 'n' Lou'siana hell
>
> Boll weevil told his wife: says, "I believe I may go north
> Let's leave Louisiana: we can go to Arkansas"
>
> Boll weevil told the farmer: "I ain't got ticket fare"
> Suck all the blossom and leave you half your square
>
> Boll weevil, boll weevil, where your native home?
> "Most anywhere they raise cotton and corn"

Patton's lyrics revealed the devastation, upheaval, and uncertainty caused by the insect but also his grudging admiration for it. In effect Patton was saying, "the boll weevil could go anywhere it wanted; the poor tenant farmworker could not. The boll weevil had power over the plantation owner; the farmworker did not."

Even before Patton had made his recording, scientists were searching for ways to destroy the insect. Although it was known that a copper-arsenic compound called "Paris green" could kill large numbers, it was toxic, costly, and difficult to apply. Powdered lead arsenic was also found to be effective and did not harm the cotton, but applying it was impractical as well as inefficient. By 1926 the Department of Agriculture began experimenting with aerial crop-dusting, using yet another pesticide, calcium arsenate, but it turned out to harm people as well as insects. Farmworkers, when exposed to the chemical, experienced a range of ailments, "including gastrointestinal pain, diarrhea, irritability, headache, drowsiness, confusion, vomiting, and toxic psychosis." And those symptoms resulted even from short-term exposure.

In time, means would be found to eradicate the boll weevil, but the process was both expensive and time-consuming. Sophisticated trapping and monitoring devices were developed, and in the 1960s the male boll weevil pheromone was identified, thereby making it possible to lure females into traps and reduce their reproduction. In 1978, eradication programs began in Virginia and North Carolina, and were extended into the Southeast and Southwest during the 1980s. Then a new, effective insecticide, Malathion, was developed. Sprayed by airplanes that were equipped with global positioning systems and guided by computers, the poisons could be placed in precise locations. By 2009, boll weevils remained on a tiny fraction—only 2 percent—of the nation's nine million acres of cotton. Eradication was complete in all regions, even in west Texas; the insects remained only in the southern and eastern areas of that state, where they had first found a home, and where treatment was ongoing. "It looks really good," commented the president of the Texas Boll Weevil Eradication Foundation.

For well over a century, boll weevils caused vast destruction, hardship, and misery throughout the South. Nowadays, however, they represent a minor regional problem, attracting attention chiefly when they are publicized at festivals designed to boost regional economies. Marshville, North Carolina, for example, hosts an annual "Boll Weevil Jamboree," noting, for the record, that "back in the 1920s, the thought of a festival honoring the boll weevil probably didn't cross too many minds"; and Enterprise, Alabama, advertises its yearly celebration, complete with amusement rides, food, and games, as "a family-friendly event for all to enjoy." Enterprise, too, is the home of the Boll Weevil Monument, dedicated in 1919. Prominently displayed in the downtown business district, it was vandalized in 1998, the boll weevil ripped out of the statue's hands. So the original is now in a museum, replaced by a polymer-resin replica, which yet serves as "a symbol of man's willingness and ability to adjust to adversity. Citizens continue to remind visitors and newcomers to the city the lesson of the boll weevil."

As the years have passed, that lesson has largely been forgotten. Songs about the boll weevil continue to be recorded on folk and country music albums, but in most versions, the farmer puts the boll weevil in the sand, only to hear it say, "I can stand it like a man," or in the ice, only to have it declare, "this is mighty cool and nice," or even in the fire: "here I are, here I are." In the song—if not in the modern world of traps, insecticides, and GPS systems—the boll weevil still has the final boast, "this'll be my home," or more defiantly: "this is my home, it is my home."

> Boll weevil said to the farmer
> You'd better leave me alone
> I done eat all your cotton out
> I'm goin' to start on your corn
> I'll have a home, I'll have a home.

Martyrs

CHAPTER 26

JOE HILL (1915)

I dreamed I saw Joe Hill last night
Alive as you and me
Says I, "But Joe you're ten years dead"
"I never died," says he
"I never died," says he

In September 1934, several verses of a poem titled "I Dreamed I Saw Joe Hill Again" were published in the leftist journal the *New Masses*. Alfred Hayes, a young man in his twenties, had written it, and in the summer of 1936, while at Camp Unity in Wingdale, New York—which called itself "the first proletarian summer colony"—he handed the poem to the composer Earl Robinson, who recalled, "I went into the tent with the lyric and came out 45 minutes later with the tune." The song was printed in the *Daily Worker* in 1936, copyrighted in 1938, and recorded a year later by Samuel Isaac Mirviss, a rabbi's son who had recently embarked on a career as a singer under the stage name Michael Loring. In the decades that followed, Paul Robeson, Joan Baez, Pete Seeger, and countless others would sing "Joe Hill" before audiences all around the world.

The man about whom the song was written—Joel Emmanuel Hägglund—was born in Gävle, Sweden, on October 7, 1879, the son of Olaf, a railroad conductor, and Catharina Hägglund. The couple had nine children, three of whom died in infancy or early childhood. His father passed away when Joel was eight, and although Catharina took in ironing, the family barely scraped by, and so the older children had to work to help make ends meet. Joel, a shy, introverted boy, took a job in a rope mill when he was only twelve. He also learned to play the organ and the violin, but in 1896, when he was seventeen, he developed tuberculosis of the skin and was unable to hold a steady job. X-ray therapy at a nearby hospital was of little help, so in 1898 he went to Stockholm for further treatment and finally in April 1900 underwent surgery. After recuperating for six months, he was discharged in October just before his twenty-first birthday. Soon there-after his mother died, and the children sold the family's home and went off in separate directions. In October 1902 Joel and his brother Paul boarded ship for the United States.

They were among the thirty-three thousand Swedish immigrants who arrived that year. Like many newcomers, Joel changed his name, from Häg-glund to Hillstrom. "His was an itinerant, uncertain life," his biographer Wil-liam M. Adler wrote, "the only constant the hunt for another job, a meal, a bed, a toehold in industrializing America." He moved from state to state—New York, Illinois, Pennsylvania, North Dakota, Colorado, Wyoming, Nevada, California—and from job to job, working in mines, on ranches, and on the railroads. He happened to be in San Francisco on April 18, 1906, during the great earthquake, and wrote about it for a Swedish newspaper. Although he was not injured, some three thousand people lost their lives, and hundreds of thou-sands were left homeless. By 1910, he was in Portland, Oregon, and had joined the Industrial Workers of the World (IWW), a revolutionary union that sought improved working conditions but was better known for favoring the overthrow of capitalism. As the preamble to its constitution said: "The working class and the employing class have nothing in common. There can be no peace so long as hunger and want are found among millions of the working people and the few, who make up the employing class, have all the good things of life." The class struggle would go on, the "Wobblies" believed, until the workers created a cooperative commonwealth.

During the next few years, Hill took part in the IWW's "free speech" cam-paigns, holding forth in public spaces chiefly in California and Washington State, and also began writing songs. In 1911, he spent six weeks in Mexico, joining a group of rebels who had fought against the government of Porfirio Díaz and then against the current leader, Francisco Madero. It appears that Hill took part in some battles, and perhaps came to know the brothers, both of them revolutionar-ies, Enrique and Ricardo Flores Magón. One of the verses Hill wrote at the time was: "Should I ever be a soldier / Neath the Red Flag I would fight / Should a gun I ever shoulder / It's to crush the tyrant's might." In all, Hill spent about six weeks in Mexico, slipping back into the United States late in June.

In July 1911 and thereafter his songs began to appear in the IWW's song-book. One of them, "The Preacher and the Slave," began

> Long-haired preachers come out every night
> Try to tell you what's wrong and what's right
> But when asked how 'bout something to eat
> They will answer with voices so sweet

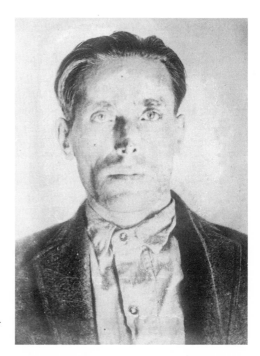

Joseph Hillstrom, 1915. Courtesy of
the Library of Congress.

"You will eat by and by
In that glorious land above the sky
Work and pray, live on hay
You'll get pie in the sky when you die"

In September, Hill wrote "Casey Jones—the Union Scab," a song about the engineer Casey Jones who—in Hill's version—opposes a railroad strike and remains
loyal to his Southern Pacific employers. When his train crashes, he goes to
heaven, is told by St. Peter that "you can get a job a'scabbin any time you like,"
but is promptly evicted by the angels: "Casey Jones went to Hell a-flying / Casey
Jones the devil said 'oh fine' / Casey Jones get busy shoveling sulphur / That's
what you get for scabbing on the S. P. line."

Although he remained on the West Coast, Hill wrote verses about a textile
strike in Lawrence, Massachusetts, which had begun in January 1912 and ended
in March when the workers gained a pay increase. He took part in a free-speech
campaign in San Diego, speaking for the first time before a large crowd, and
then headed north across the border where an IWW railroad strike was in
progress in British Columbia. There he composed another song—"Where the
Fraser River Flows"—hoping in the process to energize the workers who were

demanding better wages and safer working conditions. "Where the Fraser river flows, each fellow worker knows / They have bullied and oppressed us, but still our union grows. / And we're going to find a way, boys, for shorter hours and better pay, boys / And we're going to win the day, boys, where the Fraser river flows." Despite Hill's efforts, the strike failed. By July, 250 workers had been arrested, and many others had been deported.

Hill spent much of 1913 in San Pedro, California, working wherever he could and writing songs, many of which found their way into IWW publications. He wrote "Mr. Block," about a worker who snubbed the union ("His head is made of lumber, and solid as a rock") and dutifully went to fight in the war against Spain, only to lose a leg ("And now he's peddling shoestrings and is walking on a peg"). He wrote "Scissor Bill" about a worker—alcoholic, xenophobic, racist—who refused to join a union ("He says he never organized and never will"). To the tune of "My Old Kentucky Home" he wrote "We Will Sing One Song"—a song of "the greedy master class," "the politician sly," "the preacher, fat and sleek"—and a verse about the injustice of child labor:

> We will sing one song of the children in the mills
> They're taken from playgrounds and schools
> In tender years made to go the pace that kills,
> In the sweatshops, 'mong the loom and spools

And he wrote "The Tramp," about migratory workers who had no place to call home: "Tramp, tramp, tramp, keep on a-tramping / Nothing doing here for you / If I catch you 'round again, you will wear the ball and chain / Keep on tramping that's the best thing you can do." There were many other songs as well, some militant labor ballads, and some that were nonpolitical, romantic, and deeply sentimental, among them: "Oh, Please Let Me Dance This Waltz with You" ("and look in your dreamy eyes of blue"); or "My Dreamland Girl" ("And my heart is ever pining for my Dreamland Girl so fair").

While in San Pedro, Hill was arrested, first on a robbery charge that was dismissed, and then for vagrancy that resulted in a month in jail. At about this time he became concerned about proliferating deportation proceedings, not to mention the difficulty of finding work, and so, after meeting three Swedish seamen—Otto Appelquist and John and Ed Eselius—he decided to go with them to Utah. He arrived in Salt Lake City in the summer of 1913 but was there for only six months when he was arrested and charged with murder. On the night of January 10, 1914, two men shot and killed John G. Morrison and his seventeen-year-old son, Arling, in their grocery store. The only witness was Morrison's thirteen-year-old son, Merlin, who said the men shouted, "We have got you now!"

Later that night, Joe Hill appeared at the home of Dr. Frank M. McHugh with a bullet wound in his left lung, claiming that he had been shot in an argument over a woman. He was telling the truth. Both he and Otto Applegate had been courting twenty-year-old Hilda Erickson, who for a time had been engaged to Applegate, but decided not to go ahead with the marriage. Many years later, she recalled that Hill told her, "Otto shot him in a fit of anger." A remorseful Applegate had then taken Hill to see Dr. McHugh, and another physician who happened to be visiting noticed that Hill had a gun in a shoulder holster. The incident was reported to the police, who assumed, as did the prosecution, that Hill's wound had been received during the holdup, and on January 14 Joe Hill was taken into custody.

His trial began in June before Judge Morris L. Ritchie, "whose partiality toward the prosecution," according to Adler, "was manifest at every step of the trial." The judge took it on himself personally to select three members of the jury. Although Hill was represented by two attorneys—Ernest D. MacDougall and Frank B. Scott—he informed the judge he wished to conduct his own defense, telling the lawyers: "See that door? Get out. You're fired." The lawyers remained, though, in the capacity of friends of the court. Hill chose not to take the stand in his own behalf, and while the testimony of others was complex and often contradictory, the jury was prepared to convict him on flimsy evidence. The judge's prejudicial summation made that task even easier. After deliberating for only two hours, the jurors returned a guilty verdict. The judge offered Hill an unenviable choice: a firing squad or the hangman's noose. "I'll take shooting," Hill replied.

An execution date was set for early in September, but Hill, now represented by a new attorney, Orrin N. Hilton, appealed his conviction, first to Judge Ritchie, who turned him down, and then to the Utah Supreme Court. While the case was under consideration, Hill continued to write, not only letters, but also songs, one of them a paean to workers who committed industrial sabotage so as to win shorter hours and better pay: "Ta-ra-ra boom de-ay / it made a noise that way / And wheels and bolts and hay / Went flying every way." He corresponded with twenty-five-year-old Elizabeth Gurley Flynn, a fellow radical, and wrote songs for her, too, including "The Rebel Girl." Early in May 1915, she was permitted to visit him in the sheriff's office, and reported that he continued to write songs "that sing, that lilt and laugh and sparkle, that kindle the fires of revolt in the most crushed spirit and quicken the desire for fuller life in the most humble slave."

On May 28, 1915, the Utah Supreme Court finally heard Hill's appeal, which his new attorney, Judge Orrin N. Hilton, presented. The conviction had been based on "inconclusive, disjointed fragments of suspicion," Hilton argued, and

Elizabeth Gurley Flynn. Courtesy
of the Library of Congress.

the trial judge had erred in not appointing a new defense attorney after Hill had
dismissed his lawyers, thereby effectively depriving him of proper counsel. But
on July 3, the justices unanimously affirmed the lower court ruling. Hill decided
not to appeal to the United States Supreme Court since he did not wish to "drain
the resources of the whole organization and weaken its fighting strength just on
account of one individual." On August 2, after having been resentenced and
having again opted for the firing squad, he explained, "I never did like the ring
of the word 'pardon,' and I think I'd rather be buried dead, than buried alive."
He had already told his lawyer that he would show the world "how a MAN
should die."

In September, Hill appeared before the Utah Board of Pardons. Three of its
five members, however, were the same Supreme Court justices who had already
rejected his appeal, and if anything he sealed his fate by not asking for a pardon
but rather for a new trial, a request that was immediately rejected. Then, at the
last minute, President Woodrow Wilson asked Utah's governor, William Spry,
for a postponement until the Swedish minister could present a further argument for clemency. Spry reluctantly agreed, but the pardon board met again and

decided against any delay. Despite many appeals, including another from Wilson—which the governor termed "unwarranted interference"—the execution went forward on November 19, 1915. Just before facing the firing squad, Hill had written, "I will die like a true-blue rebel. Don't waste any time in mourning—organize."

He had also written a last will in the form of a poem that, as the years went by, would frequently be recited whenever radicals got together:

> My will is easy to decide
> For I have nothing to divide
> My kin don't need to weep and moan
> Moss does not cling to a rolling stone
>
> My body? oh, if I could choose
> I would to ashes it reduce
> And let the merry breezes blow
> My dust to where some flowers grow
>
> Perhaps some fading flower then
> Would soon rise up and grow green again
> This is my last and final will
> Good luck to all of you,
> Joe Hill

Through his songs and poetry, Joe Hill came to be considered a working-class martyr. Following his death, his body was sent to Chicago, where it was cremated; the ashes were given to IWW locals in every state—except Utah—and even to countries around the world. One envelope, however, was seized by the Post Office, later winding up in the National Archives. Eventually, in the 1980s, it was turned over to the IWW, which arranged to scatter a packet of Hill's ashes on the graves of six Wobbly coal miners who had been killed by the state police in the Columbine Mine Massacre of 1927 in Serene, Colorado.

Meanwhile, the song that Alfred Hayes had composed about Joe Hill—he later recalled writing it "in about a half-hour, and it just came like that—and there it was"—continued to be sung in left-wing circles. Then, in 1947, Woody Guthrie, who was nearing the end of his career as a songwriter, composed his own version that he called "Joe Hillstrom." Sixteen verses long, and written in the first person, the song provided explicit details of the crime, the arrest, the trial, and even the execution—all, naturally, through Joe Hill's eyes. Guthrie mentioned the site where the robbery had occurred; the names of the victims, the prosecuting attorney, the defense lawyers, and the governor; the place where

Hill was arrested; his decision, as Guthrie wrote, to "take away these attorneys you picked for me / My own lawyer now I'm going to be"; President Wilson's futile last-minute intervention; and the support offered to Hill by Flynn. "It's because I'm a union organizer in the copper mines," Guthrie has Hill declare, "You've got me on your killing floor to die."

Two years later, Paul Robeson sang a significantly altered version of Hayes's "Joe Hill" in Moscow. Robeson had recorded the song as early as 1942, had performed it at the Workers' Theater in England, and in March 1947 had sung it before two thousand people at the University of Utah in Salt Lake City, where he received a chilly response. But the response was strikingly different when he visited the Soviet Union in 1949, where his rendition was received with great applause. By then Robeson had modified the lyrics—changing "Joe says, 'What they forgot to kill'" to "Joe says 'what they can *never* kill,'" and also changing "where workingmen are out on strike" to "where workers fight and organize"—thereby giving the song a distinctly more militant tone. In 1952, Robeson's passport had been revoked, but he appeared in Blaine, Washington, on the Canadian border, to sing before more than thirty thousand people. The union official who introduced him declared that "Joe Hill" "is a song of the struggle of the hard rock miners."

People still sing about Joe Hill, and new songs are still being written about him. Pete Seeger recorded "Joe Hill" many times. Bob Dylan modeled his song that began "Hey, hey, Woody Guthrie, I wrote you a song / 'Bout a funny ol' world that's a-comin' along" on Guthrie's "Joe Hillstrom": "Hey, Gurley Flynn, I wrote you a song / To the dove of peace, it's coming along." Joan Baez performed "Joe Hill" at Woodstock in 1969 and has included renditions of the song on nearly a dozen albums. Phil Ochs wrote a lengthy song called "Joe Hill" that used the melody of "John Hardy": "For his songs that he made, he was carefully paid / With a rifle bullet buried in his head." Long after his death, Joe Hill became the subject of Si Kahn's song "Paper Heart" and of Louis Ludwig's "Joe Hill Cryin'"—"well I heard today the one big union's dyin' / that ain't rain boys, it's Joe Hill cryin'"—and of an entire album by Otis Gibbs entitled *Joe Hill's Ashes*.

Toward the end of his life, Joe Hill wrote "I have done what little I could to bring the flag of freedom closer to its goal." That goal has not been reached, and may never be, but many who strive to achieve it remain stirred by his songs, and by songs about him, that always hold out the hope of a brighter future. In the refrain to "We Will Sing One Song," he wrote

> Organize! Oh, toilers, come organize your might
> Then we'll sing one song of the workers' commonwealth
> Full of beauty, full of love and health.

CHAPTER 27

SACCO AND VANZETTI (1927)

Bart Vanzetti and Nicola Sacco
Bart Vanzetti and Nicola Sacco
Come here looking for the land of freedom
I just want to sing your name

In 1946, Woody Guthrie decided that that he wanted to write and record songs about Nicola Sacco and Bartolomeo Vanzetti, Italian American anarchists who many believed had been wrongly convicted of robbery and murder in Massachusetts in 1921 and then executed in 1927. With an advance of a few hundred dollars from Moses Asch, the owner of Folkways Records, Guthrie set out for Boston with his friend the folksinger Cisco Houston. They visited South Braintree, where the crime had been committed, and Bridgewater, where the trial had been held. In January 1947 Guthrie recorded what he called "the most important dozen songs I ever worked on," but, dissatisfied with the result, he told Asch they should not yet be released since "I just feel rushed, and I don't want this album about Sacco and Vanzetti to feel rushed, to smell rushed, to taste rushed, nor to sound like something rushed."

Guthrie also composed a long, blistering letter to Judge Webster Thayer, who had tried the case (but who had passed away years earlier): "You set their souls free with a spark of Massachusetts electricity because you were so unwise as to think that this would hold and silence their voices." Yet to judge from the number of books and articles that even now continue to appear about the case—as well as the numerous songs and poems that have been written about it, and the many motion pictures and television documentaries that have been made—the voices of Sacco and Vanzetti have neither been held or silenced. In fact, the publication of many of their prison letters within a year after their deaths ensured that their voices would live on.

Woody Guthrie, 1943. Courtesy of the Library of Congress.

Both men had left Italy for the United States in 1908. Sacco had arrived at the age of seventeen. Born and raised in Torremaggiore, he recalled having had a pleasant childhood, but he was eager to make a fresh start in America. He eventually moved to Milford, Massachusetts, and began working in a shoe factory. In 1912 he married seventeen-year-old Rosa Zambelli. A son, Dante, was born in 1913, and a daughter, Ines, in 1920, after Sacco's arrest. A skilled worker who earned a good living, Sacco nevertheless became a revolutionary. He later explained to his daughter, "The nightmare of the lower classes saddened very badly your father's soul." In the spring of 1917, shortly after the United States entered World War I, he joined a band of revolutionaries and spent several months in Mexico, preparing to return to Italy to take part in a revolution that, in any event, never happened. It was while planning the move to Mexico that he met Bartolomeo Vanzetti.

In many respects, the two men were quite different. Sacco came from southern Italy, Vanzetti from Villafalletto, in the northwest. Sacco was a family man with a steady job and a stable home; Vanzetti, three years older than Sacco, remained single, a roomer in boardinghouses who barely managed to make ends meet, working, when work was to be had, as a dishwasher, a pastry chef, a laborer in stone quarries, and, finally, a fish vendor. He hoped he would "never lose the joy of that vagabond freedom of working and living in the open," and, as an anarchist, he wanted to see that "the social wealth would belong to every [hu]umane creature." At the time of their trial, both men had only an uncertain command of English and required a translator's services when testifying.

What they had in common was a fervent belief in anarchism. The abolition of government, law, and private property, they thought, far from leading to chaos or disorder, would permit men and women to live on terms of perfect equality. In such a world, they believed, cooperative instincts would overcome competitive ones, liberty would replace repression, and mutual respect would flourish. Ardent revolutionaries, both men believed in the violent overthrow of capitalism. As the historian Paul Avrich has explained: "Far from being the innocent dreamers so often depicted by their supporters, they belonged to a branch of the anarchist movement which preached insurrectionary violence and armed retaliation, including the use of dynamite and assassination."

Sacco and Vanzetti never tried to conceal their radicalism, their militancy, or their implacable hatred of their oppressors. To one of his supporters, Sacco wrote in June 1927 that he "have try to hit at the centres of this decrepid society." Vanzetti said that while he abhorred "useless violence," he endorsed purposeful, revolutionary violence: "I will ask for revenge—I will tell that I will die gladly by the hands of the hanger after having known to have been vindicated. . . . to win it is necessary that 100 enemies fall to each of us." "To progress, even a little," he said in April 1925, "we have to destroy a world." Just a few weeks before the date set for execution, he wrote: "We are and will remain innocent, our execution would be the same as murder, our blood will call for revenge."

These themes, however, were not the predominant ones in their prison letters. Rather, Sacco and Vanzetti were also idealists and humanitarians, men who loved justice and hated oppression. Close to nature, in touch with their own truest feelings, they were deeply grateful for the support of friends, and even while bemoaning the isolation of prison life they managed to find humor in the hand fate had dealt them. They dwelt lovingly on their fondest memories of freedom, with Vanzetti referring to himself and his comrade as "two poor Christs." Vanzetti, indeed, attained an extraordinary eloquence. As early as 1921, as he was being moved from Charlestown State Prison to the jail in Dedham, he observed two young women trudging to work, their pale faces etched with "lines of sorrow and distress," the "suffering in their big, deep, full eyes. Poor plebian girls," he remarked, "where are the roses of your springtime?"

Both men were followers of Luigi Galleani, who had immigrated to the United States in 1901. As editor of the anarchist newspaper *Cronaca Sovversiva*, Galleani was known for advocating violence to eliminate those who he believed oppressed the working class. Never having acquired citizenship, though, he was at risk of being deported. In June 1919, he was arrested following a wave of bombings in eight major cities, including Cleveland, Pittsburgh, and New York, and within three weeks was sent back to Italy. Then, in February 1920, federal agents in New York, who had infiltrated Galleani's movement, arrested two of his followers, Roberto Elia and Andrea Salsedo, and, although lacking a warrant, secretly detained them for questioning, claiming the two men were only being "watched" and not "held."

Somehow, Salsedo managed to smuggle a letter to Vanzetti in which he played down what he had told the authorities. But anarchists in Massachusetts, still worried about what he might have revealed, sent Vanzetti to New York City to see what he could find out. He spent four days there late in April, without seeing Salsedo. On his return, fearing further raids, he decided to get rid of his anarchist literature. Early on the morning of May 3, 1920, Salsedo fell to his death from the fourteenth floor of the building in which he was being detained. (His comrade, Ella, was soon deported.) A Boston newspaper reported: "Salsedo Gives Names of all Terrorist Plotters Before Taking Death Leap."

Fearing that the law enforcement net was tightening, Sacco and Vanzetti began making plans to return to Italy. But on the evening of May 5, they were arrested while on a streetcar, since, in the eyes of the authorities, they seemed to be "suspicious characters." Both were found to be carrying concealed weapons and cartridges: Sacco a loaded .32 Colt Model 1903 automatic pistol, and Vanzetti a .38-caliber Harrington & Richardson revolver. The two men assumed they were being held because they were radicals, but in fact they were accused of robbery and murder: the holdup of the Slater and Morrill Shoe Company on April 15 in South Braintree, in which two guards, Frederick Parmenter and Alessandro Berardelli, were murdered and more than $15,000 was stolen. Vanzetti was also charged with an earlier crime (for which Sacco had an airtight alibi): the unsuccessful payroll robbery of the L. Q. W. White Shoe Company in Bridgewater on December 24, 1919.

> 'Twas nineteen and twenty, the fifth of May
> The cop and some buddies took these two men away
> Off of the car and out and down
> Down to the jail Brockton town

Vanzetti was tried in June 1920 for the Bridgewater crime, found guilty, and sentenced to twelve to fifteen years in prison. The judge was Webster Thayer, who also presided a year later when both men stood trial for the South Braintree crime. That trial began on June 22, 1921, with District Attorney Frederick G. Katzmann as the prosecutor, and Fred H. Moore, who had represented radical defendants in the past, serving as defense attorney. At the time, and for years afterward, the defense would claim that the proceedings were marred by numerous errors: that the jury foreman had been prejudiced (once responding to a comment that the defendants might be innocent by sneering, "Damn them, they ought to hang them anyway!"); that the prosecution had induced a witness to make a false identification; and that the district attorney had encouraged a firearms expert to give misleading testimony that led the jury to believe that Sacco's gun was the murder weapon. After three weeks of testimony, the jury found both men guilty.

> Judge Thayer told his friends around
> That he had cut the radicals down
> "Anarchist bastard" was the name
> Judge Thayer called these two good men

Despite the verdict, no credible evidence linked Vanzetti to the South Braintree crime. Several eyewitnesses claimed to have seen a man resembling him in the getaway car, but many other observers who failed to make a positive identification were simply dismissed by the prosecution. Katzmann misled the jury by purportedly reading excerpts from the transcripts of Vanzetti's interrogation after his arrest, but the actual transcripts were not introduced into

Bartolomeo Vanzetti handcuffed to Nicola Sacco, Dedham, Massachusetts, 1923.

evidence, and Vanzetti was at times misquoted and thereby made to appear deceptive. Worse, prosecutors claimed the Harrington & Richardson revolver found on Vanzetti belonged to one of the murdered guards, Alessandro Berardelli, even though they knew that the serial numbers did not match. Rather than making such exculpatory evidence available to the defense, the prosecution concealed it.

The case against Sacco, although better substantiated, did not prove his guilt beyond a reasonable doubt. The eyewitness testimony was, as in Vanzetti's case, shaky, and Sacco's police-station interrogation was similarly misrepresented to make it seem he had made damaging statements. Katzmann maintained that one of the bullets—it became known as Bullet III—retrieved from Berardelli's body had been fired from Sacco's .32-caliber Colt, and that one of the shells found at the scene had also come from that revolver. While Bullet III indeed appears to have been fired from Sacco's pistol, there is good reason to suspect that it was not the actual bullet taken from the murdered man, but rather one that was used in a test firing of the weapon in the period between the arrest and trial, substituted for the original, and then offered as a genuine exhibit.

Nevertheless, by October 1924 Judge Thayer had rejected all motions made by the defense. In January 1926, William G. Thompson and Herbert B. Ehrmann, the lawyers who now represented the two men (Moore having been replaced), submitted an appeal to the Supreme Judicial Court of Massachusetts, but in May the justices upheld the verdict. In January 1927, a further appeal was made, based largely on a statement by Celestino Madeiros, in prison at the time, who came forward, confessed to the crime, and claimed that Sacco and Vanzetti had not been involved; but in April, the court ruled that Judge Thayer "has decided that no reliance can be placed upon the alleged confession; that its truth is not substantiated by other affidavits." Moreover, the court said, "a confession made out of court by a third party is not admissible."

Once the verdict had been upheld, Thayer, as expected, imposed the death penalty. But in view of what had become a national, indeed a worldwide, protest movement, Massachusetts governor Alvan T. Fuller appointed a blue-ribbon advisory panel made up of A. Lawrence Lowell, president of Harvard University; Samuel W. Stratton, president of the Massachusetts Institute of Technology; and Robert Grant, a retired jurist. The Lowell Committee—William Carlos Williams later branded it "a triumvirate of inversion"—reported to the governor on July 27 and made its report public on August 7. It concluded that the trial had been fair: the facts showed Sacco was guilty, and "on the whole" the evidence supported Vanzetti's conviction. It was not known at the time that the commission had begun writing its report before all the evidence was presented to it or that the defense attorneys had not been given an opportunity to answer questions. Nevertheless, Fuller turned down a petition for clemency and set August 10 as the execution date. Thirty minutes before the switch was thrown, however, the governor granted a twelve-day stay to permit further appeals.

There was one last hope for the defense: that a justice of the United States Supreme Court might be persuaded to grant a stay of execution. Louis D. Brandeis was the most liberal member of the Court, but he recused himself because his wife, Alice, had supported the efforts of the defense. So the attorneys for the condemned men turned to Justice Oliver Wendell Holmes Jr. While on summer vacation he granted them an audience; but on August 19, 1927, after hearing their arguments, he ruled: "This is a case of a crime charged under state laws and tried by a State Court. I have absolutely no authority as a judge of the United States to meddle with it." Holmes added: "I do not consider that I am at liberty to deal with this case differently from the way in which I should treat one that excited no public interest and that was less powerfully presented. I cannot say that I have a doubt and therefore I must deny the stay."

With all avenues of appeal exhausted, the execution was set. The protests, marches, and vigils in many American cities and all around the world, the pleas for clemency from writers, politicians, and scientists—made no difference in the end. Nor did last-minute appeals to Fuller from Sacco's wife, Rosa, and Vanzetti's sister, Luigia, who had come all the way from Italy. Shortly after midnight on August 23, Sacco bid a last farewell; Vanzetti said, "I wish to forgive some people for what they are now doing to me"; and the electrocutions took place. One of the many people who gathered outside the gates of Charleston Prison that night was the writer Katherine Anne Porter. She remembered commenting to a man nearby that she felt as if "we were all of us soiled and disgraced and would never in this world live it down." "What on earth are you talking about," a man said. "There's no such thing as disgrace any more."

> You souls of Boston, bow your heads
> Our two most noble sons are dead
> Sacco and Vanzetti both have died
> And drifted out with the Boston tide

On the day he died, Sacco wrote a letter to his son. "Don't cry Dante, because many tears have been wasted, as your mother's have been wasted for seven years, and never did any good." Pete Seeger later put those words to music, and, many years later recorded the song on Guthrie's Folkways album *Songs of Sacco and Vanzetti*, altering only a word here or there: "So, son, instead of crying, be strong, so as to be able to comfort your mother, and when you want to distract your mother from the discouraging soulness, I will tell you what I used to do. To take her for a long walk in the quiet country, gathering wild flowers here and there, resting under the shade of trees, between the harmony of the vivid stream, and the gentle tranquility of the mothernature, and I am sure that she will enjoy this very much, as you surely would be happy for it." Combining tender advice with revolutionary zeal, Sacco implored his son: "Help the weak ones that cry for help, help the prosecuted and the victim, because they are your better friends; they are the comrades that fight and fall as your father and Bartolo fought and fell yesterday for the conquest of the joy of freedom for all and the poor workers. In this struggle of life you will find more love and you will be loved."

Besides Woody Guthrie, many poets, playwrights, novelists, and artists made use of the case. More than one hundred poems were written about it in the days just before and after the execution, the authors often noting reverentially the precise moment of composition—"midnight" or "after midnight" or "execution day." Lesser-known poets wrote much of the verse, but so did the more renowned, among them Malcolm Cowley, James Rorty, Countee Cullen, and Babette Deutsch. "Evil does overwhelm / The larkspur and the corn," wrote Edna St. Vincent Millay: "We have seen them go under." Maxwell Anderson coauthored a book about the two men, *Gods of Lightning* (1928), and later won a Pulitzer Prize when he returned to the theme in *Winterset* (1935). Upton Sinclair wrote a highly regarded novel, *Boston* (1928), about the case, while writers as diverse as Nathan Asch, John Dos Passos, Bernard DeVoto, Ruth McKenney, and James T. Farrell would be drawn to its pathos and human drama.

Songs, too, and not only Guthrie's, were written about the two anarchists. In 1927, as the execution date approached, Alfredo Bascetta, a Neopolitan tenor who had emigrated to New York City, recorded "Lacrime 'e cundannate" (Bitter tears and two condemned men)

> The whole world is turned upside down
> for Sacco and for Vanzetti both found guilty
> And those villains who scorned them
> Should never find a minute's rest!
>
> Everyone has been so cold-hearted
> Even the jury—what a cruel company!
> No they don't listen to reason or to innocence
> No this is not justice, this is only wicked vileness!

Bascetta expressed a keen sense of outrage, as did several other songs recorded shortly after the men's deaths, including "Morte di Sacco e Vanzetti" (The death of Sacco and Vanzetti) and "I martiri d'un ideale" (The martyrs of an ideal).

A well-known tenor, Raoul Romito, who had sung with the Boston Opera, also recorded a tribute to the two men.

By the 1960s, as the case became more widely known, other songs about it were also recorded. One of the most beautiful was "Sacco e Vanzetti" by the Italian folksinger Giovanna Daffini, who was accompanied on the violin by her husband, Vittorio Carpi. Born in 1913 in north central Italy, Daffini made her living chiefly by working in the rice fields. Fortunately, in 1962 ethnomusicologists sought her out, and in the few years she had left—she died in 1969—she recorded many folk songs, including some that she had learned from peasant women. The song she recorded about the anarchists began "*il ventitré Agosto . . .*"

> On the 23rd of August in Boston in America
> Sacco and Vanzetti went to the electric chair
> And with a shot of electricity
> They were sent to the next world.

Later in the song came the line, "the whole world proclaims their innocence," and then

> Sacco and Vanzetti calm and serene
> "We are innocent. Open up your jail"
> But they replied, "There is no mercy
> You must go to your death"

By far the most frequently recorded song about Sacco and Vanzetti remains "Here's to You." Joan Baez wrote the lyrics in 1970; they were set to music by Ennio Morricone, and a year later served as the sound track for a film about the two men. Baez's version would receive millions of hits on YouTube. Only one verse in length, the words were repeated over and over again:

> Here's to you, Nicola and Bart
> Rest forever here in our hearts
> The last and final moment is yours
> That agony is your triumph

Eventually, the lyrics were recorded by singers all around the world and were later used, oddly enough, in the video game Metal Gear Solid 4: Guns of the Patriots.

Baez also wrote the "Ballad of Sacco and Vanzetti," a song in which she said the men stood convicted only of "the crime of love and brotherhood." Indeed, that seems to be the way they are now remembered. On August 23, 1977, Massachusetts governor Michael Dukakis declared the fiftieth anniversary of their execution to be "Nicola Sacco and Bartolomeo Vanzetti Memorial Day." They had been unfairly convicted, he said, and so "any disgrace should be forever removed from their names." By now, several sites in the former USSR have been named for the two men, Italy has roads named Via Sacco-Vanzetti both in Torremaggiore and in Villafalletto, and there are other memorials as well. Certainly the two anarchists could not have imagined that they would still be remembered more than a century after they set foot on American soil, or that their names would be enshrined in song:

> Two good men a long time gone
> Two good men a long time gone
> (Two good men a long time gone, oh, gone)
> Sacco, Vanzetti a long time gone
> Left me here to sing this song.

EPILOGUE

Hear My Sad Story

"Oh, beat the drum slowly and play the fife lowly
And play the dead march as you carry me along
Take me to the green valley, and lay the sod o'er me
For I'm a young cowboy and I have done wrong"

In the early 1920s, Frank Maynard, now in his seventies, continued to make his home in Colorado Springs, Colorado. Over the years, he had joined the Pikes Peak Chapter of the Modern Woodmen of America, and had invested in a speculative gold-mining venture near Cripple Creek. But he had chiefly earned his living as a carpenter and furniture repairman, traveling, when necessary, to construction projects in various parts of the state. Having retired, he still puttered in his workshop and occasionally wrote poetry. In February 1924 he published a wistful poem, a lament for "the days of the old frontier." "Where now are the boys who rode the range," he asked, "in the far-off days when the west was young?" Many had died, he said, and many more were likely to be occupied with "the sober prosaic tasks of life."

In 1924, during the annual Pikes Peak or Bust rodeo in Colorado Springs, Elmo Scott Watson, a journalism instructor at the University of Illinois with an interest in western history, happened to discover that Maynard was working there as a night watchman. He knew that Maynard had written "The Dying Cowboy"—by then generally known as "The Cowboy's Lament"—and the encounter led Watson to write an article about Maynard's many adventures. Maynard naturally expressed his thanks, but shortly thereafter he began to suffer from serious ailments, including cardiovascular disease. On March 28, 1926, he passed away at the age of seventy-three.

He was not so terribly old, and yet the changes that had occurred during his lifetime were truly immense. Born in 1853 when Franklin Pierce was president and the country was on the road to civil war, he died in 1926 when Calvin

Coolidge was president and the country was a few years away from the Great Depression. When Maynard was born, Martin Van Buren, John Tyler, and Millard Fillmore were still alive; when he died, Ronald Reagan, Jimmy Carter, and George H. W. Bush had already appeared on the scene, although not having yet begun their political careers.

The songs that were written, sung, listened to, and sometimes even recorded during Maynard's lifetime could not, and certainly did not, tell the whole story of the American people, but they could—and did—tell a significant part of it. Songs described the work that people did and what they thought about it. Songs explained what made them happy and what made them sad. Songs announced their triumphs and their failures. Songs expressed their hopes and their fears. Songs made heroes of some and villains of others. Songs told about tragedies, disasters, and love gone wrong, but also of recurrent efforts to make things better.

In many ways, the history of American folk music is the history of the American people. Over the years, through the lyrics of songs—and the joyful, mournful sounds—we not only discover names, dates, and facts, but also feel the emotions, often very intense, of those who lived that history and wanted to remember it. As Carl Sandburg once said, the songs that people sing contain "love and hate in many patterns and designs, heart cries of high and low pitch." Along with those heart cries, though, there have been joyful cries—of bravery, hope, and courage. Songs not only enable us to learn about the past: they also allow us to learn about ourselves.

Sources for Readers and Listeners

Preface

For Francis Child, and links to more than three hundred ballads he collected, see http://www.contemplator.com/history/childbio.html and http://www.sacred-texts.com/neu/eng/child/.

On Cecil Sharp see Michael Yates, "Cecil Sharp in America: Collecting in the Appalachians," 1999, at http://www.mustrad.org.uk/articles/sharp.htm.

For a video of Sharp dancing in 1912 see http://www.vwml.org/vwml-projects/vwml-the-full-english/vwml-full-english-collectors/vwml-cecil-sharp, and for Sharp's list of songs see http://www.bbc.co.uk/programmes/profiles/38g95mzGrM3GQzrgbNJbMxk/radio-2s-cecil-sharp-collection.

St. Louis

1. St. Louis Blues (1914)

There is a superb biography by David Robertson, *W. C. Handy: The Life and Times of the Man Who Made the Blues* (New York, 2009), which can be supplemented by W.C. Handy, *Father of the Blues: An Autobiography* (New York, 1941); the fine account in Adam Gussow, *Seems Like Murder Here: Southern Violence and the Blues Tradition* (Chicago, 2002), chapter 2; and David A. Jasen and Gene Jones, *Spreadin' Rhythm Around: Black Popular Songwriters, 1880–1930* (New York, 1998). An important article by Lynn Abbott and Doug Seroff is " 'They Cert'ly Sound Good to Me': Sheet Music, Southern Vaudeville, and the Commercial Ascendancy of the Blues," *American Music* 14 (Winter 1996): 402–454, reprinted in David Evans, ed., *Ramblin' on My Mind* (Urbana, IL, 2008), chapter 2.

On Mayor Edward H. Crump see G. Wayne Dowdy, *Mayor Crump Don't Like It: Machine Politics in Memphis* (Jackson, MS, 2006); on Edward Abbe Niles see Elliott S. Hurwitt, "Abbe Niles: Blues Advocate," in Evans, *Ramblin' on My Mind*, chapter 3, and the interesting essay by Mario Dunkel at http://commons.trincoll.

264 SOURCES FOR READERS AND LISTENERS

edu/rring/2013/03/06/jazzed-about-an-archive/; and on Harry Pace see http://www.americansongwriter.com/2009/07/behind-the-song-st-louis-blues/.

Several websites contain useful information, among them http://msbluestrail.org/blues-trail-markers/the-enlightenment-of-w-c-handy; http://www.american bluesscene.com/2013/12/mississippi-blues-trail-recognized-enlightenment-of-w-c-handy/; and Paul Slade's "Black Swan Blues: America's first Motown," at http://www.planetslade.com/black-swan-blues1.html.

For the violence against blacks in 1917 that affected Handy see "Memphis May 22, A.D. 1917," *Crisis* 14, no. 4 (July 1917): 1–4.

For a collection of Handy's blues—the lyrics and music to fifty-three songs—see Abbe Niles, *Blues: An Anthology* (New York, 1926, rev. ed., 1972), with Niles's essay, "The Story of the Blues," 12–45. For Thomas Cunniffe's essay on forty-eight versions of "St. Louis Blues" consult http://jazzhistoryonline.com/St_Louis_Blues_1.html.

2. Duncan and Brady (1890)

The finest account of Duncan and Brady is chapter 3 of John Russell David's doctoral dissertation, "Tragedy in Ragtime: Black Folktales from St. Louis" (St. Louis University, 1974). The background is provided by another dissertation, Lawrence O. Christensen, "Black St. Louis: A Study in Race Relations, 1865–1966" (St. Louis University, 1972). The legal documents concerning Duncan's trial and appeals are available online: "Reports of Cases Determined by the Supreme Court of the State of Missouri," 116:288–312; "State v. Duncan," *Southwestern Reporter*, 22:699–705; and *Duncan v. Missouri*, 152 U.S. 377 (1894). There is a short account in J. Elbert Jones, *A Review of Famous Crimes Solved by St. Louis Policemen* (St. Louis, n.d.), 43–48, and the case may also be followed in the *St. Louis Post-Dispatch*. There is a highly informative three-part essay by Patrick Blackman at the Murder Ballad Monday website, "Duncan and Brady / 'Been on the Job Too Long,'" http:mbmonday.blogspot.com/2013/01.

3. Stagolee (1895)

For the story of Lee Shelton see Cecil Brown, *Stagolee Shot Billy* (Cambridge, MA, 2003), and http://cecilbrown.net/stagolee/; the superb essay by George M. Eberhart, "Stack Lee: The Man, the Music, and the Myth," in *A Question of Manhood: A Reader in U.S. Black Men's History and Masculinity*, ed. Darlene Clark Hine and Ernestine Jenkins (Bloomington, IN, 2001), 2:387–440; and chapter 4 of John Russell David's doctoral dissertation, "Tragedy in Ragtime: Black Folktales from St. Louis (St. Louis University, 1974).

Many websites also contain useful information: http://www.staggerlee.com/, which includes a "definitive list" of songs; http://www.stagolee.org/; James P.

Hauser's "Original Stagger Lee Essay," https://sites.google.com/site/thestagger leefiles/original-stagger-lee-essay; http://www.planetslade.com/stagger-lee1.html; http://mbmonday.blogspot.com/2013/03/stagolee-digital-compendium-classics. html; http://prezi.com/vho0gyqo8u79/stagolee/; http: www3.clearlight.com/~acsa/ stagroot.htm; Max Haymes's essay "Got the Blues for Mean Old Stack O'Lee," at http://www.earlyblues.com/essay_stack_o_lee.htm; Tony Kullen, "Staggerlee Roots," at http://blueslyrics.tripod.com/dictionary/stagolee.htm; and Dave's Stagger Lee Database at www.stackolee.net.

See also Jamie Pamela Rasmussen, *The Missouri State Penitentiary: 170 Years inside the Walls* (Columbia, MO, 2012).

Early recordings of "Stagolee" by Harvey Hull and Cleve Reed, Mississippi John Hurt, and others are available on iTunes or YouTube.

4. Frankie and Johnny (1899)

For the story of Frankie and Johnny, and the court cases, see Cecil Brown, "We Did Them Wrong: The Ballad of Frankie and Albert," in *The Rose and the Briar: Death, Love and Liberty in the American Ballad*, ed. Sean Wilentz and Greil Marcus (New York, 2005); John David's doctoral dissertation, "Tragedy in Ragtime: Black Folktales from St. Louis" (St. Louis University, 1974); and Bruce Redfern Buckley's doctoral dissertation, "Frankie and Her Men: A Study of the Interrelationships of Popular and Folk Traditions" (Indiana University, 1962). There is also an excellent essay by Bruce Olson, "Frankie and Johnny: He Done Her Wrong Right Here in St. Louis," http://www.stlouisbluessociety.org/ files/1413/7420/2791/BluesLetter_July2013.pdf, pp. 4–11.

On John Huston's use of the song see his *Frankie and Johnny* (New York, 1930); Jeffrey Meyers, *John Huston: Courage and Art* (New York, 2011); and Graham Daseler, http://brightlightsfilm.com/74/74huston_daseler.php.

On the film *Frankie and Johnny* see Larry Wood, *Murder and Mayhem in Missouri* (History Press, Kindle ed., 2013); on the painting by Thomas Hart Benton see Leo G. Mazow, "Thomas Hart Benton: Painting the Song," https:// www.monmouth.edu/the_space_between/articles/LeoMazow2011.pdf; on the musical score by Jerome Moross see http://www.naxos.com/mainsite/blurbs_ reviews.asp?item_code=8.559086&catNum=559086&filetype=About%20 this%20Recording&language=English; and on the use of the song in modern dance see George Dorris, "Frankie and Johnny in Chicago and Some Problems of Attribution," *Dance Chronicle* 18 (1995).

Additional information is available in Jessie Carney Smith, ed., *Encyclopedia of African American Popular Culture* (Santa Barbara, CA, 2011), 542–546; and Jill Watts, *Mae West: An Icon in Black and White* (New York, 2003). Mae West sings the song at https://www.youtube.com/watch?v=40TkmE3_xNc.

Useful websites include "She Loved Her Man but He Done Her Wrong," http://www.ipernity.com/doc/285591/21005065; Paul Slade, "It's a Frame-up: Frankie and Johnny," http:www.planetslade.com/Frankie-and-johnny.html; and "Frankie Baker—'He Done Her Wrong,'" http:www.murderbygaslight. com/2010/03/he-done-her-wrong.html.

Mississippi John Hurt's recording of "Frankie and Johnny" can be heard at https://www.youtube.com/watch?v=VtxyjOFLXSg.

Charlie Patton's recording of "Frankie and Albert" is at https://www.you tube.com/watch?v=U39R94i_338, and Jimmie Rodgers's is at https://www.you tube.com/watch?v=kNq532Cyhu0. Other recordings and references are listed at http://www.fresnostate.edu/folklore/ballads/LI03.html.

Lying Cold on the Ground

5. Omie Wise (1807)

The fullest account is Robert Thomas Roote, "'Naomi Wise': A Study of a North Carolina Murder Ballad" (master's thesis, North Carolina State University, 1982). For early descriptions see the poem by Mary Woody, at http:// en.wikisource.org/wiki/A_true_account_of_Nayomy_Wise, and Baxter Craven's 1851 essay, "The Story of Naomi Wise," http://archive.org/details/lifeof naomiwiset00crav.

For an excellent analysis see Edward E. Baptist, "'My Mind Is to Drown You and Leave You Behind': 'Omie Wise, Intimate Violence and Masculinity," in *Over the Threshold: Intimate Violence in Early America*, ed. Christine Daniels and Michael V. Kennedy (New York, 1999), 94–110. Other books and articles include Eleanor R. Long-Wilgus, *Naomi Wise: Creation, Re-creation, and Continuity in an American Ballad Tradition* (Chapel Hill, NC, 2003); Gerald Milnes, "West Virginia's Omie Wise: The Folk Process Unveiled," *Appalachian Journal* 22 (Summer 1995): 376–389; and Richard Williams, "'Omie Wise': A Cultural Performance," *Kentucky Folklore Record* 23 (January–March 1977): 7–11. Manly Wade Wellman's essay from *Dead and Gone* (New York, 1954) is at http://allred family.com/naomiwise.htm. See also Matthew Burns, "Little Omie Wise," http://appalachianlifestyles.blogspot.com/209/02/little-omie-wise.html; "Notes on the History of Randolph County, NC," http://randolphhistory.wordpress. com/2009/06/03/naomi-wise/; and Kevin Griffin Moreno's essay at http://mob townblues.com/2012/05/16/the-trueish-tale-of-the-murder-of-poor-omie-wise/. As Paul Clayton sang, "No pity, no pity," this monster did cry / "In Deep River bottom your body will lie."

6. *The Ballad of Frankie Silver (1831)*

For a full account of the story of Frankie Silver see Perry Deane Young, *The Untold Story of Frankie Silver: Was She Unjustly Hanged?* (Asheboro, NC, 1998); Daniel W. Patterson's superb study, *A Tree Accurst: Bobby McMillon and Stories of Frankie Silver* (Chapel Hill, NC, 2000); and Gwen McNeil Ashburn, "Silence in the Courtroom: Language, Literature, and Law in 'The Ballad of Frankie Silver,'" in *Literature and Law*, ed. Michael J. Meyer (New York, 2004), 67–81. Three short articles in the *Journal of American Folklore* 113 (Spring 2000): 200–210, are also helpful, especially Daniel Patterson, "The Ballad and the Legends of Frankie Silver: A Search for the Woman's Voice." Finally, the *North Carolina Folklore Journal* 47 (2000) contains more than a half dozen informative essays on the subject and includes the full text of the ballad.

For a novel about the case see Sharyn McCrumb, *The Ballad of Frankie Silver* (New York, 1998). For a thirty-minute documentary video by Legacy Films, *The Ballad of Frankie Silver* (2000), see http://www.youtube.com/watch?v=1oaoWPaFlVc, and for Bobby McMillon's view of the case see http://www.youtube.com/watch?v=qAFT4OwNhSg. Useful and informative websites include Susan Graham Erwin Helm, http://deweyfox.com/frankiesilverhistory.htm; http://www.murderbygaslight.com/2010/04/ballad-of-frankie-silver.html; Beverly Patterson, "Give Me the Truth! The Frankie Silver Story in Contemporary North Carolina," http://www.folkstreams.net/context,160, and Lyle Lofgren's essay on the song, at http://www.lizlyle.lofgrens.org/RmOlSngs/RTOS-FrankieSilvers.html. Several versions of "Frankie Silver" are available on YouTube, including the recording by Byrd Moore and His Hot Shots.

7. *Tom Dooley (1866)*

Two excellent studies of Tom Dula are John Foster West, *Lift Up Your Head, Tom Dooley* (Asheboro, NC, 1993), and John Edward Fletcher, *The True Story of Tom Dooley* (Charlotte, NC, 2013). Much of the trial transcript can be found in West's volume, but I also consulted the original record at https://familysearch.org/pal:/MM9.3.1/TH-1951–20393–3947–97?cc=1878751&wc=MMYG-G1 K:n726718435. See also the original transcripts of the Tom Dula Case, 1866–1868, Supreme Court Case No. 8923 (61 NC 437) at http://digital.ncdcr.gov/cdm/ref/collection/p16062coll3/id/458.

Several websites contain crucial information on the case, among them http://www.kronsell.net/tom_dooley_the_legend.htm; Chuck Shuford, http://www.dailyyonder.com/tom-dula-murder-sold-10–000-guitars; http://www.fmoran.com/wilkes/anny2.html, which contains much of the testimony at Dula's second trial in 1868; and "Tom Dooley: An Investigative Report," at http://www. papiotom.com/dooleyp1.html. Additional information as well as video clips of songs may be found at http://wunc.org/post/hang-down-your-head-tom-dooley; a useful essay by Harry McKown, with an audio clip of Grayson and Whitter, is at http://www2.lib.unc.edu/ncc/ref/nchistory/may2008/; and see also http:// www.murderbygaslight.com/2010/01/hang-down-your-head-tom-dula.html; Peter J. Curry's 1998 essay, "'Tom Dooley': The Ballad That Started the Folk Boom," http://kingstontrioplace.com/tdooleydoc.htm; the informative essay by Paul Slade, "Infectious: Tom Dooley," http://www.planet slade.com/tom-dooley. html; and Rob Neufeld, "The Tom Dula Story," http://thereadonwnc.ning.com/ forum/topics/the-tom-dula-story.

For the Kingston Trio's version of "Tom Dooley" see William J. Bush, *Greenback Dollar: The Incredible Rise of the Kingston Trio* (Lanham, MD, 2013).

See also *The Frank C. Brown Collection of North Carolina Folklore*, 7 vols. (Durham, NC, 1952–1964).

There is a Tom Dooley Museum in Ferguson, North Carolina, at the Whippoorwill Academy and Village.

8. Poor Ellen Smith (1892)

The most important source is the decision of the North Carolina Supreme Court in *State v. Peter DeGraff*, which is available in *North Carolina Reports* (September term, 1893, 688–697). See also Frances H. Casstevens, "A Crime of Passion: The Murder of Ellen Smith," in *Death in North Carolina's Piedmont* (Charleston, SC, 2006), 43–52. I consulted the 1880 North Carolina census returns, as well as several newspapers on microfilm, especially the *Roanoke Times* and the *Richmond Dispatch*. Additional information is available at these websites: http://murderby gaslight.bogspot.com/20010.07poor-ellen-smith.html and http://appalachianlife styles.blogspot.com/2009/poor-ellen-smith.html (August 26, 2009), by Matthew Burns, and http://www.examiner.com/article/before-fire-murder-at-the-hotel-zinzendorf (May 15, 2012) by Guy Montgomery.

9. Pearl Bryan (1896)

There are several excellent books about Pearl Bryan: James McDonald and Joan Christen, *The Perils of Pearl Bryan: Betrayal and Murder in the Midwest in 1896* (Bloomington, IN, 2012); Anne B. Cohen, *Poor Pearl, Poor Girl! The Murdered Girl Stereotype in Ballad and Newspaper* (Austin, TX, 1973); and a ninety-six-page essay by Paul Slade, "Please Tell Me Where's Her Head": Pearl Bryan in Song and Story," http://www.planetslade.com/pearl-bryan.html.

Also useful is "The Mysterious Murder of Pearl Bryan, or, the Headless Horror: A Full Account of the Mysterious Murder Known as the Fort Thomas

Tragedy, from Beginning to End; Full Particulars of All Detective and Police Investigations: Dialogues of the Interviews between Mayor Caldwell, Chief Deitsch and the Prisoners" (Cincinnati, 1896). It is available online at http://www.gutenberg.org/files/29569/29569-h/29569-h.htm.

In addition see Larry Rouse, "The True Story of Pearl Bryan," at http://voices.yahoo.com/the-true-story-pearl-bryan-297177.html?cat=10, and "The Mysteries of Pearl Bryan," at http://www.murderbygaslight.com/2012/01/mysteries-of-pearl-bryan.html, which was originally published as "Pearl Bryan: Headless Corpse Found on Northern Ky. Farm," by Robert Wilhelm in *Kentucky Explorer* 26 (November 2011). Additional information is available at http://hauntedohiobooks.com/news/pearl-bryans-shoes-mr-poock-and-the-clew-that-solved-her-murder/.

For an informative story in the *Los Angeles Herald*, February 7, 1896, see the California Digital Newspaper site, http://cdnc.ucr.edu/cgi-bin/cdnc?a=d&d=LAH18960207.2.2#. Two YouTube videos tell something of the story of Pearl Bryan, though in a melodramatic fashion: https://www.youtube.com/watch?v=viMjtGOlZ_I and https://www.youtube.com/watch?v=5iZxgPmR4_w, which also contains many excellent photographs.

To hear Bradley Kincaid's version of the song go to https://www.youtube.com/watch?v=yS7uYc38nII. And for Burnett and Rutherford's, https://www.youtube.com/watch?v=iyw8DTeuxec.

10. Delia's Gone (1900)

Crucial documentation—the prison file of Moses Houston, which includes his clemency appeals and excerpts from the trial testimony—is available in the Georgia State Archives in Morrow, Georgia. (Adam Goldstein copied the file for me, and I am deeply indebted to him.) The story may also be followed in the *Savannah Daily News*.

Sean Wilentz has written about the background of "Delia's Gone" in chapter 7 of *Bob Dylan in America* (New York, 2010) and in *The Rose and the Briar* (New York, 2004), a book he edited with Greil Marcus. An early but useful essay is Chapman J. Milling, "Delia Holmes—a Neglected Negro Ballad," in *Southern Folklore Quarterly* 1 (December 1937): 1–8. Some biographical information on Raiford Falligant is available at http://dlg.galileo.usg.edu/centennialcatalog/html/FALLIGANT_Raiford_page1.html.

Useful articles include http://www.murderbygaslight.com/2010/03/delias-gone-one-more-round.html, March 21, 2010; a 2007 entry at http://weeniecampbell.com/yabbse/index.php?topic=4397.0, which includes a list of recordings as well as the lyrics sung by Blind Willie McTell, Pete Seeger, Johnny Cash, and Bob Dylan; see also http://expectingrain.com/discussions/viewtopic.

php?f=6&t=65833, and http://realdeepblues.blogspot.com/2010/09/delias-gone-letter-from-mr-johnson.html; informative statements by John Garst can be found at http://dylanchords.info/36_wgw/ballad_of_delia_green.htm and in his brief *Delia* (Northfield, MN, 2012).

For background see Robert E. Perdue, *The Negro in Savannah, 1865–1900* (New York, 1973); Charles Lwanga Hoskins, *Yet with a Steady Beat: Biographies of Early Black Savannah* (Savannah, 2001); Jacqueline Jones, *Saving Savannah* (New York, 2008); Franklin M. Garrett, *Atlanta and Environs: A Chronicle of Its People and Events, 1880s–1930s*, vol. 2 (Atlanta, 1969); Debora Kodish, *Good Friends and Bad Enemies* (Urbana, IL, 1986), a biography of Robert Winslow Gordon; and Laurie A. Stout, *Somewhere in Time: A 160 Year History of Missouri Corrections*, 2nd ed. (Missouri Department of Corrections, 1991).

Bold Highwaymen and Outlaws

11. Cole Younger (1876)

Several books about Cole Younger are particularly helpful: John Koblas, *When the Heavens Fell: The Youngers in Stillwater Prison* (St. Cloud, MN, 2002); Marley Brant, *The Outlaw Youngers: A Confederate Brotherhood* (Lanham, MD, 1992); and Homer Croy, *Cole Younger: Last of the Great Outlaws* (Lincoln, NE, 1999 [1956]). Younger's autobiography, originally published in 1903, *The Story of Cole Younger by Himself* (St. Paul, MN, 2000), is also useful. A portion of Younger's prison file, available at the Minnesota Historical Society (no. 699, 1900–1903) is available at http://www2.mnhs.org/library/findaids/gr00206/pdf/gr00206-000001-1.pdf.

Several articles provided additional information, including John Q. Anderson, "Another Texas Variant of 'Cole Younger,' Ballad of a Badman," *Western Folklore* 31, no. 2 (April 1972): 103–115; Burton J. Williams, "Quantrill's Raid on Lawrence: A Question of Complicity," *Kansas Historical Quarterly* 34 (Summer 1968): 143–149; and the chapter on Younger in Norm Cohen, *Long Steel Rail: The Railroad in American Folksong* (Urbana, IL, 2000), 117–121.

On Minnesota's Stillwater State Prison see Denise Suzette Hesselton, *Crisis and Reform at Minnesota's Stillwater Prison, 1960–2000* (Minneapolis, MN, 2007); James Taylor Dunn, "The Minnesota State Prison during the Stillwater Era, 1853–1914," *Minnesota History Magazine*, December 1960, 137–151; and William Casper Heilbron, "Convict Life at the Minnesota State Prison, Stillwater, Minnesota" (1908), available on Kindle, which includes Younger's account "Real Facts about the Northfield, Minnesota Bank Robbery," 125–147.

The ballad about Cole Younger in John A. Lomax's 1910 volume, *Cowboy Songs and Other Frontier Ballads*, can be found at https://archive.org/details/

cowboysongsother00lomarich. Many references to other recordings are available at "The Old Weird America" website, http://www.fresnostate.edu/folklore/ballads/LE03.html.

For the first recording of "Cole Younger," by Marc Williams, see https://www.youtube.com/watch?v=5HGKt-1r_SE, and for information about Edward L. Crain, http://www.fresnostate.edu/folklore/ballads/LE03.html.

12. Jesse James (1882)

Of the many books written about Jesse James, the one I relied on most is T. J. Stiles's superb biography, *Jesse James: The Last Rebel of the Civil War* (New York, 2002). Other useful studies include Ted P. Yeatman, *Frank and Jesse James: The Story behind the Legend* (Nashville, TN, 2000); William A. Settle Jr., *Jesse James Was His Name* (Columbia, MO, 1966); and James P. Muehlberger, *The Lost Cause: The Trials of Frank and Jesse James* (Yardley, PA, 2013). I also consulted Ronald J. Pastore and John O'Melveny Woods, *Jesse James' Secret* (Kirkland, WA, 2011); the relevant chapter in Norm Cohen, *Long Steel Rail: The Railroad in American Folksong*, 2nd ed. (Urbana, IL, 2000); and Louis Proyect, "Jesse James: The Myth and the Man," at http://www.swans.com/library/art14/lproy47.html.

There are many websites devoted to the James brothers. Among the more informative are http://www.jessejamesintexas.com/index.htm, subtitled "Death Hoax and Buried Treasures"; Betty Dorsett Duke's 2012 analysis of handwriting: http://www.jessejamesintexas.com/handwriting.pdf; http://jessewjames.wordpress.com/tag/exhumation, the title of which speaks for itself; and a site devoted to James's wife, http://www.legendsofamerica.com/we-zeejames.html.

For a detailed account of the 1883 trial of Frank James, and many links to additional information—including a chart listing all twenty-six robberies attributed to the James gang—see http://www.civilwarstlouis.com/history/jamesgangfrankjamestrial.htm.

The lyrics to most of the songs written about Jesse James can be found, and often heard, either on iTunes or YouTube. For Woody Guthrie's view of James see Joe Klein, *Woody Guthrie: A Life* (New York, 1980). His view of the 1939 film about James is cited in Marjorie Guthrie et al., eds., *Woody Sez* (New York, 1975).

13. John Hardy (1894)

The most complete account of the career of John Hardy was written by John Harrington Cox and published in the *Journal of American Folklore* 32 (October–December 1919): 505–520; see also his *Folk Songs of the South* (1925), 175–188, which may be consulted online at https://archive.org/stream/folksongsofsouth00coxj#page/174/mode/2up; useful information may be found in Richard Ramella, "John Hardy: The Man and the Song," *Goldenseal* 18

(Spring 1991): 47–50; John Douglas, "John Hardy: A Desperate Little Man," *Southern Cultures* 10, no. 2 (Summer 2004): 77; and Bryan K. Garman, *A Race of Singers: Whitman's Working-Class Hero from Guthrie to Springsteen* (Ames, IA, 2001), 120–123.

See also the following websites: http://kidnappingmurderandmayhem.blogspot.com/2008/06/murder-ballad-john-hardy-was-desperate.html; and http://www.wvculture.org/history/thisdayinwvhistory/0119.html, with several newspaper articles from the time. For capital punishment in West Virginia see http://www.wvculture.org/history/wvhs941.html.

A great many recorded versions of "John Hardy" are available at http://old weirdamerica.wordpress.com/2009/03/05/17-john-hardy-was-a-desperate-little-man-by-the-carter-family/ and http://www.deaddisc.com/songs/John_Hardy.htm.

The recordings of "John Hardy" cited in the chapter may be found on YouTube.

14. Railroad Bill (1896)

Information about Morris Slater can be found in the 1885 Florida census returns. Burgin Mathews has written a fine scholarly essay, "Looking for 'Railroad Bill': On the Trail of an Alabama Badman," *Southern Cultures* 9 (Fall 2003): 66–88. Also useful is John W. Roberts, "'Railroad Bill' and the American Outlaw Tradition," *Western Folklore* 40 (October 1981): 315–328; and Norm Cohen, *Long Steel Rail*, 2nd ed. (Urbana, IL, 2000), 122–131. A few pages are devoted to the topic in Annie C. Waters, *History of Escambia County, Alabama* (Huntsville, AL, 1983).

Short articles are "Railroad Bill," http://jayssouth.com/florida/mccoy/; http://www.brewtonstandard.com/2007/05/23/forgotten-trails-saga-of-outlaw-railroad-bill-continues/; "That Hoodoo That You Do So Well!—Alabama's Railroad Bill," http://blog.al.com/strange-alabama/2012/03/post.html; and Azizi Powell, ed., a five-part series with the earliest recordings, at http://pancocojams.blogspot.com/2013/09/riley-puckett-railroad-bill-information.htm.

Some information may also be found in the *Encyclopedia of Alabama*. Slater's grave in Pensacola was located by Larry Massey as part of his research for a book about Railroad Bill: St. John's Cemetery Foundation *Summer Newsletter*, 2012.

15. Betty and Dupree (1921)

The indispensable source for the story of Betty Andrews and Frank Dupre is the *Atlanta Constitution*, which covered the crime, the trial, and the aftermath in great detail. The Supreme Court of Georgia's opinion in the case may be found online in *DuPre v. the State*, "Reports of Cases Decided in the Supreme Court of the State of Georgia" (March term, 1922), 798–826; and *DuPre v. Humphries, Judge*, 884.

Contemporary articles may be located through an online search: "Bandit Kills Detective and Robs Store," the *Jewelers' Circular*, December 21, 1921, 85; and the *Spartanburg (SC) Herald*, September 1, 1922. For state death penalty statistics see http://deathpenaltyusa.org/usa1/date/1922.htm.

Two articles on the case by Chris Smith appeared in the journal *Blues and Rhythm* (February and March, 1995), based in part on an article titled "The Last Man to Hang in Georgia," in *Master Detective*, March 1993. For background on Atlanta in the 1920s see William Bradford Willford, *Peachtree Street, Atlanta* (Athens, GA, 1962), and Steve Goodson, *Highbrows, Hillbillies, and Hellfire: Public Entertainment in Atlanta, 1880–1930* (Athens, GA, 2002).

Information about the song "Betty and Dupree" is available in Howard W. Odum and Guy B. Johnson, *Negro Workaday Songs* (Chapel Hill, NC, 1926), at http://www.bluegrassmessengers.com/negro-workaday-songs—odum—johnson-1926.aspx.

Fortunately Blind Willie Walker's version can be heard at http://www.you tube.com/watch?v=AYGLShUQX, while other versions are available at http://pancocojams.blogspot.com/2013/03/five-versions-of-blues-rhythm-blues.html.

Railroads

16. John Henry (1870s)

Important books about John Henry include Scott Reynolds Nelson, *Steel Drivin' Man: John Henry, the Untold Story of an American Legend* (New York, 2006); Brett Williams, *John Henry: A Bio-Bibliography* (Westport, CT, 1983); Guy B. Johnson, *John Henry: Tracking Down a Negro Legend* (Chapel Hill, NC, 1929); and Louis W. Chappell, *John Henry: A Folk-Lore Study* (Jena, Germany, 1933).

Important articles, essays, and book chapters are Norm Cohen, *Long Steel Rail: The Railroad in American Folksong*, 2nd ed. (Urbana, IL, 2000), 61–89; MacEdward Leach, "John Henry," in *Folklore and Society*, ed. Bruce Jackson (Hatboro, PA, 1966), 93–106; two articles by John Garst, "Chasing John Henry in Alabama and Mississippi: A Personal Memoir of Work in Progress," *Tributaries: Journal of the Alabama Folklife Association* (2002): 92–129, and "On the Trail of the Real John Henry," *History News Network*, http://hnn.us/article31137 (November 27, 2006), http://en.wikipedia.org/wiki/George_Mason_University, including a rebuttal by Scott Nelson; and Richard M. Dorson, "John Henry," *Western Folklore* 24 (July 1965): 155–163.

Several websites also contain useful information, including: "John Henry: The Steel Driving Man," at http://www.ibiblio.org/john_henry/; Paul Garon, "John Henry: The Ballad and the Legend," at http://hq.abaa.org/books/antiquarian/

news_fly?code=49; a three-part series, "Resistance and Rebellion in the Legend of John Henry," at https://sites.google.com/site/johnhenrytherebelversions/home; also http://www.loc.gov/folklife/guides/BibJohnHenry.html; and http://www.mattesonart.com/the-history-of-the-song-john-henry.aspx.

Carl Sandburg's *The American Songbag* can be downloaded at https://archive.org/details/americansongbag029895mbp.

On Lawrence Gellert see Steven Garabedian, "Reds, Whites, and Blues: Lawrence Gellert, 'Negro Songs of Protest,' and the Left-Wing Folk-Song Revival of the 1930s and 1940s," *American Quarterly* 57, no. 1 (2005): 179–206; and Bruce M. Cornforth, *African American Folksong and American Cultural Politics: The Lawrence Gellert Story* (Lanham, MD, 2013); on Hugo Gellert see http://newdeal.feri.org/gellert/wechsler.htm.

For an extraordinarily full listing of songs about John Henry see http://bruce.orel.ws/seegersessions/songs/john_henry.html.

Videos of Fiddlin' John Carson, and Gid Tanner and the Skillet Lickers singing "John Henry," are available on YouTube.

17. Engine 143 (1890)

The most useful sources are Norm Cohen, *Long Steel Rail: The Railroad in American Folksong*, 2nd ed. (Urbana, IL, 2000), 183–196; Alfred Frankenstein, "George Alley: A Study in Modern Folklore," *John Edwards Memorial Foundation Newsletter*, June 1967, 46–47, reprinted from *Musical Courier*, April 16, 1932; Katie Letcher Lyle, *Scalded to Death by the Steam: Authentic Stories of Railroad Disasters and the Ballads That Were Written about Them* (Chapel Hill, NC, 1988), 34–49; and several websites: http://oldweirdamerica.wordpress.com/2009/05/25/23-engine-143-by-the-carter-family/, including recordings of many versions of "Engine 143" and a news story from the Huntington *Daily Advertiser*; http://forums.randi.org/archive/index.php/t-55132.html, with excerpts from several newspaper accounts of the train crash; http://hin.stparchive.com/Archive/HIN/HIN01012002p02.php, the newspaper archives of the *Hinton (WV) News*; and the Chesapeake and Ohio Historical Society website at http://cohs.org.

I also consulted the *Fifth Annual Report of the Interstate Commerce Commission*, December 1, 1891 (Washington, DC, 1892); John F. Shover, *American Railroads* (Chicago, 1961), and http://en.wikipedia.org/wiki/Fast_Flying_Virginian. Information on the musicians who recorded "Engine 143," from George Reneau to Johnny Cash, is available at Wikipedia and other Internet sources.

18. Casey Jones (1900)

A fine study of railroad mishaps is Mark Aldrich, *Death Rode the Rails: American Railroad Accidents and Safety, 1828–1965* (Baltimore, 2006). For an excellent account of Casey Jones, and the songs about him, see the relevant chapter in Norm Cohen, *Long Steel Rail: The Railroad in American Folklore*, 2nd ed. (Urbana, IL, 2000). An older but still useful account with facsimiles of a few of Jones's letters is Fred J. Lee, *Casey Jones: Epic of the American Railroad* (Kingsport, TN, 1939). Those I found most useful are the website of the Casey Jones Railroad Museum, which has newspaper articles, official reports, and photographs, http://www.watervalley.net/users/caseyjones/casey.htm; John D'Angelo, "Casey Jones, the Legend, the Man, the Facts," www.virtualreader.com/vol ume_1/casey.html; and the Grateful Dead's website, "The True Story of Casey Jones," http://www.taco.com/roots/caseyjones.html. Versions of the song about Casey Jones, including Wallace Saunders's, and one that allegedly was his wife's favorite—"His wife and three children were left to mourn / The tragic death of Casey on that April morn. / May God through His goodness keep them by His grace / 'Til they all meet together in that heavenly place"—can be found at http://kristinhall.org/songbook/USFolk/BalladOfCaseyJones.pdf.

19. Wreck of the Old 97 (1903)

There are several excellent studies of the 1903 train wreck, including Larry G. Aaron, *The Wreck of the Old 97* (Charleston, SC, 2010); the first chapter of Katie Letcher Lyle, *Scalded to Death by the Steam* (Chapel Hill, NC, 1991); and Norm Cohen, *Long Steel Rail: The Railroad in American Folksong*, 2nd ed. (Urbana, IL, 2000), 197–226, as well as his essay, "Robert W. Gordon and the Second Wreck of 'Old 97,'" *Journal of American Folklore* 87 (January–March 1974).

The case involving the Victor Talking Machine Company and David Graves George led to decisions in Federal District Court, the Court of Appeals, and the Supreme Court. The decisions can be found in Court of Appeals, 3rd Circuit (January 3, 1934); U.S. Supreme Court (December 17, 1934), 55 Supreme Court 229; U.S. District Court New Jersey (July 6, 1938); Court of Appeals, 3rd Circuit (July 14, 1939); U.S. Supreme Court (December 11, 1939), 60 Supreme Court 294; and U.S. Supreme Court (January 29, 1940), 60 Supreme Court 466.

Excerpts from the rulings and additional information are available in Henry M. Belden and Arthur Palmer Hudson, eds., *Folk Ballads from North Carolina* (Durham, NC, 1952), vol. 2 in *The Frank C. Brown Collection of North Carolina Folklore*, at https://archive.org/details/frankcbrowncolle02fran.

Several websites contain useful information, including http://www.blue ridgeinstitute.org/ballads/old97news.html, which has newspaper accounts of the 1903 crash; and http://www.blueridgeinstitute.org/ballads/old97news.html, with good photographs of the accident. More can be found at http://www. rdricketts.com/pittsco/wreckold97.html.

Also helpful is Charles Francis Adams, *Notes on Railroad Accidents* (New York, 1879), at https://archive.org/details/notesonrailroad02adamgoog.

Henry Whitter's recording of "The Wreck of the Old 97" is at https://www. youtube.com/watch?v=5b8fUJT_ZNA, and additional information about him is at http://www.bluegrassmessengers.com/henry-whitter--1923.aspx. Vernon Dalhart's recording can be heard at https://www.youtube.com/watch?v= PKN1_yN3sgs.

Workers

20. Cotton Mill Blues (1930s)

Two superb books by John A. Salmond provided a wealth of information about labor struggles in the cotton mills: *Gastonia 1929: The Story of the Loray Mill Strike* (Chapel Hill, NC, 1995), and *The General Textile Strike of 1934: From Maine to Alabama* (Columbia, MO, 2002). Other important works are Vincent J. Roscigno and William F. Danaher, *The Voice of Southern Labor: Radio, Music, and Textile Strikes, 1929-1934* (Minneapolis, MN, 2004); Beth English, *A Common Thread: Labor, Politics, and Capital Mobility in the Textile Industry* (Athens, GA, 2006); Janet Irons, *Testing the New Deal: The General Textile Strike of 1934 in the American South* (Urbana, IL, 2000); and Bryant Simon, *A Fabric of Defeat: The Politics of South Carolina Millhands, 1910-1948* (Chapel Hill, NC, 1998).

Other useful books were Mildred Gwin Andrews, *The Men and the Mills: A History of the Southern Textile Industry* (Chapel Hill, NC, 1998); Gary M. Fink, *The Fulton Bag and Cotton Mill Strikes of 1914-1915* (Ithaca, NY, 1993); David L. Carlton, *Mill and Town in South Carolina, 1880-1920* (Baton Rouge, LA, 1982); Stephen Yafa, *Big Cotton* (New York, 2009); and D. Clayton Brown, *King Cotton in Modern America* (Jackson, MS, 2011). Two older books also were helpful: Melvin Thomas Copeland, *The Cotton Manufacturing Industry of the United States* (Cambridge, MA, 1912, reissued in 1923); and Broadus Mitchell, *The Rise of Cotton Mills in the South* (Baltimore, 1921), reprinted in 2001 by the University of South Carolina Press with an introduction by David L. Carlton.

For Lewis Hine's photographs of child labor in the textile mills see Child renoftheCottonIndustry2.htm and http://docsouth.unc.edu/nc/childlabor/ menu.html.

Information about Ella May Wiggins is available at http://ncpedia.org/ biography/wiggins-ella and in an essay by Patrick Huber at http://www.old hatrecords.com/ResearchGGEMWiggins.html.

Much information about the 1929 strike at the Loray Mill in Gastonia, including participants' accounts and lyrics to some songs, can be found at http://www.weisbord.org/Gastonia.htm, which appeared originally in *Southern Exposure* 1, nos. 3/4 (Winter 1974). The article was written by Vera Buch Weisbord and edited by Dan McCurry and Carolyn Ashbaugh. On methods and

techniques of cotton production see http://www.spinningtheweb.org.uk/inter
actives/cotton production.php.

For Sinclair Lewis's pamphlet *Cheap and Contented* see Richard R. Linge-
man, *Sinclair Lewis: Rebel from Main Street* (St. Paul, MN, 2005). Examples of
cotton mill songs can be found in Doug DeNatale and Glenn Hinson, "Southern Textile Song Tradition Reconsidered," *Journal of Folklore Research* 28,
nos. 2/3 (May–December 1991): 103–133; and Patrick Huber, *Linthead Stomp:
The Creation of Country Music in the Piedmont South* (Chapel Hill, NC, 2008).
Lyrics to other songs are in Alan Lomax, ed., *Hard Hitting Songs for Hard-Hit
People* (New York, 1967), and also at http://www.folkarchive.de/mills.html, a
website with many songs by Dorsey and Howard Dixon and by Dave McCarn.

21. Chain Gang Blues (1930s)

Two fine books on Parchman Farm are David M. Oshinsky, *"Worse Than Slav-
ery": Parchman Farm and the Ordeal of Jim Crow Justice* (New York, 1996), and
William Banks Taylor, *Down on Parchman Farm: The Great Prison in the Mis-
sissippi Delta* (Columbus, OH, 1999). For useful background information see
Alex Lichtenstein, *Twice the Work of Free Labor: The Political Economy of Con-
vict Labor in the New South* (New York, 1996); Robert Perkinson, *Texas Tough:
The Rise of America's Prison Empire* (New York, 2010); and Matthew J. Mancini,
One Dies, Get Another: Convict Leasing in the American South, 1866–1928
(Columbia, SC, 1996).

On Huddie Ledbetter see Charles Wolfe and Kip Lornell, *The Life and Leg-
end of Leadbelly* (New York, 1992), and on his relationship with John and Alan
Lomax see chapter 4 of Marybeth Hamilton, *In Search of the Blues* (New York,
2008), and chapter 12 of Amanda Petrusich, *It Still Moves* (New York, 2008).
Also useful is Bruce M. Conforth, *African American Folksong and American
Cultural Politics: The Lawrence Gellert Story* (Lanham, MD, 2013). For the
Lomaxes see Nolan Porterfield, *Last Cavalier: The Life and Times of John A.
Lomax, 1867–1948* (Urbana, IL, 2001), and John Szwed, *Alan Lomax: The Man
Who Recorded the World* (New York, 2010).

Two important essays are Tessa M. Gorman, "Back on the Chain Gang:
Why the Eighth Amendment and the History of Slavery Proscribe the Resur-
gence of Chain Gangs," *California Law Review* 85 (1997): 441–478; and on the
Georgia Prison system, Stephen Garton, "Managing Mercy," *Journal of Social
History* 36 (2003): 675–699. The U.S. Court of Appeals decision in *Gates v. Col-
lier* is at 501 F.2d 1291 (1974).

See also the prison songs at "No Mo Freedom: Prison Blues," http://sunday
blues.org/archives/156, and "Angola Bound: The Blues of Harry Oster," http://
sundayblues.org/archives/tag/harry-oster.

22. Only a Miner (1930s)

There is a rich historical literature on coal mining and workers' efforts to join unions. I relied on several books: David McAteer, *Monongah: The Tragic Story of the 1907 Monongah Mine Disaster* (Morgantown, WV, 2007); George F. McGovern and Leonard F. Guttridge, *The Great Coalfield War* (Boston, 1972), a study of the Ludlow, Colorado, strike; Michael Punke, *Fire and Brimstone: The North Butte Mining Disaster of 1917* (New York, 2006); Lon Savage, *Thunder in the Mountains: The West Virginia Mine War, 1920–1921* (Pittsburgh, 1990); Robert Shogan, *The Battle of Blair Mountain* (New York, 2004); John W. Hevener, *Which Side Are You On? The Harlan County Coal Miners, 1931–1939* (Urbana, IL, 1978, 2002); Tony Bubka, "The Harlan County Coal Strike of 1931," *Labor History* 11 (1970): 41–57; and Irwin M. Marcus et al., "Confrontation at Rossiter: The Coal Strike of 1927–1928 and Its Aftermath," *Pennsylvania History* 58 (October 1992): 310–326. A 1932 pamphlet, *The Kentucky Miners' Struggle*, by the American Civil Liberties Union is at http://books.google.com/books/about/The_Kentucky_Miners_Struggle.html?id=Sw9BAAAAIAAJ.

Two other useful studies are Keith Dix, *What's a Coal Miner to Do? The Mechanization of Coal Mining* (Pittsburgh, 1978), and Crandall A. Shifflett, *Coal Towns: Life, Work, and Culture in Company Towns of Southern Appalachia, 1880–1960* (Knoxville, TN, 1991). For "Harlan Miners Speak," by John C. Hennen, see https://appalachiancenter.as.uky.edu/sites/default/files/Harlan%20Miners%20Speak%20-%20Hennen%20Intro.pdf. Some websites I found helpful are the Centers for Disease Control and Prevention's list of mining disasters, 1839 to the present, http://www.cdc.gov/niosh/mining/statistics/content/all miningdisasters.html; the U.S. Department of Labor exhibition of mining disasters, http://www.msha.gov/DISASTER/MONONGAH/MONON6.asp; http://www.historyinsidepictures.com/Pages/MonongahCoalMineExplosion MemorialPhotographsoftheWorstMiningDisasterinUSHistory.aspx; and a website with information on the coal strike of 1927, http://patheoldminer.rootsweb. ancestry.com/indrossiter2.html.

For coal-mining songs see Archie Green, *Only a Miner* (Urbana, IL, 1972); and for Woody Guthrie's songs about mine disasters see Mark Alan Jackson, *Prophet Singer: The Voice and Vision of Woody Guthrie* (Jackson, MS, 2007). Guthrie sings "Ludlow Massacre" at https://www.youtube.com/watch?v=XDd64suDz1A; for songs about mine strikes in general see http://noclexington.com/?p=6379; for Blind Alfred Reed's "Explosion in the Fairmount Mines" see http://www.folkarchive.de/explo.html; Florence Reece can be heard singing "Which Side Are You On?" at https://www.youtube.com/watch?v=Nzudto-FA5Y; and Pete Seeger sings "The Death of Harry Simms" at https://www.youtube.com/watch?v=FU5f4xj-Xeg.

Aunt Molly Jackson's song "I am a Union Woman" and her testimony before the Dreiser committee can be found at http://www.historyisaweapon.com/def con1/unionwomanmollyjackson.html; and see Shelly Romalis, *Pistol Packin' Mama: Aunt Molly Jackson and the Politics of Folksong* (Urbana, IL, 1999).

23. House of the Rising Sun (1930s)

There are several excellent studies of prostitution in New Orleans, including Emily Epstein Landau, *Spectacular Wickedness: Sex, Race, and Memory in Storyville, New Orleans* (Baton Rouge, LA, 2013); Alecia P. Long, *The Great Southern Babylon: Sex, Race, and Respectability in New Orleans, 1865–1920* (Baton Rouge, LA, 2004); and Mara L. Keire, *For Business and Pleasure: Red-Light Districts and the Regulation of Vice in the United States, 1890–1933* (Baltimore, 2010). Al Rose, *Storyville, New Orleans: Being an Authentic, Illustrated Account of the Notorious Red-Light District* (Tuscaloosa, AL, 1974), provides not only the fullest account of the red-light district, but also reprints some of the most important ordinances, court decisions, and legal briefs. Many other legal documents relating to the case of *L'Hote v. City of New Orleans* can be found in the *Southern Reporter* 24, Supreme Court of Louisiana (November 21, 1898): 608–611.

For the Supreme Court ruling in *L'Hote v. New Orleans*, 177 U.S. 587 (1900) see http://supreme.justia.com/cases/federal/us/177/587/. A book that I found indispensable is Ted Anthony, *Chasing the Rising Sun: The Journey of an American Song* (New York, 2007).

For Jelly Roll Morton see Howard Reich and William Gaines, *Jelly's Blues: The Life, Music, and Redemption of Jelly Roll Morton* (Cambridge, MA, 2003). And for Morton's reminiscences, recorded by Alan Lomax at the Library of Congress, see http://www.doctorjazz.co.uk/locspeech3.html, and for his lyrics, http://www.lyricsbox.com/jelly-roll-morton-lyrics-cgt5p.html.

Among the most helpful websites were http://musiccourtblog.com/2011/06/28/the-house-of-the-rising-sun-a-folk-evolution/; http://www.fresnostate.edu/folklore/ballads/RL250.html, which lists early versions of the song; http://www.shmoop.com/animals-house-rising-sun/meaning.html; a short essay by Kevin Herridge at http://www.risingsunbnb.com/the-song; and for the song's history, http://h2g2.com/edited_entry/A12460772.

Many of the photographs of Storyville taken by Ernest J. Bellocq were reprinted in *Smithsonian Magazine* on March 28, 2012, and are available at http://www.smithsonianmag.com/history/the-portrait-of-sensitivity-a-photographer-in-storyville-new-orleans-forgotten-burlesque-quarter-166324443/?no-ist.

Recordings of "House of the Rising Sun" by Clarence Ashley, the Callahan Brothers, the Animals, Dolly Parton, and others are accessible on YouTube.

Disasters

24. The Titanic (1912)

Of the many books written about the *Titanic*, I found three indispensable: Steven Biel, *Down with the Old Canoe: A Cultural History of the* Titanic *Disaster* (New York, 1996); Jennifer Hooper McCarty and Tim Foecke, *What Really Sank the* Titanic: *New Forensic Discoveries* (New York, 2008); and Paul Heyer, Titanic *Century: Media, Myth, and the Making of a Cultural Icon* (Santa Barbara, CA, 2012). Also useful is Hugh Brewster, *Gilded Lives, Fatal Voyage: The* Titanic's *First-Class Passengers and Their World* (New York, 2012). There are also many extraordinarily detailed websites, among them http://www.titanicinquiry.org/, which includes the testimony offered at both the American and British investigations of the disaster; http://www.boston.com/bigpicture/2012/04/the_titanic_at_100_years.html, which has many superb photographs; http://ngm.nationalgeographic.com/2012/04/titanic/sides-text; and http://ultimatetitanic.com/the-sinking/, and http://adventure.howstuffworks.com/titanic2.htm. An informative essay by Erwin Bosman may be found at http://www.nodepression.com/profiles/blogs/blues-and-black-folk-music-shine-on-the-american-titanic. Many of the songs written about the *Titanic* are available at http://oldweirdamerica.wordpress.com/2009/05/07/22-when-that-great-ship-went-down-by-william-versey-smith/. And others can be found at http://www.fretboardjournal.com/features/online/songs-paying-tribute-titanic. On Richard "Rabbit" Brown see http://www.bluesworld.com/RabbitBrown.html; on Blind Willie Johnson see Michael Corcoran's essay, http://www.austin360.com/news/entertainment/arts-theater/he-left-a-massive-imprint-on-the-blues-but-little-/nRzPM/. And on Huddie Ledbetter see Charles K. Wolfe and Kip Lornell, *The Life and Legend of Leadbelly* (New York, 1992). A fine essay, by Chris Smith, "The *Titanic*: A Case Study of Religious and Secular Attitudes in African American Song" (1991), can be found online.

25. The Boll Weevil (1920s)

There are several excellent accounts of the boll weevil and its impact on American life: James C. Giesen, *Boll Weevil Blues: Cotton, Myth, and Power in the American South* (Chicago, 2011); Willard D. Dickerson et al., *Boll Weevil Eradication in the United States through 1999*, published by the Cotton Foundation (Memphis, 2001); L. O. Howard, *The Insect Menace* (New York, 1931); and the U.S. Department of Agriculture's *The Boll-Weevil Problem*, by W. D. Hunter and B. R. Coad (Washington, DC, 1923). Websites, too, are useful, especially "Boll Weevil Blues" at http://uncensoredhistoryoftheblues.purplebeech.com/2009/01/show-40-boll-weevil-blues.html, and Fabian Lange and Alan L. Olmstead, "The Impact of the Boll Weevil, 1892–1932" (2008), at http://www.econ.ucdavis.edu/faculty/alolmstead/Working_Papers/BOLL%20WEEVIL%20.pdf.

Many songs can be found at "Boll Weevil Here, Boll Weevil Everywhere," described at http://www.document-records.com/fulldetails.asp?ProdID= DOCD-5675. See also Robert K. D. Peterson, "Charley Patton and His Mississippi Boweavil Blues," *American Entomologist* (Fall 2007): 142–44, at http://entomology.montana.edu/historybug/Peterson_2007.pdf, and Gates Thomas, "South Texas Negro Work-Songs: Collected and Uncollected," University of North Texas Digital Library, 173–175, http://digital.library.unt.edu/ark:/67531/metadc67654/m1/158/.

Martyrs

26. Joe Hill (1915)

There is a superb book about Joe Hill: William M. Adler, *The Man Who Never Died: The Life, Times, and Legacy of Joe Hill, American Labor Icon* (New York, 2011); it can be supplemented by Philip S. Foner, ed., *The Letters of Joe Hill* (New York, 1965), which contains forty-five letters written in 1914 and 1915. Three other informative biographies are Gibbs Smith, *Joe Hill* (Salt Lake City, 1969), and Franklin Rosemont, *Joe Hill: The IWW and the Making of a Revolutionary Workingclass Counterculture* (Chicago, 2003); and Philip S. Foner, *The Case of Joe Hill* (New York, 1965).

Several highly informative essays are Archie Green, "Singing Joe Hill," in his *Wobblies, Pile Butts, and Other Heroes* (Urbana, IL, 1993), 77–94; Lori Elaine Taylor, "Joe Hill Incorporated: We Own Our Past," and Sam Richards, "The Joe Hill Legend in Britain," both in *Songs about Work*, ed. Archie Green (Bloomington, IN, 1993); and James O. Morris, "Philip Foner and the Writing of the Joe Hill Case," *Labor History* 12 (January 1971): 81–114. See also Archie Green et al., eds., *The Big Red Songbook: 250-Plus IWW Songs* (Chicago, 2007).

Several websites contain important information, among them http://www.fresnostate.edu/folklore/ballads/Arn175.html; http://www.joehill.org/joesbio.htm; http://www.folkarchive.de/hillstro.html, with Joe Hill's lyrics as well as those to Woody Guthrie's "Joe Hillstrom" and other songs; http://themanwhoneverdied.com/, a blog by William M. Adler; and http://www.dailykos.com/story/2011/11/29/1040950/-Joe-Hill-the-man-and-the-myth-Protest-Tuesday.

Earl Robinson's posthumously published autobiography, written with Eric A. Gordon, *Ballad of an American* (Lanham, MD, 1998), describes the origins of the song. On Alfred Hayes see Alan Calmer, "The Wobbly in American Literature," the *New Masses*, September 18, 1934, 21–22; an essay by A. S. Hamrah, http://www.criterion.com/current/posts/2901-alfred-hayes-screenwriter; and for an evaluation of several of Hayes's books see Paul Bailey, "Chronicles of Dust and Sin," at http://www.theguardian.com/books/2005/oct/29/featuresreviews.guardianreview10.

For Elizabeth Gurley Flynn's autobiography see *The Rebel Girl* (New York, 1955). Michael Loring's 1939 rendition of "Joe Hill," accompanied by Earl Robinson, can be heard at http://www.youtube.com/watch?v=VjRqPH530mQ.

For Paul Robeson's singing of "Joe Hill" see Laurel Sefton MacDowell, "Paul Robeson in Canada: A Border Story," *Labor / Le Travail* 51 (Spring 2003): 177–221; Martin Duberman, *Paul Robeson* (New York, 1995); and Paul Robeson Jr., *The Undiscovered Paul Robeson: Quest for Freedom, 1939–1976* (New York, 2009).

27. Sacco and Vanzetti (1927)

I have adapted some of the material here from my introduction to the 1997 edition of Gardner Jackson and Marion Denman Frankfurter, eds., *The Letters of Sacco and Vanzetti* (New York, 1928). For an exhaustive bibliography see Jerry Kaplan's compilation (2008) prepared for the Sacco and Vanzetti Commemoration Society, http://saccoandvanzetti.org/saccovanzetti_bibliography.pdf.

Among the most important books on the case are Louis Joughin and Edmund M. Morgan, *The Legacy of Sacco and Vanzetti* (New York, 1948); David Felix, *Protest: Sacco-Vanzetti and the Intellectuals* (Bloomington, IN, 1965); Herbert B. Ehrmann, *The Case That Will Not Die: Commonwealth vs. Sacco and Vanzetti* (Boston, 1969); Roberta Strauss Feuerlicht, *Justice Crucified: The Story of Sacco and Vanzetti* (New York, 1977); Francis Russell, *Tragedy in Dedham: The Story of the Sacco-Vanzetti Case* (New York, 1962), and *Sacco and Vanzetti: The Case Resolved* (New York, 1986); William Young and David E. Kaiser, *Postmortem: New Evidence in the Case of Sacco and Vanzetti* (Amherst, MA, 1985); Paul Avrich, *Sacco and Vanzetti: The Anarchist Background* (Princeton, NJ, 1995); Bruce Watson, *Sacco and Vanzetti* (New York, 2007); Moshik Temkin, *The Sacco-Vanzetti Affair: America on Trial* (New Haven, CT, 2009); Theodore W. Grippo, *With Malice Aforethought: The Execution of Nicola Sacco and Bartolomeo Vanzetti* (i-universe books, 2011); Susan Tejada, *In Search of Sacco and Vanzetti: Double Lives, Troubled Times, and the Massachusetts Murder Case That Shook the World* (Boston, 2012).

There are many useful websites devoted to the case, among them http://law2.umkc.edu/faculty/projects/ftrials/saccov/saccov.htm, which includes the appellate court and clemency decisions; and http://jurist.law.pitt.edu/famous trials/sacco.php. Recordings of songs about the case are available at http://www.antiwarsongs.org/categoria.php?id=23&lang=it, and music devoted to it, including videos, can be found at http://www.saccoandvanzetti.org/sn_display1.php?row_ID=50. The Sacco and Vanzetti commemoration website is at http://www.saccoandvanzetti.org/index.php. Valuable material compiled by Doug Linder is at http://law2.umkc.edu/faculty/projects/ftrials/saccov/s& vaccount.html.

For the liner notes and lyrics to Woody Guthrie's *Ballads of Sacco and Van-zetti*, and a copy of Guthrie's letter to Judge Webster Thayer, see http://media.smithsonianfolkways.org/liner_notes/smithsonian_folkways/SFW40060.pdf.

For substantial excerpts from the trial testimony, and many other documents, see Richard Newby, ed., *Kill Now, Talk Forever: Debating Sacco and Van-zetti* (1st Books Library, 2001).

An exceptionally beautiful collection is Alejandro Anreus, *Ben Shahn and the Passion of Sacco and Vanzetti* (New Brunswick, NJ, 2001).

Index